Hollywood Party

HOLLYWOOD PARTY

How Communism Seduced

the American Film Industry

in the 1930s and 1940s

Kenneth Lloyd Billingsley

FORUM

An Imprint of Prima Publishing

For Irene, my wife.

FORUM is an imprint of Prima Publishing, 3875 Atherton Road, Rocklin, California 95765

PRIMA PUBLISHING and colophon are registered trademarks of Prima Communications, Inc.

Photographs and publications in photo insert courtesy of Roy Brewer.

"Confessions of a Red Screenwriter" by Richard Collins. Reprinted with Permission of *New Leader*.

LIBRARY OF CONGRESS CATALOGING-IN-PUBLICATION DATA

Billingsley, Kenneth Lloyd.
  Hollywood Party : how communism seduced the America film industry in the 1930s and 1940s / Kenneth Lloyd Billingsley.
     p.   cm.
  Includes bibliographical references and index.
  ISBN 0-7615-1376-0
  1. Screenwriters—California—Los Angeles. 2. Communism and motion pictures—United States. 3. Blacklisting of entertainers—United States. 4. Motion pictures—Political aspects—United States. I. Title.

PN1998.2.B53 1998
384'.8'79494'09043—dc21   98-27188
                                                                          CIP

98 99 00 01 02 AA 10 9 8 7 6 5 4 3 2 1
Printed in the United States of America

HOW TO ORDER
Single copies may be ordered from Prima Publishing, P.O. Box 1260BK, Rocklin, CA 95677; telephone (916) 632-4400. Quantity discounts are also available. On your letterhead, include information concerning the intended use of the books and the number of books you wish to purchase.

Visit us online at *www.primapublishing.com*

Contents

Acknowledgments

THIS BOOK DEALS with some of the most complicated events ever to take place in American labor, politics, and show business, and it would not have been possible without the cooperation of Roy Brewer, who was there for all of it and opened his archives to me. Peter Collier provided guidance and thoughtful criticism. Herb Romerstein and Stephen Schwartz made available their expertise in Soviet espionage, the American labor movement, and the history of the Communist Party. The author wishes to thank officials in the former Soviet Union for opening the Comintern archives to Western scholars, and to current and former members of the Communist Party for being so forthcoming in their interviews with sympathetic journalists.

Steven Hayward passed on details of Hollywood's political wars along with steady encouragement. Friends and colleagues John Tregaskiss, Rick Michalski, Peter Faulkner, Cristopher Rapp, Joe Sloan, Jack Hafer, Robert Gillespie, Jennie Gillespie, John Seitz, Michael Cromartie, Ternot MacRenato, Robert Caldwell, Randall Kuhl, and many others supplied both encouragement and inspiration. Steven Martin of Prima Publishing provided careful oversight for the project, and the author wishes to acknowledge the editorial work of Jennifer Fox. Responsibility for the content of this work remains mine alone.

Partial Cast of Characters

CHARLES BAKCSY — Private investigator; infiltrated Ella Winter–Lincoln Steffens circle in Carmel, California

AVERILL BERMAN — Radio broadcaster; CSU supporter

ALVAH BESSIE — Writer for *Daily Worker;* screenwriter; Communist Party member; one of the Hollywood Ten

HERB BIBERMAN — Screenwriter; Communist Party member; one of the Hollywood Ten

WILLIE BIOFF — Racketeer; representative of Hollywood IA, 1936–1940

BETSY BLAIR — Actress; Communist Party supporter; wife of actor–dancer Gene Kelly

HUMPHREY BOGART — Actor; member of Hollywood Fights Back, group that protested the HCUA hearings

BERTOLT BRECHT — German dramatist and Communist; one of the Nineteen unfriendly witnesses before the HCUA

ROY M. BREWER — New Deal Liberal; anti-Communist Hollywood labor leader; IA representative

HARRY BRIDGES — Leader of the Longshoreman's Union; secret member of Communist Party; engineered the 1934 San Francisco waterfront strike

EARL BROWDER — Communist Party leader during 1930s and 1940s

CHARLIE CHAPLIN	Actor; supporter of Communist Party and USSR
MORRIS CHILDS	American Communist leader; double agent
LESTER COLE	Writer; Communist Party member; one of the Hollywood Ten
RICHARD COLLINS	Writer; Communist Party member; one of the Nineteen unfriendly witnesses before the HCUA
HUGH DeLACY	Popular Front congressman from Washington State
MARTIN DIES	Democratic house representative from Texas; first chairman of the HCUA, 1938–1944
WALT DISNEY	Cartoon magnate; friendly witness before the HCUA
EDWARD DMYTRYK	Director; Communist Party member; one of the Hollywood Ten
FATHER GEORGE DUNNE	Catholic priest; public speaker; broadcaster; CSU supporter
PHILIP DUNNE	Liberal anti-Communist writer; director; one of the founders of Hollywood Fights Back, group that protested the HCUA hearings
GERHART EISLER	Comintern official
WILLIAM Z. FOSTER	Hard-line Communist Party leader and Stalinist; author of *Toward a Soviet America*
BEN GITLOW	Onetime Communist Party member; twice ran for vice president of the United States
MIKE GOLD	Writer; Communist Party "literary enforcer"

STERLING HAYDEN Actor; Communist Party member; witness before the HCUA

LILLIAN HELLMAN Playwright; screenwriter; Communist Party supporter

KATHARINE HEPBURN Actress; CSU supporter

PAUL JARRICO Screenwriter; Communist Party member

V. J. JEROME Cultural Commissar, Communist Party USA

GORDON KAHN Writer; one of the Nineteen unfriendly witnesses before the HCUA

ELIA KAZAN Director; actor; writer; novelist; onetime Communist Party member who later publicly recanted; won Oscar for *On the Waterfront* (1954)

JEFF KIBRE Hollywood labor organizer; Communist Party member; attempted in the 1930s to organize the craft guilds into one broad union

HOWARD KOCH Writer; one of the Nineteen unfriendly witnesses before the HCUA

ARTHUR KOESTLER Writer; onetime Communist Party member who later abandoned Marxism and was reviled by the Party; author of *Darkness at Noon*

RING LARDNER JR. Screenwriter; Communist Party member; one of the Hollywood Ten; won Oscars for *Woman of the Year* (1943) and *M*A*S*H* (1970)

STANLEY LAWRENCE Communist Party organizer in Hollywood

JOHN HOWARD LAWSON Playwright; screenwriter; Hollywood Communist leader; one of the Hollywood Ten

JAY LOVESTONE American Communist Party leader, deposed by Stalin

ALBERT MALTZ	Screenwriter; novelist; Communist Party member; one of the Hollywood Ten; won Oscar for *The House I Live In* (1945)
LOUIS B. MAYER	Head of Metro-Goldwyn-Mayer movie studios; friendly witness before the HCUA
ADOLPHE MENJOU	Anti-Communist actor; friendly witness before the HCUA
LEWIS MILESTONE	Director; one of the Nineteen unfriendly witnesses before the HCUA
ROBERT MONTGOMERY	Anti-Communist actor; SAG leader
SAMUEL ORNITZ	Screenwriter; Communist Party member; one of the Hollywood Ten
LARRY PARKS	Actor; one of the Nineteen unfriendly witnesses before the HCUA
IRVING PICHEL	Actor and director; one of the Nineteen unfriendly witnesses before the HCUA
WILLIAM POMERANCE	NLRB official and secretary of Screen Cartoonists Guild
AYN RAND	Anti-Communist novelist and screenwriter
MAURICE RAPF	Mogul's son; writer; Communist
RONALD REAGAN	Actor and Hollywood labor leader; SAG president; friendly witness before the HCUA; president of the United States, 1981–1989
PAUL ROBESON	Actor; singer; Communist supporter
FRANKLIN D. ROOSEVELT	President of the United States, 1933–1945
ROBERT ROSSEN	Writer; director; producer; Communist Party member; one of the Nineteen unfriendly witnesses before the HCUA

WALDO SALT Writer; one of the Nineteen unfriendly witnesses before the HCUA; won Oscars for *Midnight Cowboy* (1969) and *Coming Home* (1978)

BUDD SCHULBERG Novelist; screenwriter; former Communist Party member; won Oscar for *On the Waterfront* (1954)

ADRIAN SCOTT Producer; Communist Party member; one of the Hollywood Ten

HERBERT K. SORRELL Hollywood labor leader; Communist Party member and collaborator; founder and head of the Conference of Studio Unions

JOSEF STALIN Leader of USSR 1929–1953

LINCOLN STEFFENS Muckraking journalist; Communist supporter; first husband of Ella Winter

DONALD OGDEN STEWART Screenwriter; Communist Party member; first chair of the Hollywood Anti-Nazi League; second husband of Ella Winter

ANNA LOUISE STRONG American journalist, editor of *Moscow News;* Communist Party supporter

PARNELL THOMAS Republican house representative from New Jersey; Chairman of House Committee on Un-American Activities during Hollywood hearings

LEON TROTSKY Soviet revolutionary; rival of Stalin; assassinated in 1940

HARRY TRUMAN President of the United States, 1945–1953

DALTON TRUMBO Screenwriter; Communist Party member; one of the Hollywood Ten

RICHARD WALSH President of IA during 1940s and 1950s

JACK WARNER   Head of Warner Brothers studios; friendly witness before the HCUA

ELLA WINTER   Journalist for *New Masses*; author; Communist Party supporter; wife of Lincoln Steffens and, later, Donald Ogden Stewart

JOHN WEBER   Communist Party organizer in Hollywood; department head at William Morris Agency

Abbreviations and Organizations

Abbreviations

AFI	American Film Institute
AFL	American Federation of Labor
APM	American Peace Mobilization
AVC	American Veterans Committee
CIO	Congress of Industrial Organizations
Comintern	Communist International
CPUSA	Communist Party USA
CSU	Conference of Studio Unions
HICCASP	Hollywood Independent Citizens Council of the Arts, Sciences and Professions
HCUA	House Committee on Un-American Activities
IATSE/IA	International Alliance of Theatrical Stage Employees
MPA	Motion Picture Alliance for the Preservation of American Ideals
MPDC	Motion Picture Democratic Committee
MPPA	Motion Picture Producers Association
NLRB	National Labor Relations Board
PCA	Progressive Citizens of America
SAG	Screen Actors Guild

USSR   Union of Soviet Socialist Republics
USTG   United Studio Technicians Guild
WFTU   World Federation of Trade Unions

Organizations

Committee for the First Amendment
Hollywood Anti-Nazi League
Hollywood Fights Back
Hollywood League for Democratic Action
League of American Writers
League of Hollywood Voters
Screen Writers Guild
Society of Motion Picture Interior Decorators

World

1917	1933	1939	1940
USSR founded world's first socialist state.	Adolf Hitler appointed chancellor in Germany.	World War II begins.	Trotsky assassinated.

Soviet Union

1917	1919	1924	1929	1932	1936	1939	1940
Bolshevik Revolution occurs.	Communist International (Comintern) founded in Moscow.	Vladimir Lenin dies.	Stalin Era begins.	Forced famine in Ukraine.	Josef Stalin stages show trials, purges rivals, and imprisons millions in labor camps.	Stalin signs pact with Hitler. Stalin invades Finland.	Stalin annexes Baltic states.

United States

1919	1929	1932	1933	1934	1935	1936	1937	1938	1939
Communist Party of America founded in United States.	American Communists purge followers of Leon Trotsky.	Communists call for a Soviet America.	Franklin Delano Roosevelt begins first term as president of the United States.	Earl Browder becomes general secretary of Communist Party USA.	Communists pro-claim Popular Front against fascism.	Communists support Roosevelt and the New Deal. Branch of Communist Party established in Hollywood.	American Communists fight in Spanish Civil War.	Congress establishes House Committee on Un-American Activities.	CPUSA abandons anti-fascism, opposes aid to Allies, leads strikes at U.S. defense industries.

Shifts in the Communist Party Line

New Revolutionary Period, 1929–1935
Party maintains militant stance, denouncing liberals and socialists as "social fascists," calls for a Soviet America and separate Communist-dominated trade unions.

Popular Front Period, 1935–1939
Communists make common cause with liberals, calling for a common front and collective security against fascism. Party urges boycott of German and Japanese goods, inter-venes on side of the Republicans in Spain, supports flow of U.S. armaments to victims of fascist aggression. Party supports work within mainstream trade unions.

Nazi-Soviet Pact, 1939–1941
Communist Party charges that England and France started the war, which it denounces as an "imperialist" struggle. Party supports Hitler's proposal for ending the war, including the settlement of the "Jewish problem." Party opposes

1941	1945	1948	1949	1950	1952	1989
Hitler invades USSR.	World War II ends.	Communist coup in Czechoslovakia.	Mao Tse-Tung seizes power in China.	North Korea invades South Korea.	In Czech purge trials, eleven Jews are convicted as "Zionist Trotskyite enemies of the people" and executed.	Collapse of Communism in Eastern Europe.

1945	1948	1949	1953	1956
USSR returns to anti-Western stance. Cold War begins.	Stalin launches wave of postwar purges.	Soviet Union explodes atomic bomb.	Stalin dies.	Nikita Khrushchev denounces Stalin's crimes. USSR invades Hungary.

1941	1943	1944	1945	1947	1948	1951	1956	1959	1980	1989	1991
CPUSA abandons isolationism, revives popular front against fascism, supports war effort.	Comintern dissolved.	CPUSA changed to Communist Political Association. Browder preaches accommodation with the West.	Roosevelt dies. Harry S. Truman sworn in as president of the United States. Browder removed as Party leader.	House Committee on Un-American Activities holds hearings on Hollywood.	Spy scandals in United States. Truman reelected.	HUAC Hollywood hearings resume.	Communist Party membership begins decline.	Gus Hall becomes leader of American Communist Party.	Ronald Reagan elected President of the United States.	USSR reduces subsidies to Communist Party USA.	Hall supports coup attempt against Mikhail Gorbachev

the draft, opposes U.S. aid to victims of Nazi aggression, and uses the slogan "The Yanks Are Not Coming." Party spearheads strikes in American defense industries.

Accommodation Period, 1941–1945
The Party supports the Allied war effort, now a "people's war," urges a second front, dissolves the Comintern, urges a no-strike pledge for duration of the conflict. Party changes its slogan to "The Yanks Are Not Coming Too Late."

Cold War, 1945–thereafter
The Party attacks the United States as an aggressive enemy of peace, promotes armed uprisings in Greece and French Indo-China, demands withdrawal of American troops from China, opposes the Truman Doctrine of containment, opposes the Marshall Plan, opposes NATO, and denounces "American imperialism" as the aggressor in the Korean conflict.

Introduction: The Official Story

ON OCTOBER 27, 1997, A STEADY STREAM OF PEOPLE filed into the Motion Picture Academy of Arts and Sciences on Wilshire Boulevard in Beverly Hills, California. It was mostly an older, show-business crowd, but the younger set was well represented and television cameras were at the ready. The crowd had ventured out on a Monday evening, not a busy time except for Oscar night, even in the entertainment capital of the world. The mood that evening was not festive but serious, more like that of a conference than a gala event.

They had come to see *Hollywood Remembers the Blacklist,* a production of the American Federation of Radio and Television Artists, the Directors Guild of America, the Screen Actors Guild, and the Screen Writers Guild of America, with cooperation from the Association of Motion Picture and Television Producers. For those old enough to remember, the show would bring back memories. For those new to the story, no expense had been spared to make everything perfectly clear, in fine multimedia style.

A collage of headlines from the 1940s forms a backdrop to the stage. The lights go down in the posh Academy theater, nearly packed to capacity. As the film begins, big-band jazz swells, saxophone section booming, and a swift procession of images from the forties and fifties, including American icons Marilyn Monroe and Joe DiMaggio, flashes upon the screen. The smiling faces radiate postwar optimism: jobs, opportunity, and new cars for all. It was a great time to be an American, the narrator says, and a great time to be in Hollywood. But his tone suddenly turns ominous. Even during that upbeat and idyllic time, he intones, there was trouble in the dream factories.

The presentation cuts to black-and-white still photos of testimony before the House Committee on Un-American Activities (HCUA), which fifty years ago to the day was holding hearings on Communist infiltration of the motion picture industry. On Monday, October 27, 1947, in Washington, D.C., the Committee began hearing testimony from a group of nineteen unfriendly witnesses. The nineteen were eventually pared down to a group known as the Hollywood Ten: Alvah Bessie, Herb Biberman, Lester Cole, Edward Dmytryk, Ring Lardner Jr., John Howard Lawson, Albert Maltz, Samuel Ornitz, Adrian Scott, and Dalton Trumbo.

The narrator describes the Hollywood Ten as an "award-winning group of writers and directors who had given voice and structure to hundreds of memorable films." For many in the audience, the names hold meaning, but others draw a blank. Images of screenwriters Herb Biberman, Samuel Ornitz, and John Howard Lawson appear on the screen. The film fades, and the lights come up, stage left, on some live action.

Five actors, playing members of the House Committee on Un-American Activities, sit high on a raised platform, rigid, aloof, like a bank of inquisitors. In front of them, facing the audience, sits a solitary witness who is playing himself. In 1947, screenwriter Ring Lardner Jr. had been a dashing thirty-two-year-old with a Clark Kent look. Now, half a century later, at eighty-two, the wizening, slightly stooped writer still sounds lively, reading a list of his accomplishments and proudly telling the audience that his brother fought in the Abraham Lincoln Brigade during the Spanish Civil War. The audience responds with warm applause. Lardner then reads the speech the Committee prevented him from giving fifty years before.

"My record includes no antidemocratic word or act, or opposition to American democratic principles as I understand them," Lardner proclaims. "Compared to what I have seen in this room, Hollywood is a citadel of freedom. . . . Here there is such fear of free speech that men are forbidden to read statements."

Brisk applause rewards his lines as the theater darkens and the film footage resumes.

"Many in Hollywood were outraged," explains the narrator, "so a planeload of celebrities who weren't willing to conform flew into Washington to lend their support, but the Committee was in no mood to let the witnesses speak. Under the relentless pounding of the Committee's gavel, idealism crumbled and fear began to take its place."

The group that flew to Washington included the biggest box-office draw of the day, Humphrey Bogart, along with his wife Lauren Bacall, and a young actress named Marsha Hunt. On screen, the camera zooms in to a close shot of Marsha Hunt in 1947; then image yields to reality as the lights come up, stage right, on Marsha Hunt, 1997, now a stately, dignified woman, still poised and elegant. Like Ring Lardner Jr. she had been there and could speak with authority.

"We were all fired up with our mission, to defend our industry's good name and to defend, not Communism or Communists, but all Americans' right to privacy of opinion and freedom of advocacy," Hunt explains.

"We were flying to keep the First Amendment alive. In that year, after weeks of a headline circus that was nationwide, all Hollywood seemed to be outraged at the charges against our industry that were coming from the HCUA hearings. And they were rallying behind the nineteen talented film people who were now being called the unfriendly witnesses. But only days after our return from Washington, our film colony was rapidly turning into a different town."

People began to play it safe, she says, and were reluctant to express an opinion in a climate of suspicion, lest they lose their jobs. The fear and tension, as she recalls it, were not limited only to those who were targets of the Committee's efforts to hunt down Communists in Hollywood movies.

"As the virus spread across the nation," Hunt concludes, "for over a decade, this was no longer the land of the free, nor the home of the brave."

Applause thunders through the theater, but *Hollywood Remembers the Blacklist* has yet to marshal its contemporary star power. Actor Billy Crystal is here, but not as a wisecracking master of ceremonies.

The action moves to center stage, where Crystal, seated before the Committee, is playing the late Larry Parks, an actor who gained a measure of fame for his screen renditions of singer Al Jolson. Larry Parks was one of the nineteen unfriendly witnesses and the first actor to testify. Tonight, in a clip from *The Jolson Story,* the handsome Parks lip-synchs "I'm Sitting on Top of the World." The diminutive Billy Crystal, departing from his usual glib comedic style, delivers lines taken straight from Parks's testimony in a soft voice trembling with emotion:

"I would appreciate not having to. . . . Don't present me with the choice of either being in contempt of this Committee and going to jail or forcing me to really crawl through the mud to be an informer; for what purpose? I think to do something like what is happening in Russia today. . . . So I beg of you not to force me to do this."

But the Committee wants names. The crowd senses the actor's agony and a hush falls over the theater. Then, after a few beats of silence, speaking barely above a whisper, the witness reluctantly gives the Committee some names of other people whom he knows to be Communists. As he names names, Committee members boorishly interrupt him to request correct spellings. Audience members can be heard gasping at the audacity of it.

Actor John Lithgow turns in an emotional performance as Sterling Hayden, the tall, strapping actor best known for his role as General Jack Ripper in Stanley Kubrick's *Dr. Strangelove*, the classic Cold War black comedy. Hayden had also named names, an act that left him guilt-stricken for life.

"I was a real daddy longlegs of a worm when it came to crawling," Lithgow says, speaking lines that Hayden himself had written.

Academy Award–winner Kevin Spacey, fresh from roles in *The Usual Suspects, Breakout,* and *L.A. Confidential,* in tonight's performance stars as screenwriter Paul Jarrico, who was not one of the nineteen or the Hollywood Ten but was nonetheless a blacklisted veteran of the times.

"One man's subversion is another man's patriotism," he tells the Committee. "I consider the activities of this Committee subversive of the Constitution of the United States."

The audience applauds as Spacey delivers Jarrico's lines to the Committee.

"I believe that this country was founded on the doctrine of freedom, the right of a man to advocate anything he wishes, advocate it, agitate for it, organize for it, attempt to win a majority for it. And I think any Committee that intimidates people, that makes it impossible for people to express their opinions freely, is subverting the basic doctrine of the United States and of its Constitution. And I hope that some day, the stand the Hollywood Ten took will be recognized historically along with the stand that Jefferson took against the Alien and Sedition Act."

The ovation is long and loud, but there is more to come. In film footage, John Randolph, Jeff Corey, and other actors tell how they suffered under the blacklist. Dalton Trumbo, one of the Ten, explains how he beat the blacklist by writing under fake names, a tactic that enabled him to take credit for good films and avoid blame for bad ones. The film cuts to scenes from *The Front,* starring Woody Allen, the first studio-released movie about the blacklist, and *Spartacus,* written by Dalton Trumbo.

Later, in a brief film scene, former Screen Actors Guild president Ronald Reagan appears, eliciting instant, Pavlovian hostility from the crowd. The appearance of actor Adolphe Menjou, like Reagan a friendly witness before the Committee, also draws jeers. In footage Menjou is shown saying, "If it came here I would move to the state of Texas because I think the Texans would shoot them on sight." The audience responds with mocking laughter.

At the end of the footage, the names of those blacklisted scroll slowly up the screen, with the plaintive strains of violins providing an emotional backdrop. The mood has been established for penance.

Jack Shea of the Directors Guild officially restores the screen credits of Herb Biberman, one of the Hollywood Ten. Officials from the other guilds indulge in flagellation about the time when, as Marsha Hunt told them, the country was no longer the land of the free nor the home of the brave. They are immediately rewarded.

Paul Jarrico is there in a live appearance, gnomelike but still sprightly at eighty-two, with the genial demeanor and smooth voice of a game-show host.

"There has been a mistake," he says. "I *am* Kevin Spacey."

The line gets big laughs, but Jarrico swings back to the somber themes at hand.

"The Guilds have come a long way since they failed to protect the Hollywood Ten," he says. He tells a story from Budd Schulberg's novel *What Makes Sammy Run?*, about how Sammy has lied and cheated and knifed his way up the ladder and finally becomes head of a major studio. When asked how he feels about it, Sammy thinks and then responds, "Patriotic."

Back then, Jarrico continues, patriotism had been defined as "a willingness to betray others." The octogenarian outlines two strands of American history, one of them brutal. "The genocide witnessed on Native Americans, the ugly wave of know-nothing bigotry that has greeted every wave of immigration . . . labor strikes broken by force of arms . . . periodic repression of dissent."

The other strand, he tells the audience, is "noble" history, "the abolition, the suffragettes, the fight to end racism, to end sexism, to end the obscene chasm between poverty and wealth. Our brutal history defines patriotism as my country right or wrong. Our noble history defines it as my country, right the wrong. It may take another fifty years, but we shall overcome. The good guys will win."

By this time during the evening, many names, events, and insider references have been mentioned. They are lost on the younger members of the audience, but Jarrico's payoff line, "The good guys will win," brings it all back, in the most basic language of cinema. And tonight's show leaves no doubt as to who the good guys are.

Daniel Petrie of the Screen Writers Guild presents Paul Jarrico with a plaque engraved with the words of the First Amendment to the United States Constitution. As Jarrico accepts, other formerly blacklisted victims in the audience stand to a rousing ovation.

The crowd files out through the Academy's wide corridors, lined with movie memorabilia, toward a lavish buffet in the lobby. Camera crews corner the blacklisted writers, and reporters hang on their every word, like sportswriters in the winners' locker room. Around the food tables, the conversation buzzes with "Red scare," "witch hunt," and "McCarthyism."

For the show-business crowd, at least, the evening was an experience in validation, a combination documentary, stage play, award ceremony, and western, in stark black and white, with easily identifiable victims and heroes in a simple-to-follow plot. The bad guys—a committee of political bullies, goose-stepping zealots, and opportunists—had ridden into town, smearing everything that moved as un-American, blacklisting those who failed to cooperate, and ruining many careers. The good guys defended freedom of expression, overcame adversity, and prevailed in the end. The industry that so shamefully collaborated in their persecution had now publicly repented and had received absolution from the victims themselves. For this crowd, *Hollywood Remembers the Blacklist* was the feel-good hit of fall 1997.

Fiftieth anniversaries tend to be the last celebrated, and the audience got the feeling that this show intended to be the final, authoritative, and above all official entertainment-industry last word. Produced by the major show-business guilds, backed by the producers, and staged at the prestigious Academy, it attempted to establish for all time who were the good guys and the bad guys. Featuring Billy Crystal, the regular host of the Oscar broadcast, in a brilliant piece of casting, it played as a kind of lifetime achievement award for those it portrayed as heroes.

What the show revealed was interesting, but what it concealed was crucial, and no one knew that better than those who had performed so convincingly onstage. When the carefully contrived emotional payoff had faded, even casual observers could not help noticing that something was missing. As they moved out onto Wilshire Boulevard, many people knew full well that what they had seen was full of secret passageways and escape hatches and gaps vast enough to swallow entire decades.

"There were Communists in Hollywood, and I was one of them," Paul Jarrico had proudly stated at a Screen Writers Guild forum a decade earlier. But tonight he left the subject unexplored. Jarrico had mentioned screenwriter Budd Schulberg, another Party member, but did not tell the audience how, long before *The Front,* Schulberg had won an Oscar for a screenplay dealing with Communism, Communists, and the Committee. Why had this important information been left on the cutting-room floor?

The House Un-American Activities Committee came along in 1947, but why had Hollywood captured their attention? What had happened there during the preceding quarter-century? Marsha Hunt had provided the evening's sole reference to Communism and Communists. Were there any actual Communist Party members among that talented group of writers and directors who were persecuted by the Committee?

What did it mean to be a Communist in the thirties and forties, and what had the Communists done in the studios? What had they said about Josef Stalin and his totalitarian regime? What had they done when Stalin and Hitler were allies against the West? What had Ronald Reagan done to earn the disdain of the show-business crowd? Why had Humphrey Bogart and Lauren Bacall criticized the Hollywood group that had defended the First Amendment?

With the programs they received at the Academy on October 27, 1997, members of the audience were given a 1961 tract called "Red Stars," which had been written by a man named Myron Fagan. His list of Reds included Steve Allen, Lauren Bacall, Lucille Ball, Marlon Brando, Lloyd Bridges, Charlie Chaplin, Kirk Douglas, Melvyn Douglas, José Ferrer, Henry Fonda, Burt Lancaster, Peter Lorre, Groucho Marx, Burgess Meredith, Henry Morgan, Sidney Poitier, Edward G. Robinson, Frank Sinatra, Jessica Tandy, Orson Welles, and many others. But these stars were not mentioned in the show, and there was nothing mentioned about where they stood now. Was "Red Stars" an example of hysterical false accusation, or had some of these actors actually been members of the Communist Party?

Had tonight's show included all those who might have had full recall of those dark days, or had some important players been deliberately excluded? Was there more to the story? Perhaps another side that had been left out?

Paul Jarrico had never told the whole story and now would never do so. He died in an automobile accident the following day on the way to another southern California blacklist remembrance.

Another Communist Party member, Abe Polonsky, screenwriter for *Body and Soul,* was onstage and had a brief speaking role in *Hollywood Remembers the Blacklist*. The slender eighty-six-year-old writer knew the full story too and like Jarrico had been present at some key scenes. But he wasn't providing any full-length narration. Polonsky, in fact, had taken his name off *Guilty by Suspicion* (1991), the most recent cinematic attempt to tell the story of the blacklist, when the producer changed the hero, played by Robert De Niro, from a Communist to a liberal.

Many people in the Academy audience had little way of knowing that what actually happened fifty years before was not as simple as a black-and-white Western, but was in fact a longer-running and infinitely more complex and colorful production. It didn't involve only a group of ten award-winning writers and directors; it bustled with a cast of thousands, domestic and international, from national leaders to moguls to grips, who played roles as spies, clowns, traitors, heroes, and victims. Many switched sides after sudden, unexpected plot twists. The players were not restricted to the narrow confines of Hollywood but moved on a global stage, against a backdrop of the great events of our time.

The story of the Hollywood blacklist wasn't just a morality play about people testifying to government committees. It was a cultural and political thriller, a story of war on constantly changing fronts, with pitched battles, blood flowing in the streets, and even a brief use of air power. It wasn't just about whether a small group of people lost their jobs because of false accusations. It was the story of how the central conflict of this century affected the American movie industry, and ultimately, decisions about who controlled Hollywood.

During the fifty years since the 1947 hearings, the Cold War ended, and Ronald Reagan, the first union leader to hold the office, became President of the United States. The Soviet Union passed into history, and its former leader, Mikhail Gorbachev, who presided over the demise, did commercials for Pizza Hut. Since 1947 a number of books and documentaries have echoed the inquisitorial themes of *Hollywood Remembers the Blacklist,* but no one has told the entire story of why the Communist Party came to Hollywood, and what it accomplished there. The blacklist was both a sideshow and a sequel to that "back story" and could not be understood without it.

Part I

The Back Story

Of all the arts, the cinema is the most important.
—Vladimir Lenin

Communism, Communists, and Cinema

WORKERS OF THE WORLD, arise, you have nothing to lose but your chains. From each according to his ability, to each according to his need. The dictatorship of the proletariat ruling over a classless society, based not on the blind forces of the market but on scientific socialism. Progressing onward and upward, abolishing ignorance, oppression, poverty, injustice, and disease, until the state itself withers away, leaving humankind in a pristine, pre-Edenic condition of pure Communism . . . forever.

Such was the vision—biblical in force, with the lowly and downtrodden rising up to displace the powerful—prophesied by the German political philosopher and socialist Karl Marx. Marx believed that the Communist ideal would first become reality in a modern, industrial nation—in Germany, France, or even America. In fact, it took shape in a backward, mostly agricultural country, the largest on Earth and, as it turned out, an ideal base for the most significant mass movement of the twentieth century.

In Vladimir Lenin's design, Communism would achieve a "new man" and would replace the exploited bourgeois relic of the past.

In this utopian vision, the state would fade away, but in reality the state came to wield more power over its citizens than any other regime in history. In theory society might be classless, but in practice it was the most rigid class system ever conceived, a dictatorship *over*, not of, the proletariat.

Lenin died in 1924, and by the end of the 1920s, the reins of the revolutionary state had passed to the man who would be the impresario for all Communist Party activity over the next three decades. This man was a character no scriptwriter could invent, but from the beginning he fit the category of a "heavy," and he remained a towering figure throughout the Party's involvement in the Hollywood studios.

Iosif Vissarionovich Dzhugashvili, a Georgian seminary student who had never held a legitimate job, converted to Marxism and became a professional revolutionary. Around the turn of the century, he took part in hold-ups ("expropriations," the Bolsheviks called them) and often escaped from custody, disappearing into the underground. Standing five-foot-four and speaking Russian with a heavy Georgian accent, in 1910 he took the name Stalin, or "man of steel." Once in power he lived up to the name and methodically eliminated potential rivals, many of whom had played more important roles in the revolution than he. He sent Leon Trotsky, who had once referred to Stalin as "our party's outstanding mediocrity," into exile. Stalin remained true to Leninist principles by using terror as a means of policy.

Marxist dogma called for the collectivization of agriculture, which Stalin set out to accomplish by any means necessary, whatever the cost in human life. He engineered a man-made famine in Ukraine, during which more than 5 million peasants died at the rate of 25,000 a day—a rate higher than in World War I, when 6,000 soldiers perished daily.[1] Hitler killed his enemies, but Stalin eliminated his friends and associates as well as "enemies of the people." The three-step process was "arrest, try, shoot"; the purges claimed Lev Kamenev, head of the Red Army, and Grigory

Zinoviev of the Party's Central Committee. As Vladimir Pozner, for years the Soviets' primary apologist in America, explained, "There were no dissidents; they were shot *before* they ever came close to dissenting."[2] As one account had it, Stalin's execution squads worked day and night, but the shots were drowned out by the noise of the machines that were excavating new mass graves.[3] By the end of the 1930s, the purges had claimed 10 million victims, a number greater than that of the Nazi holocaust victims, but only about one-quarter of the final death tally.

With their penchant for secrecy and their closed society, the Soviets were able to conceal most of their crimes. Those who broke the story of the Ukraine famine were called liars, while Walter Duranty of the *New York Times* won a Pulitzer for his stories that covered up the atrocity. Duranty and other defenders of the regime justified the action by saying, "You can't make an omelet without breaking eggs." Others went beyond that position.

Bertolt Brecht, a German Communist and dramatist who practically invented the propaganda play, had traveled to America, where Communist Party cultural officials such as V. J. Jerome helped him stage his works. Marxist scholar Sidney Hook, who had come to know Brecht in Berlin, asked him about the purges. Brecht maintained that it was the Soviet Party that counted. "As for them," he said of Zinoviev, Kamenev, and the other purge victims, "the more innocent they are, the more they deserve to be shot."[4]

The industrialization of the Soviet Union proved more of a success, not because of Stalinist policy but in spite of it. A burst of industrialization and modernization in the Soviet Union took place during the Great Depression in America, when one-fourth of American workers could not find jobs, and people, their stomachs gnawing with hunger, scavenged for food in garbage cans. For many, the Depression seemed to provide evidence that capitalism, as the Communists so confidently proclaimed, was doomed and that the scientific socialism practiced in the USSR was indeed the wave of the future. Americans began to visit this great new experiment, touching off a wave of adulation for the Soviet Union and its leader, who was now considered the living embodiment of socialism and was known throughout his own vast domains as "Father," "the Sun," "Wise Leader," "Immortal Genius," "Great Helmsman," and "Unbending Commander." As Soviet historian Dmitri Volkogonov has noted, Stalin was "a great actor" and played the roles of commander, prophet, and statesman to the hilt.[5] His performance drew rave reviews in America.

"One must not make a god of Stalin, he was too valuable for that," wrote American journalist Anna Louise Strong, a headstrong Nebraskan who edited *Moscow News*, an English-language Soviet publication, and whose writings on the USSR were widely publicized in the United States.[6] The most memorable phrase, however, came from one of Strong's colleagues, who would soon find himself stationed on Communist Party supply lines that led to Hollywood.

Lincoln Steffens, born in San Francisco in 1866 and educated at the University of California, had pioneered the muckraking school of journalism, exposing corruption in American business and government in such articles as "Shame of the Cities." His widely influential *Autobiography of Lincoln Steffens* found fans in Hollywood, including actor James Cagney. A one-time admirer of Mussolini and his Fascist regime, Steffens did as much as any American to swing the idealistic youth of the thirties toward what Max Eastman called the "pro-Soviet parade." Steffens told Marxist scholar Sidney Hook that his own motive for supporting Communism was emotional, that he had given up trying to think things out and simply "felt" that the Communists were right.

After visiting the Soviet Union, Steffens proclaimed the much-quoted line for which he is most remembered: "I have been over into the future and it works." He inspired thousands of others to step into the future for themselves. When the Americans arrived, the Soviets gladly led them on carefully staged tours, complete with fake building fronts, like those on Hollywood sets, that the

Russians had used to convince the czar that all was well when it wasn't. The American visitors included screenwriter and novelist Budd Schulberg, son of mogul B. P. Schulberg, who made the trip and came away impressed, and writer Maurice Rapf, son of Metro Goldwyn Mayer executive Harry Rapf, whose tour of the USSR was sponsored by the National Student League. On his tour Rapf met fellow screenwriter Ring Lardner Jr., like him an impressionable young man, open to new ideas.

These pilgrims, like thousands of others, had made their first contact with Communism not in the USSR but through Communism's outreach campaigns in the United States. In 1919 the Soviets had established the Communist International, known as the Comintern, to control the national Communist parties outside of Russia, including the one in the United States. The Comintern selected Party leaders, set Party strategy, disciplined wayward members, and funded Party operations.[7] The Communist Party of the United States not only accepted Moscow's control—no records exist of them disobeying an order—but actively sought it.

"The Communist movement was psychologically a movement of political colonists determined to place the world, or as much of it as possible, country by country, under the sway of their government in Moscow," wrote Ben Gitlow, who ran for vice president as a Communist in 1924 and 1928. "We were volunteer members of a militarized colonial service, pledged to carry out the decisions of our supreme rulers resident at Moscow anywhere in the world but particularly in the land we were colonizing for Communism, the United States."[8]

The joke that the Communist Party was like the Brooklyn Bridge—suspended by cables—originated with the Party organizers themselves. "Moscow gold," as Party men called it, subsidized between one-third and one-half of Party operations, providing the American Communists with an infrastructure, including daily newspapers on both coasts, far beyond what their membership could hope to support. Russian-born Morris Childs, a graduate of the International Lenin School in Moscow and a former *Daily Worker* editor, headed the Communist Party apparatus in Chicago and came to be regarded by the Soviets as the American foreign minister. During a twenty-year period, Morris and his brother Jack transported $28 million in Soviet subsidies for the American Communist Party.[9]

Soviet money meant Soviet control, and even for high-placed officials, policy came from Moscow and was to be obeyed without question. Morris Childs himself had been assigned to Chicago by Comintern official Gerhart Eisler, who would later play a role in Hollywood's political intrigue. That intrigue began as a result of a change in tactics following a shift of the Communist Party line, which was diligently followed.

"If the Party says you're going to China, you'll be on the next train or boat to China," Childs later explained. "If the Party tells you to climb a flagpole at midnight and hoist a banner saying 'Power to the Peasants,' you'll scrape your balls climbing that flagpole at midnight. If the party tells you to quit and go underground, at that instant you're underground."[10] In that underground, as decoded Soviet intelligence transmissions have revealed, Soviet agents referred to American, Mexican, and Canadian Communists as *zemlyaki*, "compatriots" or "fellow-countrymen," direct confirmation of Soviet control.[11] Those who resisted that control or attempted to pursue an independent policy quickly found themselves purged.

While some on America's homegrown Left urged evolution and ballots, the Bolsheviks had burst from the gates preaching revolution and bullets. The Communists made no appreciable inroads into American society until they softened their line. Instead of preaching class hatred and violent revolution, they adopted the strategy of the popular front, camouflaging class struggle with populist pieties and co-opting liberals to their causes. Instead of assaulting from without, both the open and secret Party members would bore from within.

Marxist–Leninist doctrine taught that industrial workers were the key to the revolutionary transformation of society. Not surprisingly, then, the Party sought to champion the workers of the world. The Party played a leading role in protesting American unemployment, a condition that had led many to join the Party itself. By the late 1930s, a quarter of the total membership of the Congress of Industrial Organization's (CIO) members were in unions led by Communists. Harold Ware, a Communist farm–policy specialist, worked for the New Deal's Agricultural Adjustment Administration (AAA). Lee Pressman, lead counsel for the CIO, was a Communist who belonged to the Ware group. Another member of the Ware group was John Abt, chief counsel for the Civil Liberties Subcommittee of the Senate Education and Labor Committee.

Nathan Witt, a secret Communist and former member of the Ware group, became the first secretary and a staff director of the National Labor Relations Board (NLRB). In that powerful federal post he hired many secret Communists, leading the NLRB to tilt toward the Communist-dominated CIO. Edwin S. Smith, one of the first NLRB commissioners, also became a close ally of the Communist Party, and after departing that post under pressure, he became a professional lobbyist for the Soviet Union.[12]

"The curiosity is not that there were undoubtedly many Reds that made government their vocation," wrote "Man from U.N.C.L.E." actor Robert Vaughn years later in a study of blacklisting, "but that the entire Communist Party was not on the federal payroll."[13] For Eugene Lyons, former Party member, this was not much of an exaggeration.

"Never before—or since—had all areas of American society been so deeply penetrated by a foreign nation and a foreign ideology," wrote Lyons. "Never before had the country's thinking, official policies, education, arts, and moral attitudes been so profoundly affected by the agents, sympathizers, and unwitting puppets of a distant dictatorship."[14]

The Communist Party enjoyed great success with "front groups," organizations they controlled without that control being publicly recognized. One of the major front groups, the League of American Writers, had been an outgrowth of the American Writer's Congress, an affiliate of the International Union of Revolutionary Writers, headquartered in Moscow. During the 1930s, at the height of its success, the League even managed to enlist Franklin Delano Roosevelt, the President of the United States.[15]

But the Communist Party had visions of something bigger. The founders of the Union of Soviet Socialist Republics were fascinated with the cinema because they recognized that it allowed limitless alteration of reality, the very goal that they were attempting to achieve in real life. "Communists must always consider that of all the arts the motion picture is the most important," said Lenin, who sent cinema trains into the Russian countryside during the 1920s. As he explained in his 1936 address to the Commissariat for Cinematography, Stalin too was fascinated by cinema's endless possibilities, at home and abroad. "The cinema is not only a vital agitprop device for the education and political indoctrination of the workers," Stalin said, "but also a fluent channel through which to reach the minds and shape the desires of people everywhere."

In 1926, Sergei Eisenstein, the USSR's premier *cinéaste*, made *The Battleship Potemkin*, a film about a sailors' mutiny. The Soviets used the movie as part of their labor organizing efforts. Joseph Goebbels praised the picture and said it should be the model for Nazi cinema. French actor Yves Montand, who was born to Communist Italian parents who fled to France from Mussolini's Fascist regime, said it was the dramatic *Potemkin*, not the turgid *Das Kapital*, that stirred his loyalties to Marxism and the USSR.

The American Communist Party's early cinematic efforts with groups such as Frontier Films produced some documentaries of interest, but, despite praise for such movies in the *Daily Worker,* none of them captured the interest of America's moviegoing public. Even during hard times, doubtless partly because of them, Americans lined up and plunked down their money for the certified magic that Hollywood served up. In 1933, at the nadir of the Depression, impoverished New Yorkers paid $89,931 in four days to see *King Kong*, at the time a record draw for an indoor attraction.[16] Party cultural officials, eager as Stalin to influence people "everywhere," duly took notice of Hollywood's clout.

Hollywood was adapting the American dream, in which all men are created equal, into the view that all people's dreams should be created equal. Not long after the American film industry was established, Hollywood's entries were written large in the household books of virtually every nation outside the Soviet Union, and even Stalin enjoyed American gangster movies.

The implications of such influence were staggering to those who were seeking to extend this major mass movement of their time. Stalin reportedly claimed that he could easily convert the world to Communism if he controlled the American movie industry.

"One of the most pressing tasks confronting the Communist Party in the field of propaganda," wrote Comintern boss Willie Muenzenberg, "is the conquest of this supremely important propaganda unit, until now the monopoly of the ruling class. We must wrest it from them and turn it against them."[17]

There, in the starkest terms, was the "back story" as the Communists saw it. A more daunting task could hardly be imagined, but based on their successes in controlling unions and entering other areas from within the New Deal, it was, in their minds, an entirely achievable goal. By the mid-1930s the tectonic shifts of history, and certainly the social and political conditions of the time, were all favorable to the Party, which was then moving from triumph to triumph. Hollywood loomed as one of its easier targets.

2

Hollywood:
The Dream Factory

HOLLYWOOD BECAME THE MOVIES' COMPANY TOWN partly for economic reasons. Since the dawn of cinema, movies had been produced in London, Paris, and New York. Some of the first filmmakers to move west were "pirates" who were using bootleg equipment copied from a design patented by Thomas Edison. When Edison began to drag these rip-off artists into court, they fled to southern California precisely because of its isolation; it was then a sunny Siberia thousands of miles from the nation's cultural center in New York and its political center in Washington, D.C. The California climate and terrain were ideal, and there was a steady supply of eager actors and extras, enabling the filmmakers to churn out westerns all year round. And when the Edison trust was eventually broken and different equipment was in use, the movies had found a permanent home.

In 1913, while living in a barn at the corner of Vine and Selma, Cecil B. DeMille made *The Squaw Man*, starring Dustin Farnum. By 1925 Hollywood had formed a veritable film factory with Paramount, United Artists, Columbia, Warner Brothers, Universal,

Fox, MGM, and assorted independents working overtime to meet the demands of an entertainment-starved populace. Public demand for movies skyrocketed after the introduction of the talkies. This proved very fortunate for the early moguls, who, having triumphed over the Edison trust, proceeded to form a trust of their own, controlling production, distribution, and exhibition through their theater chains. Hollywood wasn't so much an artistic colony producing movies as a business community making money—lots of it.

Before coming to Hollywood, Louis B. Mayer had picked rags in New Brunswick, Canada. By 1937 he had become the highest-paid man in the United States, making $1,300,000 a year.[1] Samuel Goldwyn had been a glove salesman and Adolph Zukor a furrier. The Cohn brothers were sons of a tailor and the Warner brothers sons of a cobbler. Perhaps because of this early penury, once in power the moguls vied with each other in extravagance while intermarrying their families like royalty. The studio system over which they ruled may be the closest version of an absolute monarchy ever to exist in America.

In *Hollywood: The Dream Factory*, anthropologist Hortense Powdermaker called the studio system "totalitarian," a closed system of complete top-down control, in which the individual's will counted for little or nothing. In some aspects it was worse than slavery, because its inmates chose to be part of it, selling themselves, in effect, to the highest bidder.[2] And in few industries was the gap between the haves and the have-nots so vast.

By the end of the 1930s, stars such as Bing Crosby and Claudette Colbert earned nearly $500,000 a year, with Douglas Fairbanks pulling down $37,000 per week and Walter Huston $40,000. Money formed a rigid dividing line in the Hollywood class system. Stars earning hundreds of thousands of dollars a year socialized with other stars who earned similarly high incomes. B-picture actors hung around at nightclubs and restaurants with other B-picture actors. Directors at Paramount kept company with other directors at Paramount. Writers at MGM socialized with other writers at MGM, and when writers earning thousands of dollars per week threw parties, they generally did not invite writers who were earning merely hundreds of dollars per week. The most basic division was the line dividing the so-called "talent"—groups of actors, writers, and directors, the above-the-line costs of a movie—from the below-the-line assortment of back-lot and technical workers that Budd Schulberg had captured in *What Makes Sammy Run?*

"The studio street was full of the pretty girls in slacks going home in twos and threes and carpenters and painters in overalls carrying their lunchboxes and cat-calling to each other; a director exhausted from the day's shooting and already worrying with a couple of assistants about the camera set-ups for the next; a star clowning as he climbs over the door into his silver Cord; the crazy-quilt processional of laborers, extras, waitresses, cutters, writers, glamour-girls, all the big cogs and the little ones that must turn together to keep a film factory alive."[3] At the dawn of the film age, those below-the-line cogs cost less in Los Angeles.

Around 1920, labor costs in Los Angeles were 25 to 50 percent below those in New York, and the prevailing climate in the West Coast city was decidedly antilabor. Union men John and James McNamara, though represented by the great radical lawyer Clarence Darrow, pleaded guilty in 1911 to bombing the headquarters of the then antilabor *Los Angeles Times*. The case proved devastating to the union cause in the state. Around 1917 some early industry bosses organized the Motion Picture Producers Association (MPPA) as an "open-shop" organization.

On July 18, 1918, five hundred craftsmen refused to work, starting the first Hollywood strike. They succeeded in closing down several studios, and the U.S. Department of Labor eventually intervened. There was another strike in July 1921, in protest of a wage reduction instituted by the studios, even though labor expenses then represented less than 5 percent of a picture's cost.[4] And in between these two strikes, the cameramen walked out. On November 29, 1926, five unions and nine companies signed the first labor agreement in the studios, but the battles were far from over. Like other industries, the movies felt the sting of the Depression, and in 1933 studio bosses responded by demanding all actors under contract and below-the-line workers to take a 50 percent pay cut, with freelancers getting docked 20 percent.

In March 1933, the International Alliance of Theatrical State Employees (IATSE or IA), the oldest show-business union, refused to accept the pay cut, calling out their electricians, engineers, and grips. The musicians union also walked out, and the studio bosses turned to nonunion labor, leading IA to call out 6,000 workers in retaliation. The pay cuts also affected the above-the-line talent groups and spurred their efforts toward union organization.

At the time, most actors made less than $2,000 a year, before deductions and agents' fees. The studios would work an actor like a slave, late Saturday night and often into Sunday. If a holiday intervened, the actor often had to work the following Sunday to make up the lost time. Meals were irregular, and there was rarely more than twelve hours of rest between calls. There was no travel time, no overtime, and no recompense for wardrobes or screen tests. As former radio announcer Ronald Reagan, who would later head the Screen Actors Guild (SAG), once explained, "There was no arbitration machinery or any other way to redress a grievance except by falling to one's knees and weeping before the producer."[5]

The studio bosses, ever attentive to the bottom line, also helped fertilize the ground for the Communists by altering what had been a relatively apolitical landscape. The major campaign involved one of their own employees.

Born in Baltimore in 1878, Upton Sinclair gained fame with his 1906 novel, *The Jungle,* about the Chicago stockyards and meatpacking industry. The book was a fictional version of Lincoln

Steffens's muckraking journalism and generated the same political fallout. The book helped touch off a federal investigation that paved the way for regulation of the food industry.

A candidate for the California Socialist Party, Sinclair worked briefly for MGM in 1932. Irving Thalberg bought *The Wet Parade*, Sinclair's book on prohibition, which the author supported, and made it into a successful movie. Sinclair also collaborated with Sergei Eisenstein, the great Soviet director who came to Hollywood in 1930 to work for Paramount, on a movie that became *Thunder over Mexico*. While promoting Eisenstein, Sinclair announced his EPIC—"End Poverty in California"—campaign, his platform for a run at the governor's office.

During the 1934 campaign, Sinclair repeatedly threatened to seize the studios or launch a state-controlled movie industry. The moguls, who leaned Republican and rejected the New Deal as intrusive big government, saw the enemy at the gates. Even Democrats such as Joe Schenk of Twentieth Century Fox enrolled in the movement. If Sinclair won, they threatened to pack up and go to Florida, which promised to welcome them with tax breaks. The moguls used the machinery of their studios for propaganda, producing and distributing free newsreels that warned of calamity should Sinclair be elected and portrayed Sinclair supporters as foreign-accented vagrants who planned to live work-free in a socialist welfare state headed by a weird, free-spending idealist. More important, they pressured their high-salaried workers to contribute one day's pay to the cause of Sinclair's Republican opponent, Frank Merriam. At Columbia, Harry Cohn demanded that all workers contribute a day's pay to a "Stop Sinclair Fund." The moves touched off an actors' rebellion led by Jean Harlow and James Cagney.

On Election Day, both Upton Sinclair and Communist Party candidate Sam Darcy were defeated. Republican Frank Merriam, the moguls' candidate of choice, carried the day with much help from a $500,000 war chest supplied by the studios, but the damage

had been done. Ironically, the studio bosses had helped to radical-
ize their own workers, a huge advantage for Communist Party organizers but far from their only asset. The Communists also held
the moral high ground and a distinct edge in propaganda.

From the Party's point of view, the studio system was the perfect
paradigm of monopoly capitalism: vast wealth for the reactionary
few, who had gained their millions, their palaces, their luxury automobiles, their furs, their stables of race horses, by the sweat and
tears of the toiling masses they controlled. During hard times,
Party men made the most of it, especially in their work with below-
the-line workers. Organizing workers takes money, but Moscow
gold was on the way.

3

"The Strategic Importance of Hollywood"

IN 1934 THE SOVIETS OPENED A CONSULATE in San Francisco, a city their intelligence operatives code-named "Babylon" and their lone official outpost on the West Coast. The consulate became a cover for the NKVD—the Soviet spy agency that eventually became the KGB—under their *rezident,* or base official, Grigory Kheifetz, code-named "Brown," and also served as a supply line for Party organizers and the state's growing number of Sovietophiles, including Lincoln Steffens—the most famous one of all.

Journalist Lincoln Steffens had seen the future in the USSR but preferred to live stateside. He set up shop in Carmel, some 100 miles south of San Francisco on the scenic central coast, then as now an upscale refuge for residents of San Francisco, Los Angeles, and the hinterlands alike. In London, Steffens had met and married Australian-born Ella Winter, a woman thirty-two years his junior and a student at the London School of Economics.

Winter had grown up a self-confessed tomboy and as a short-haired adult bore more than a passing resemblance to actor Jamie Farr. Steffens even referred to her by the masculine name Peter, the same name they gave their only son. What attracted Steffens about Ella was the burning ideologue within. Winter impressed even other Marxists as a zealot and fanatic. She too had seen the future, and it worked, prompting her to write *Red Virtue* and *I Saw the Russian People.* She described her first Soviet visit as a revelation: "Millions . . . free from squalor and disease and neglect. Health and education, literacy and knowledge were replacing the results of centuries of poverty and ignorance. . . . Public trials taught people their rights. Everyone was learning and teaching everyone."[1]

Together Winter and Steffens edited the *Pacific Weekly,* published in San Francisco, also home to the *Western Worker,* which became the *People's Daily World*—Party organ for the western United States. Steffens served as an advisor to the California Labor School. Located at 675 Minna Street in San Francisco, it billed itself as the only school in the city that based its curriculum on the theory of Marxism–Leninism and was guided by the leadership of the Communist Party of the United States of America and the Communist International.

With Steffens and Winter as chief residents in their swank vacation home, "The Getaway," the idyllic, isolated Carmel became a place of pilgrimage for the Leftist faithful, including California Communist gubernatorial candidate Sam Darcy, a former official of the Comintern. The irrepressible journalist Anna Louise Strong, a huge, loquacious woman, also came by, bringing the latest news directly from the Soviet Union. Neighbors included Albert Rhys Williams, a former Christian minister who became a zealot for Stalin after visiting the USSR and who was working on a kind of catechism that would give answers to common questions about the USSR, one of his five books about the new workers' state. Actor James Cagney, who had read Steffens's work, also rented a place nearby and often stopped by to chat. While in Carmel, Winter received money from other, unnamed, Hollywood actors who told her to dispose of it as she saw fit. She and Sam Darcy spent it on political leaflets.

Steffens and Winter agreed on basic principles but sometimes quarreled over tactics. She believed, for instance, that he lacked the wherewithal for the revolutionary task at hand. "Stef, Communists have to be sons of Bs because the capitalist system is a son of a B," she wrote to him. "The nature of the beast is coming out more and more." In another letter she challenged him: "You say you want communism in the USA. But how is it to come unless there's a fight for it? And who is to do the fighting? You know that there's a vast difference between putting yourself at odds with society and fighting for it. You never mention class struggle, you never say in your lectures, 'If it's communism we want, we must help the workers and farmers get it. . . .' Intellectuals alone won't make a revolution, you know that."[2] Befitting her orthodoxy, Winter looked to the workers to make the difference.

Months before the strike began, the Communist journal *New Masses* asked Winter to cover the 1934 San Francisco waterfront strike, a violent walkout that lasted from early May until August and involved 12,000 longshoremen from Seattle to San Diego. The strike was a project of Harry Bridges, the wiry, hawkfaced leader of the Longshoremen's Union and, as Soviet archives reveal, a secret member of the Communist Party. Bridges, who fought and successfully resisted efforts to deport him, shared not only Winter's Australian origins but also her admiration for the Soviet Union. He championed the workers' state and was in constant communication with Soviet labor leaders. For Bridges's rivals in the labor movement his involvement with the Soviets was troubling because Soviet labor unions, unlike American ones, did not exist to negotiate wages and working conditions with management, but rather to implement whatever policies the Communist leadership deemed correct. With help from the Teamsters, Bridges marshaled enough muscle to virtually shut down San Francisco and win key concessions. The victory boosted Party prestige in the labor movement and inspired organizers in central and southern California.

As Ella Winter later noted in her biography, the San Francisco industrialists believed that the money for the maritime strike came from Moscow, that the Soviet Consul brought it to Carmel, and that Lincoln Steffens gave it to Harry Bridges. According to someone who infiltrated Winter and Steffens's circle of friends, that is a close account of what actually happened. And the money did not flow only to the waterfront strikers.

Charles Bakcsy had been a detective for activist Bill Haywood of the left-wing Wobblies, the Industrial Workers of the World (IWW), in 1918, and after breaking with the Left worked for the Department of Justice as an investigator. A former boxer and sailor, the Hungarian-born Bakcsy was retained by maritime interests to conduct an undercover investigation on the San Francisco waterfront. A member of the Marine Workers Industrial Union told him to see Michael Galkovich, the Soviet consul, explaining that a woman in Carmel named Ella Winter would be able to provide financing.

Calling himself Charles Sharkey, a name he had used as a boxer, Bakcsy moved to Carmel and rented a home on Scenic Drive, one block away from the Winter–Steffens "Getaway." Bakcsy invited his neighbors to picnics on the beach and quickly struck up a friendship with Winter and Steffens, both of whom were fascinated with this new, colorful character and his sea stories about running booze during Prohibition. Bakcsy also scored points by posing as a political radical who, unlike Steffens, was willing to bring in the revolution by any means necessary. He even brought a copy of Winter's *Red Virtue* for the author to autograph. She welcomed the comrade to the fold and gave him an iron hammer and sickle made by a blacksmith with a second career as a Communist organizer.

Winter urged Bakcsy, whose house commanded a splendid view of the ocean, to set up an oceanfront light for signaling incoming ships about labor developments on the waterfront. Bakcsy, who spoke fluent Russian, went along with the scheme and before long was hosting groups of Communist functionaries in his own home. Unknown to them, he was taping the conversations.

A regular member of Winter's circle was Michael Aisenstein, a Soviet commissar for heavy industry with the Amtorg corporation, the official Soviet trading firm and a cover for Soviet intelligence. One of those dealing with Amtorg at the time was an American sea captain named Warwick Tompkins, who would later play a role in the Party's above-the-line organizing. Bakcsy learned that Aisenstein did indeed give money to Winter, which she passed on to California Communists to fund propaganda activities and labor organizing. Winter described Bakcsy as a "real live spy" and wrote that the Carmel woman he had used as his secretary sought her out to tell her that Bakcsy had been hired to find a "nest of dangerous gangsters" and had threatened to kill Winter.

In his own version of the story, Bakcsy became the hunted when Party functionaries learned they were being spied upon. The alarmed Winter sent word to the Party's Southern District Disciplinary Committee, who sent enforcers Theodore Geberder and August R. Stephens to deal with the undercover man. A contact inside the San Francisco Party tipped him off and he escaped. That proved the end of his dealings in Carmel, but while there he had learned that the money Soviet officials passed on to Winter also flowed to Hollywood.[3]

The name of another member of the Carmel group would show up in the Hollywood records of the International Alliance of Theatrical Stage Employees (IA), the major show-business union. Jeff Kibre came from a family of set decorators and graduated from UCLA in 1931. In another time he might have become a student activist or joined a motorcycle gang, but Kibre, a "social descender" who affected working-class dress, found a conduit for his rebellion in the Communist Party. Fred Rinaldo, a screenwriter and former Party member, recalled Kibre as the "official Communist" in the Hollywood trade union movement. Though younger than many of the rank and file, the leather-jacketed Kibre would show up out of nowhere, take a leadership position, act as a kind of designated troubleshooter, and then suddenly disappear.[4]

Jeff Kibre boasted an analytical mind and some literary flair. On October 7, 1937, he wrote to Harry Bridges, who had engineered the San Francisco waterfront strike in 1934:

> Throughout the country Hollywood is a magic word. It represents something apart from everyday, humdrum life; it is a world of glamour, of shadows that dance across the screen, of rose-colored romance. So unreal is the picture of Hollywood that comes to the average person's mind that few understand what makes the wheels go around; that within this world of fantasy are thousands of workers, workers of all kinds, who sweat as thousands of workers sweat, and who fight the same bitter struggles as thousands of workers to secure a decent livelihood.
>
> It is with that picture of Hollywood—the men and women who produce the glamour—that we are concerned. It is true that some are paid fabulous salaries, but for the vast majority, numbering some 35,000, of this fourth largest industry, yearly wages are low, working conditions are of the employer's own choosing, and a general atmosphere of company unionism prevails. Millions have gone to producers, to stars, but hardly a decent living to those who make the "hits," the "Garbos," the "Goldwyns," possible. . . .

Kibre knew of what he wrote. By February 1938, nearly 40 percent of studio employees were unemployed; MGM had shut down for six weeks and Paramount had laid off 1,400 workers. Kibre organized a studio unemployment conference, through which he hoped to implement a strategy that he outlined in an April 23, 1938, report to the Congress of Industrial Organizations (CIO). Here he cited "the concrete possibilities of a movement for unity within the present craft set-up." This would be a "broad anti-IA movement, representing a majority of workers in the industry." More specifically:

Correct handling of possibilities, issues, etc., may lead to the formation of a Federation in the immediate future. This will undoubtedly take the form of an independent organization—since it will involve a break with the present internationals. . . .

Despite the fact it is a fairly compact industry, operating under the direct control of Wall Street monopoly capital, Hollywood probably has the greatest Labor ramifications of any major industry in the country. There are more categories of Labor and greater variations of income than in any other single industry. . . .

Establishment of an Industrial Union in Hollywood will have repercussions far beyond the industry itself. It will open up the virtually untouched field of the amusement industry as a whole—approximating close to 300,000 workers. . . . And with Hollywood and its prestige linked to the harbor and the Longshoremen, a tremendous spurt would be given the organizing movement as a whole.

Kibre's strategy was not only bold but sound. A single major labor federation would be much easier to control than dozens of individual groups. And he was right that conditions were indeed favorable. Unemployment and wage cuts had fueled long-smoldering discontent with the studios, whose bosses lived in the wildest extravagance. The IA had also been left vulnerable by a racketeering problem and raids on other unions. And key allies were also emerging.

Kibre alluded to a meeting of the screenwriters that was "promoted by us," that is, Party labor forces, which according to Kibre organized some of the talent guilds. "A related movement for unity was immediately initiated in the Guilds," he wrote. "Through the Screen Cartoonists Guild, an independent industrial Guild organized by us, a movement for a conference of the Guilds was pushed."

Outside of the guilds, a confluence of forces also favored the plan. After the California gubernatorial elections that fall, Kibre wrote to Louis Goldblatt, then secretary of the CIO's state branch, and a close associate of Harry Bridges: "The political campaign has clearly demonstrated the strategic importance of Hollywood. Hardly anyone will question the fact that Hollywood was a dominant factor in the campaign. [Newly elected California governor Cuthbert] Olson, for example, credits the Motion Picture Democratic Committee with being the most potent force in the entire campaign. . . . Developments in Hollywood can have decisive influence on the trade union situation in California—and nationally."

Kibre conceded that "at no time during the present stage have we fooled ourselves into thinking we could establish a CIO Union overnight." His own career proved the point. He had first surfaced in Hollywood in 1937 as a member of International Alliance (IA) Local 37, where he organized a group called "IA Progressives," of which he was chairman. He chose as his lieutenant a Party zealot named Irving Hentschel.

The "Progressives" had decided to present a resolution for local autonomy to the 1937 IA convention in Cleveland. Kibre remained behind the scenes and charged Hentschel with the task. However, the IA constitution stipulated that only duly constituted unions, not ad hoc independent bodies, could present resolutions. The union quickly shot down the Progressives' resolution, embarrassing Hentschel and provoking the wrath of high Communist officials in New York.

Roy Hudson, a former seaman, was the Comintern's choice to supervise trade-union work. Hudson, based in New York, wrote to his California counterpart that, considering the Communists' strength in the IA, presenting such a resolution was "nothing short of sheer stupidity and must certainly reflect a lack of guidance upon the part of the Party to this work."[5] In the wake of this failure, Kibre took pains to network with Party officials and defend his comrade.

"Well, one thing about reds, they seldom write except on business," he wrote to Bob Reed, a Party cultural official in New York, urging Reed to discuss the matter of IA action with Jack Stachel, another Party official in New York. Kibre said he had already taken the Cleveland incident up with Paul Kline, secretary of the Party in Los Angeles County, but Kline told Kibre that to rectify the situation a "personal appeal by you or V. J. rather than communication through official channels, would get quicker results."

"V. J." was a reference to V. J. Jerome, the Communist Party cultural official who helped Bertolt Brecht stage his plays. Kibre also cited New York IA man Morris Iushewitz as "one of our people." It eventually fell to Kibre to defend Hentschel to Walter Lambert, the Communist Party's trade-union director.

"We affirm our confidence in comrade Irv Hentschel," Kibre wrote on July 12, 1938, "who is a party member of three years standing in the industry; and further state that Comrade Hentschel, despite numerous mistakes, attempted to the best of his ability to carry out the instructions of the local party organization."

On July 5, 1939, the Progressives filed a petition with the National Labor Relations Board (NLRB) claiming that the IA was a tool of the studio executives. In a bold step, they demanded the restitution of all union dues paid to the IA since 1936, a move that failed despite vigorous support. The Progressives withdrew from the IA and founded a new organization, the United Studio Technicians Guild (USTG), which was heavily funded, by their own admission, by the CIO. A confident Jeff Kibre called for an election to decide whether the IA or the new USTG would represent the workers.

One of Kibre's key allies turned out to be William Pomerance, one of the many Communists in the NLRB and, as it happened, the field organizer who supervised the 1939 USTG vote.[6] Pomerance subsequently left the NLRB and became the director of the Screen Cartoonists Guild which, as Kibre noted, the Party had organized. When he left that post to become secretary of the Screen Writers Guild, another rather astonishing move, his place at the Guild was taken by another former government employee, Maurice Howard.

In addition, a man named Milton Gotlieb moved directly from the War Labor Board in San Francisco to an important office in the Screen Publicists Guild. All these moves ran contrary to the usual practice. Gotlieb had no background for the job and had not worked his way up through the ranks, as was customary.

The IA at first resisted Kibre's call for an election but then called for a strike in response. Then IA union officials changed their minds and decided to participate—a risky strategy, considering the conditions. Alex Saunders, the USTG's duly elected recording secretary, swore to the NLRB that the petition filed by the Progressives on July 5, 1939, was not the product of the rank and file but had been drafted by Harry Bridges, Jeff Kibre, and their attorney, Charles Katz. It was this trio, he said, that really ran the Guild, with Bridges taking the primary role. And they had drafted the petition when the Guild had fewer than twenty-five members.[7]

The IA also caught a break when, shortly before the elections, copies of documents that had been confiscated from Jeff Kibre's apartment surfaced. Reports of the documents, which revealed Party labor strategy, were published in the *Los Angeles Citizen*, the organ of the American Federation of Labor's (AFL) central council in Los Angeles. Though he had many opportunities to do so, Kibre himself never challenged the authenticity of the documents. A sworn affidavit by ex-Communist Ezra Chase identified Kibre as a Communist, as did Lew Blix, the business agent of IA Local 37. Blix had seen Kibre's Party card, on which he used the alias Barry Wood.

The IA thumped the upstart USTG by a vote of 4,460 to 1,967, more than a 2-to-1 margin. Kibre made another attempt to organize studio labor under the cover of an organization called the Motion Picture Technicians Committee, but this failed, and he soon vanished from Hollywood.

THE PLAN JEFF KIBRE HAD SET IN MOTION continued under the more aggressive leadership of Herbert K. Sorrell, then business agent of AFL Painters' Local 644 and a member of Kibre's inner circle.

Herb Sorrell was born in Deepwater, Missouri, in 1897 and claimed that his ancestors had arrived on the Mayflower. His father had been a union official who once called a strike only to have management bring in black workers to break it up. The incident probably gave young Sorrell a dislike for blacks; he told a government committee that he once tried to join the Ku Klux Klan but was rejected because he had a friend who was Catholic and "they claimed they had some allegiance to the Pope or something, who was a foreigner."[8]

Sorrell's education came in the school of hard knocks: "I worked in a factory among a group of Portuguese people, some of whom were very nice and some of whom were morons," he once testified.[9] Sorrell started a painting business of his own, but after relocating to Los Angeles during the 1920s, he became curious about the movies. When he found out the films required an army of craftsmen, he sold his painting company and went to work in the studios himself. When the battles of unionization began to escalate, Sorrell found himself on the front lines.

On sunny days, the studios would set up locations on Hollywood Boulevard and Vine Street, where they would take establishing shots of building exteriors. Sorrell considered it his duty to disrupt these crews, appearing as a union organizer and demanding to see their union cards. If they failed to produce one, Sorrell said, "we usually ended by smashing the camera."[10]

Sorrell showed similar flair during a 1937 strike at Paramount, when he got arrested, but not before helping to send nineteen ambulance loads to the hospital, some coming from an IA hiring hall he and his men gleefully smashed up.[11] The strike came up later that year in Sorrell's dealings with Walt Disney, the avuncular cartoon mogul whose $3 million studio in Burbank boasted its own streets, power, and telephone systems, along with sun decks, gymnasium, and volleyball courts. Disney released *Snow White and the Seven Dwarfs* that year, which grossed $8 million, a staggering amount for the time and a foretaste of greater revenues and power to come.

One of Disney's artists told the mogul that Herb Sorrell was trying to take them over. Disney replied that that was the artists' concern, not his. As the employer, Disney had the right to demand an election to prove whether or not Sorrell had the majority, and after further persuasion by his artists, he did call for one. Herb Sorrell was not amused.

The union boss laughed at Disney, saying he would use the National Relations Labor Board as it suited his purposes. If things didn't go his way, Sorrell said, he had the tools of the trade sharpened; he told Disney he wouldn't be able to stand the pressure of a strike. Disney stuck to his guns and said he couldn't continue working with Sorrell's people if he felt he had sold them out, which brought more ridicule from Sorrell.

"I will smear you and I will make a dust bowl out of your plant," Sorrell told Disney. And it was Sorrell who brought up the issue of Communism: "You think I am a Communist, don't you?" Disney said all he knew was what he had heard. "Well, I used their money to finance my strike of 1937," Sorrell bragged.[12]

There is evidence that Herb Sorrell joined the Communist Party in 1936 or 1937 but may later have made a special arrangement to withdraw from formal membership while still serving Party purposes. The Party, in turn, may have agreed to allow him a certain latitude within the unions he controlled. Except for a brief period in 1945, Sorrell and the coalition of unions he led adhered to every shift of the Communist Party line. The case for his Party collaboration was strong, but those who accused him of Communist affiliation had problems of their own.

George E. Browne became president of IA in 1934, after the 1933 IA strike against the studios. He appointed as his Hollywood representative Willie Bioff, a Chicago hoodlum described by *True Detective* magazine as a "bull necked, blue-jowled spawn of

Chicago's underworld."[13] With his broad-brimmed hat, rimless glasses, and ever-present cigarette, Bioff would have needed no wardrobe change to line up next to James Cagney or Edward G. Robinson in a gangster movie. Like some of the studio moguls, he had worked his way up from humble beginnings. He had been brought from Russia at the age of five and worked as a newsboy before discovering that there was more money in shaking down theater owners for money, a racket he easily and eagerly transported to the dream factories.

During his stint in the studios from 1936 to 1940, Bioff won some key wage increases for his workers but backed off from negotiating others, instead extorting bribes of $100,000 from studio bosses, using the ever-present threat of labor trouble for leverage. Bioff also threatened to pull the union cards of his own members if they refused to pay a 2 percent assessment that he pocketed. This created huge resentment against Bioff in particular and the IA in general, and the Communists milked the racketeering problem to full advantage.

Martin Berkeley, a New York playwright and Communist Party member, had been brought to Hollywood by Columbia Studios after two of his works were staged on Broadway. To help undermine the IA, the leaders of the Hollywood Party named Berkeley editor of *Studio Voice*, a throwaway paper published openly in the name of the Communist Party. Party members in the IA funneled information to Berkeley, whose work helped the Party recruit new members. Berkeley also crusaded against George E. Browne and Willie Bioff.

The Communist Party and its allies readily enlisted the help of the government in their fight against labor gangsterism, pushing for an investigation of Browne and Bioff by the California Assembly. Their testimony paved the way for indictments of the racketeers in 1941 on conspiracy and extortion charges. Bioff saw himself as a victim, blaming Hollywood elitists he claimed were attacking him because he was fighting for the common man. From that time on, accusations of Communism, never popular in liberal Hollywood, were immediately linked to the corrupt pair who made the first charges.

Herb Sorrell postured as a foe of union corruption in general and of Willie Bioff in particular, but though he was not himself a racketeer, Sorrell paid tribute to the gangster when it suited him. On the signing of a 1937 agreement he conceded, "It is only through the aid of Mr. Bioff and his IA international representative that we were able to reach an agreement with the producers. I intend to thank him personally and in [sic] behalf of each member for getting our increase."[14] Screen Actors Guild president Robert Montgomery, on the other hand, not only refused to have anything to do with Browne and Bioff but spent $5,000 of the Guild's money to hire detectives to investigate them.[15] The SAG detectives found an old pandering charge that helped authorities indict Bioff for tax evasion.[16]

Herb Sorrell packed some heft and, dressed in rumpled clothes and frequently unshaven, looked as though he had just roughed someone up, or was about to. But although he liked to talk tough and could back it up, Sorrell was no mere thug. He succeeded in negotiating the first contract between the studios and a local union, the very move Jeff Kibre and Irving Hentschel had failed to make. More important, he had founded the multi-union federation that Kibre believed necessary if the Party was to make inroads in the studios.

The Conference of Studio Unions (CSU), which first emerged on October 2, 1941, was founded by Herb Sorrell; William Pomerance, previously one of the Communists on the National Labor Relations Board; and Russell McKnight, the business agent of IA Local 683. Among the CSU's first members were the Screen Cartoonists, which had been organized by the Party, the Screen Office Employees Guild, Film Technicians Local 683, Local 1185 of the Machinists, and Sorrell's Painters' Union. The original bodies were neither big nor powerful, and the membership fluctuated.

The CSU's slogan was "Autonomy and Democracy," though its constitution mandated that if one union went on strike, all the members of all the unions were duty-bound to respect the picket line. Sorrell ran the CSU like a generalissimo. His expansionist policy defied all labor logic by organizing unrelated groups under his own Painters' Union. When asked how he could include the studio publicists in a painters union, he would explain that they "paint word pictures."[17]

Later, at its height in the 1940s, the CSU embraced twelve unions and represented more than 10,000 workers. By contrast, at that time the IA represented some 60,000 workers nationally and about 17,000 in the studios. This disparity allowed the CSU to strike a David-versus-Goliath pose and use the propaganda advantage that went with it.

By the time of the CSU's founding in 1941, Lincoln Steffens had died and Ella Winter had married Donald Ogden Stewart, one of the highest-paid screenwriters of the day, known for throwing wild parties at his Bel Air mansion, where he often drank until he passed out. When Stewart accepted the Oscar for *The Philadelphia Story* he stammered: "I envy the boys who get the technical awards. They don't have to get nervously drunk before. There has been so much niceness here tonight, that I am happy to say that I am entirely—and solely—responsible for the success of *The Philadelphia Story*."[18]

As "Don's new wife," Winter wrote, she was invited to dinner parties with the Sam Goldwyns, Clark Gable and Carole Lombard, the David Selznicks, the Lewis Milestones, and other luminaries. While some thought her dangerous, others regarded Winter as a welcome curiosity, a change from the usual crowd and its film-industry banter.

"Please explain Marxism to me," Sam Goldwyn asked her during a dinner.

"Oh, not over this lovely steak," Winter responded.[19]

Donald Ogden Stewart was also a Communist Party member and a key player in many front groups. He was president of the League of American Writers, the group that had enlisted Franklin Delano Roosevelt in the 1930s. Winter's role as an apologist and courier for the Soviets suggested the marriage might have been a political arrangement. Whatever the basis for their marriage, it provided a route for Don's new wife to come to know what she called "the movement" in the Hollywood talent guilds. The Communist Party arrived in those quarters by a different route.

"The Communist Theatre Is Starting"

THE HEADQUARTERS OF THE COMMUNIST PARTY of the United States was in New York City, home to the largest American Party branch and a city whose cultural scene provided fertile ground for Party activists who were working in concert with those boring from within the New Deal, a generous funder of cultural projects. With help from the Federal Theatre Project, a government-funded program, Party organizers were able to dominate the radical theater stage in New York.

The guardian of Party cultural doctrine in America was Victor Jeremy (V. J.) Jerome. Born Isaac Romain in Poland in 1896 and naturalized in 1928, Jerome was a former bookkeeper who, according to some of his comrades, had once intended to be a rabbi. He studied in England and at New York University before teaching at Erasmus High School in New York and working as a private tutor. Short, chubby, and bald, with horn-rimmed glasses, the soft-spoken Jerome came across as a professor or perhaps the editor of an arts magazine. Bertolt Brecht, the Communist playwright whose plays he helped stage, ridiculed Jerome as an owl without wisdom, and Elizabeth Bentley, who ran a spy ring for the Soviets, compared his face to a sleepy fish. But Jerome carried a big stick, and his prodigious arrogance allowed few doubts about his infallibility, something that bothered even the faithful.

For Jerome and others on the Party's National Agitation and Propaganda Commission, the didactic plays they staged were not merely a matter of tactics but a superior artistic product. "Agitprop drama was actually better drama," Jerome explained, "because Marxists better understood the forces that shaped human beings, and could therefore write better plays."[1]

According to this vision, the dramatic medium was a weapon, and plays were to teach a lesson, sending the audience home with sweeping revolutionary insight. Current society was corrupt, in this view, and beyond redemption by peaceful change. Only the working class was to be trusted, and the USSR, with all its faults, was to be defended. Writing outside of these parameters was scorned as bourgeois art-for-art's-sake decadence.

Many writers, perhaps those not of the first rank, welcomed the notion that by writing under Marxist cultural doctrine they were producing a superior product. Whatever the quality of dramaturgy, plays written from this vision found an eager audience during the 1930s.

> "Working class unite and fight! Tear down the slaughter-house of our lives."
> The actor hoists a clenched fist.
> "Don't wait for Lefty, he might never come."

Elia Kazan cited those lines from Clifford Odets's *Waiting for Lefty* to explain how the Communists influenced others—by speaking up for the universal human desire for meaning, dignity, and security. Kazan had been born in Constantinople in 1909 to the Kazanjioglou family of Anatolian Greeks. The family came to America when he was four, but Elia, or "Gadg" as he came to be called because of his fondness for gadgets, never lost his sense of being an outsider. When his book *America America* appeared, black novelist James Baldwin wrote on the dust jacket, "Gadg, baby, you're a nigger too."

The immigrant youth with the piercing eyes and thick nest of black hair went to Williams College and moved on to the drama school at Yale. There he met a talented young writer named Albert Maltz, a Columbia University graduate, who wrote to him that "we may be able to help with the Communist theatre which is starting."[2] Other colleagues included director Joe Losey and actors John Garfield and Phil Loeb. Like others who would make the move to Hollywood, Kazan learned his craft in a milieu dominated by the Communist Party, which praised his direction of *The Young Go First*. When Kazan joined the Party, he did so for spiritual reasons.

"My hostility was no longer an alienation," he explained. "The Party had justified it, taught me that it was correct, even reasonable. I could be proud of it; it made me the comrade of angry millions all over the earth. I'd reacted correctly to my upbringing, to my social position, to the society around me, to the state of the world. I was a member of what was sure to be the victorious army of the future."

The effect of it all, he said, "made me into another person. I felt reborn, or born for the first time. The days of pain were over. I was an honored leader of the only good class, the working class, and the only real theatre, the Group."[3]

While actors and directors of the Left earned salaries on Broadway, they did their "real" work in what Kazan called "ideologically cemented collectives"—the Theatre Collective, the Theatre Union, and the Theatre of Action, all modeled on the Russian theater of the time that had influenced New York directors such as Herb Biberman. Elia Kazan took what he learned from esteemed Soviet directors such as Vsevolod Meyerhold and used it in classes he taught at the New Theatre League, a Communist-front organization. Kazan's wife, Molly, became associate editor of *New The-*

atre, a Communist-front magazine, and taught playwriting at the Theatre Union.

In those days Party affiliation, not talent, played the major role in determining who worked and who did not. Federal Theatre director Adolph Hecht, who went on to work for the Goldstone Agency in Hollywood, explained that Party affiliation was a kind of political casting couch. If the choice came down to dismissing a Communist or non-Communist, he was expected to get rid of the non-Communist, regardless of talent.[4]

One of those uneasy with the art-is-a-weapon concept was Elia Kazan's friend and comrade Albert Maltz, a serious literary man whose "The Happiest Man on Earth" won an O. Henry award as the best short story of 1938. The Party was convinced that greater achievements lay ahead for all its writers.

Kazan's colleague Clifford Odets became the prevailing radical playwright of the time, such a lofty status that the Party took away his membership card and blotted his name from Party records, reasoning that if repression came down, their man would be safe and could write on. According to Kazan, playwright Lillian Hellman and other "glamour intellectuals" enjoyed the same membership-at-large status.

Another mainstay of the radical theater was John Howard Lawson, born in 1893, an idealistic New York writer capable of demonstrating himself a man of action. In the waning days of World War I he had manned the ambulances with such luminaries as Ernest Hemingway and John Dos Passos. Lawson was twenty-four at the time of the Russian Revolution, the event that defined and inspired his life. He organized the John Reed Club in New York, named after the American author of *Ten Days That Shook the World* and a colleague of Lincoln Steffens.

A forceful, dogmatic intellectual, with an angular face to match, Lawson was known as an "extremely zealous Communist"[5] and was on record as saying that, "As for myself, I do not hesitate to say that it is my aim to present the Communist position, and to do so in the most specific manner."[6] Lawson's play *Processional* featured children in overalls and masks ranting about the "Monster of Capitalism" and screaming lines such as "Dynamo! Dynamo!" and "Kill Henry Ford!"[7] Such a slugfest of fevered rhetoric became the pattern on the radical stage.

Even those who styled themselves as artists in uniform sometimes found it difficult to work within the strictures of both the Party doctrine and the Party line, which could change in an instant. New York mayor Fiorello La Guardia, for example, had been praised by the theater before the Party position, handed down by bosses at the Twelfth Street headquarters, changed to one of ridicule. The Party also took issue with Lawson, one of its key writers, over his choice of a hero in *Gentle Woman*. Lawson was required to perform a ritual known as "crawling to the feet" of V. J. Jerome, a task that the duly chastened Lawson performed. Also as part of his penance, the Party required him to criticize others when they crossed the line, and this became Lawson's official job description. The enforcer position enabled the man of ideas to double as a man of action. There was never a shortage of work for him.

Everything that Party writers produced had to be vetted by Party officials. Rarely if ever did a first draft of a play, novel, or article run as the author had first composed it. With art as a weapon, the Party wanted to get the most bang for the buck. It was all part of the collective process.

Budd Schulberg, the writer and mogul's son who visited the USSR during the 1930s, married Virginia Ray, also known as "Jigee," a breathtakingly beautiful woman of left-wing leanings, whose sister, Anne Ray, would become a Party member. The Party gave Schulberg a list of changes for his show-business novel *What Makes Sammy Run?* Schulberg did not appreciate the suggestions, ignored them, and soon found himself attacked by Lawson and other Party leaders. One of those sympathizing with Schulberg was Kazan's friend Albert Maltz, who complained that the Party controlled too tightly the writing of its members. Writers are by nature an independent, free-spirited lot, a trend that bothered the Party so much they brought in an enforcer from Detroit to lay down the law when Kazan, one of the Party's rising stars, refused to crawl, declining suggestions that had been made to him.

"The Man from Detroit [the enforcer] had been sent to stop the most dangerous thing the Party had to cope with: people thinking for themselves," Kazan wrote. "Comrades took the floor and competed as to who could say 'Me too' best. They all did a grand job. The fact was that there was no appeal from the verdict of the Man from Detroit, so no discussion was necessary. I understood the police state from him."[8] Kazan refused to participate in the ritual of submission laid down for him. Those refusing to follow the Party script found themselves targeted for retaliation. In the USSR they simply would have disappeared without a trace, but this was not yet an option for the American Party, which nevertheless did not fail to take action against dissenters.

Kazan had played the lead in Clifford Odets's *Golden Boy* with Frances Farmer, "the blonde that you dream about," who had also been cultivated by the Communist Party. Farmer had begun her show-business career as a singing waitress at Mount Rainier National Park, in Washington State. The Communist Party was strong in the Pacific Northwest, and one of its papers, *The Voice of Action,* sponsored a talent contest and rigged it so Farmer would win.

The prize won by Frances Farmer was a trip to the Soviet Union. In return for the publicity she got for winning, Farmer was supposed to praise the USSR upon her return to America. But unlike the eager pilgrims Ella Winter, Lincoln Steffens, and others, the outspoken actress was disappointed in what she saw and described the USSR as "a land crawling and half-dead."[9] She refused other demands to support Party causes and was repaid by an ensuing campaign of harassment from the Party.

BESIDES ELIA KAZAN, other transplants from New York to California included James Cagney, actor Melvyn Douglas, known to most for his role in *Being There,* and dancer Gene Kelly. Humphrey Bogart appeared in *Cradle Snatchers* and *Saturday's Children* on the New York stage before translating his gift to Hollywood films, scoring a hit as gangster Duke Mantee in the 1936 *The Petrified Forest.* But it would be in Hollywood, not New York, where these and other actors would encounter the Communist Party, then making the same stage-to-screen transition.

When the Federal Theatre came under attack from the House Committee on Un-American Activities, James Cagney, Al Jolson, Dick Powell, Joan Blondell, Henry Fonda, John Barrymore, Gale Sondergaard, and other stars—most unaware of Party involvement—defended the program as a cultural necessity in a radio broadcast.[10] But by 1936 the Group Theatre was dying, and Hollywood's talking pictures had taken over from the stage as the main voice of popular culture. The Party had enjoyed virtual domination of the radical theater scene in New York, and that control became the model for what they sought in Hollywood, when V. J. Jerome, John Howard Lawson, Albert Maltz, and many others headed west.

5

"The Industrious Communist Tail Wagged the Lazy Liberal Dog"

BY THE MID-1930S, Los Angeles already boasted one of the nation's stronger Communist Party organizations, with as many as several thousand members in branches that included the harbor, San Padre, Echo Park, Boyle Heights, Watts, and other areas, with sectors or "cells." Members from all these cells had gained key positions in both unions and professional groups. V. J. Jerome, the Party's cultural commissar, and his fellow organizers knew the usual Party structure but opted to set up something different in Hollywood.

Jerome's designated organizer could boast no insider connections. Stanley Lawrence, a tall, tousle-headed former cab driver with Coke-bottle glasses, bragged about having worked in the Party underground in Europe. Lawrence considered that this experience qualified him for the task and so did Party leadership. Sometime in 1935, Lawrence, who held credentials from Party headquarters in New York, appeared on the Hollywood scene. He would achieve spectacular successes—gaining the Party more than 300 new members in nine months.

Lawrence's early Hollywood contacts included Harold Ashe, who had joined the Party in 1933, written for the *Western Worker,* and set up a secret Party cell that included Jeff Kibre. The circle also included screenwriter John Bright, who had been in Hollywood since 1929 and went on to write such films as *Girl of the Ozarks* and *Glamour for Sale,* and Samuel Ornitz, author of *Haunch, Paunch, and Jowl* and writer for MGM in 1929. Screenwriters became the mainstay of the Communists' organizing in the talent guilds, and Ornitz was likely the first Party scenarist to ply his trade in Hollywood.

Lawrence told his Hollywood contacts that the Party had decided to organize a Hollywood studio section that would be controlled exclusively by Party headquarters in New York City and would not be answerable to local or state officials. No other branch enjoyed such a special plan, a confirmation that the studio offensive held the highest priority. Although highly secretive and targeting above-the-line talent, the new studio section would have to follow the same rules as other Party groups on the cultural front and would be answerable to New York. Practically speaking, answerable to New York meant answerable to V. J. Jerome.

Jerome's arrogance and interminable rhetoric bothered some in the studio section, who considered themselves an independent lot. Screenwriter John Bright, for example, asked Jerome what would happen if a member disagreed with an official decision of the Party. "When the Party makes a decision, it becomes your opinion," Jerome responded.[1] By virtue of his sheer staying power, Jerome was usually able to prevail.

The Communist Party shared the view of one of its more talented members, Michael Wilson, an honors graduate in philosophy from Berkeley who went on to study English and American history. Wilson, a writer of Hopalong Cassidy movies and known for constantly curling his locks of prematurely gray hair with his forefinger, referred to Hollywood as "that big money tit."[2]

Money ranked high on the list of Party objects in the industry, highest of all in the view of some. Like the corrupt union bosses Browne and Bioff during the late 1930s, the Party hoped to shake down the studios for large amounts without attracting attention or alienating those they hoped to shake down. This was not always an easy task.

On one occasion, in the presence of studio comrades, Stanley Lawrence quipped that the Hollywood crowd was only so many "fat cows to be milked."[3] That prompted a rebuke from Jerome, who also scorned the big-money crowd, charging that "their only revolution is their bank account."[4] That barb reflected the contempt in which Party organizers, who thought of themselves as proletarians, held those in the upper-income brackets they had come to organize and fleece. According to former *Daily Worker* scribe Howard Rushmore, who had been disciplined by the Party for giving too favorable a review to *Gone with the Wind*, the general belief among the Party faithful was that 99 percent of movie people were "political morons."[5] Even so, the studio flock knew what they disliked, and that played into Party hands.

By the mid-1930s, a cracked Austrian and his National Socialist Party, backed by brownshirt thuggery, had come to power in Germany. In mass rallies with *son et lumière,* Adolf Hitler blazed a vision of a thousand-year *Reich* based on a pure, master race. Filmmaker Leni Riefenstahl, a kind of court scenarist, showcased the proceedings in documentaries such as *Triumph of the Will.* Unlike the Communists, their revolutionary socialist rivals, the Nazis did not wrap their wrath in populist pieties. They flaunted their growing military might and demonized the opposition, particularly democrats, Slavs and Jews alike. From its beginning, the swastika cast a shadow over Hollywood, an industry largely founded by Jews and a ready refuge for European Jews fleeing from Hitler.

Even the most politically naive in Hollywood knew that German fascism posed a threat and had to be opposed. Many were eager to do their part, and the Communist Party seemed to be leading the way. From 1936, the Party called for an anti-Nazi alliance of

Britain, France, the United States, and the USSR, with Communist Party support for Franklin Delano Roosevelt's New Deal as part of the package.

Max Silver, organizational secretary of the Party's Los Angeles branch, approached Jerome with a scheme that involved working with the Hollywood unit on some anti-Nazi projects. Jerome vetoed the idea on the grounds that Hollywood was special, a center of culture dealing with highly specialized fields, which therefore required "special leadership."[6]

Jerome's choice for such special leadership was John Howard Lawson, who had already proved his Marxist–Leninist orthodoxy to both V. J. Jerome and Mike Gold, one of the Party's literary stars, penning proletarian novels such as *Jews Without Money*, and an enforcer on the literary scene in his own right. Gold had been Lawson's ideological Sherpa guide, and some credit Gold with leading Lawson into the Communist Party.

Besides his plays, Lawson had contributed to the scripts of such movies as *The Ship from Shanghai* and *Our Blushing Brides*. Though his literary and artistic flair did not match that of Albert Maltz or Elia Kazan, Lawson's professional position was ideal. He became the first president of the Screen Writers Guild, which had emerged from the wage-cut wars of 1933. Dominated by leftists and Party members, the Screen Writers Guild prevailed over the rival Screen Playwrights, a group that included long-standing writers of more conservative inclinations, such as Rupert Hughes and James McGuinness. The National Labor Relations Board named the Screen Writers Guild as the official union, but this did not end the conflict between the two groups.

When Jerome retreated back to New York, John Howard Lawson became the Hollywood Party's acting commissar, with his word settling all doctrinal and disciplinary arguments. "He was the grand Poo-Bah of the Communist movement," said Martin Berkeley, who said that Lawson "speaks with the voice of Stalin and the bells of the Kremlin."[7]

Screenwriter Paul Jarrico had joined the Young Communist League while a student at UCLA and later became a force in the Hollywood Party. Jarrico regarded Lawson as an infantile leftist and a sectarian, a view for which Lawson constantly provided evidence. When fellow writer Brooks Atkinson returned from Russia and wrote articles critical of the Soviet theater, Lawson attacked him has "having become corrupt and probably senile."[8]

Lawson's dogmatic, *ad hominem* style of argument became the rule, not the exception, in the Hollywood Party. F. Scott Fitzgerald, who collaborated with Budd Schulberg on the 1939 *Winter Carnival,* discovered firsthand that discussion with Hollywood Communists tended to be one-sided. "The important thing is that you should not argue with them," Fitzgerald wrote. "Whatever you say they have ways of twisting it into shapes which put you in some lower category of mankind, 'Fascist,' 'Liberal,' 'Trotskyist,' and disparage you both intellectually and personally in the process."[9]

But despite some opposition that was doubtless based partly on jealousy, Lawson enjoyed strong support among the studio section's leadership faction.

New York writer Lester Cole had worked in theater and also as a ditch-digger for Warner Brothers. Tall, gaunt, and as a young man already losing the battle against baldness, Cole first came to Hollywood in 1926 and moved there permanently in 1932. He started as a reader at MGM, where he worked with "a young, lively" woman of considerable dramatic talent named Lillian Hellman.[10] When Cole hit town, he stayed with his old friend Archie Leach (Cary Grant) and cowboy legend-to-be Randolph Scott in an eight-room flat in fashionable Westwood, where they had hired a Filipino "boy" (Cole's description) to do the chores. While some in the studio section of the Party found Marxist theory opaque, for Cole it proved a Damascus Road experience.

"Once I read the Communist Manifesto of 1848," he said, "nothing seemed strange or unfamiliar. It was as if I had been brought up on this way of thinking from childhood."[11] Though an intellectual brawler of aggressive temperament, Cole respected and obeyed Party oracles, describing John Howard Lawson as "always brilliant, with the keenest intellect"[12] and V. J. Jerome as a "soft-spoken, learned man."[13] The former ditch-digger came to be part of a Party leadership faction along with Lawson, Yale graduate and veteran of the New York stage Herb Biberman, and Richard Collins.

Educated at the Browning School in New York and the Lycée Janson de Sailly in Paris before moving on to Stanford, Richard Collins attended a meeting of the Young Communist League in New York and then met Budd Schulberg, still glowing from his pilgrimage to the Soviet Union. Collins's first wife, actress Dorothy Comingore, was also in the Party, and the writer himself became something of a minor Party whip. Under this leadership group, the new studio section prospered, dovetailing nicely with the class structure of Hollywood. Far from changing the system, the Communists brilliantly adapted to it.

Following what Party member Jean Butler called a "rigid caste system," the Party's high-salaried writers clustered in one group, and the low-salaried writers gathered in another.[14] The same was true for directors and actors, and the approach provided advantages. The isolation of the various groups aided secrecy, the Party's strategic weapon in the talent guilds. On the other hand, Hollywood's compartmentalized structure allowed the Party to act nearly exclusively as a liaison between the groups. Under normal circumstances, a $3,000-a-week writer might never meet a $500-a-week writer or someone who worked in the back lots. But that did happen in the Party's ever-expanding circles within circles.

At exclusive parties, Marxism–Leninism was discussed beside kidney-shaped swimming pools as white-jacketed butlers circulated with drinks. Movie stars, back-lot workers, and even members of state and national committees hosted guests such as Harry Bridges, the secret Communist and West Coast labor hero who in 1934 had engineered the San Francisco waterfront strike. According to former member Sydney Davidson, the attraction for Bridges was not Party politics but female company, and the longshoreman wound up cutting "a swath of broken hearts."[15] Within all Hollywood groups, conditions for recruiting were ideal, and the Party responded with its version of the Dale Carnegie approach for winning friends and influencing people.

As many an aspiring director, actor, or writer has learned, Hollywood is an isolated and lonely town, an insulated place where newcomers and outsiders tend to be ignored or even shunned. To the aspiring player, the film colony can seem surrounded by an unscalable wall. The Communists, said former Screen Writers Guild president Leonard Spigelgass, knew this and responded accordingly. They "wined them and dined them and gave them a social life. First thing you know, they had 'em."[16]

When screenwriter Stanley Roberts arrived in Hollywood in 1936, he found that the only people who seemed to be friendly were the Communists. Like many people in the studio section, he joined the Party not so much in a quest for a better world but out of a need to be part of a powerful, inside group. "The Communists were out there in full force, with names, with people of real prestige and position," Roberts said. "They shook your hand, and that was the beginning of it."[17]

When Marc Lawrence joined the Party, his fellow actor Lionel Stander told him that "you will make out more with the dames."[18] Ring Lardner Jr. even proposed the slogan "The Most Beautiful Girls in Hollywood Belong to the Communist Party."[19]

Besides enhancing one's social and romantic prospects, joining the Communist Party conferred a certain status. In an anti-intellectual town where the major industry was the enchanted toy shop of the studios, simply to be on the political Left or to be a Party member was equivalent to being intelligent or an intellectual. The slogan "It's Smart to Be a Red"[20] reflected that position. In a town of ever-changing trends, cliques, and status-seekers, the Party became the ultimate in-group. "When Stalinism was fashionable, movie people became Stalinists the way they later became witches and warlocks," observed the critic Pauline Kael.[21]

Communist Party haunts included Stanley Rose's Bookshop, Musso & Frank's restaurant next door, the Book of the Day shop, Lucye's, the CineGrille Bar, and the Trap. For those who were educated and genuinely intellectual, the Party met other needs.

"When I joined the Party, I was handed ready-made friends, a cause, a faith, and a viewpoint on all phenomena," said Richard Collins. "A one-shot solution to all the world's ills and inequities."[22] That proved a hard package to turn down during the 1930s, when Party membership also solved some touchy professional problems.

Serious writers of the time—Hemingway, Faulkner, James T. Farrell, and others—preferred to keep their distance from the studios, even though the financial rewards were great. Some writers on the Left, particularly those who had written proletarian novels or had plays produced on the New York stage, believed that they had sold out by going to Hollywood, and joining the Party provided a way to regain self-respect. As historian Arthur Schlesinger put it, the Hollywood writer believed he had sold out his art in favor of production-line hackwork and sold out his soul in exchange for the big bucks. Therefore, the writer believed that he could "buy indulgences by participating in the Communist movement, just as men in the Middle Ages bought remission of sin from wandering monks."[23]

For the cinema revolutionaries, wrote Eugene Lyons, Communism was "an intoxicated state of mind, a glow of inner virtue, and a sort of comradeship in super-charity,"[24] a way for the wealthy to posture as proletarian wage slaves. On the other hand, the Party's triumphalist mind-set, the notion that they automatically wrote better screenplays and belonged to the victorious army of the future, led some to use ideology as a substitute for talent or even effort. According to Louis Berg, longtime Hollywood journalist, Max Youngstein of Universal circulated a memo informing all personnel that being a Communist was no longer sufficient reason to be employed there, and that doing a bit of work would also be required.[25]

Former Communist screenwriter Roy Huggins says that there were a number of "awful writers" who wouldn't have worked without their politics. For this type of person, Huggins said, becoming a member of the Communist Party "was just another way of being Sammy Glick," the hero of Budd Schulberg's novel, *What Makes Sammy Run?*[26]

One of those Huggins may have had in mind was *Daily Worker* scribe Alvah Bessie, veteran of the Abraham Lincoln Brigade, a Communist Party militia sent to fight in Spain. Though the stars of Party hagiography, according to other accounts they inflicted as much damage on their Republican comrades as the forces of General Franco. As George Orwell noted in *Homage to Catalonia*, the first order of business for the Stalinists was the elimination of other rivals on the Left, particularly the anarcho-syndicalists of the POUM, the Partido Obrero de Unification Marxista, with whom Orwell fought. One of the victims was Hollywood Communist pioneer Stanley Lawrence, who shunned Hollywood and left to fight in Spain, where he was killed under suspicious circumstances in 1938.

If Alvah Bessie, an obedient Party man and *Daily Worker* scribe, knew how Lawrence had met his end, he gave no clue. He returned from Spain venerated by the Party but without solid means of support. Then he saw an ad in *Variety* that read: "Scribblers are so scarce in Hollywood these days—most have gone into the armed forces—that anyone who can write a declarative English sentence is being inked to long-term pacts." Bessie circled the item and wrote "me" next to it.[27] According to the *Daily Worker's* Howard Rushmore, the Party's cultural commission sent Bessie to Hollywood, where the Communists' insider network was sufficiently powerful to secure him a job immediately.

Curiously, on the train west, Bessie found himself riding with Communist Party boss Earl Browder, his choice for president in

1932. Browder told Bessie he enjoyed reading Bessie's articles in the *New Masses* and was pleased to see him heading for Hollywood, "to set it on fire." Bessie replied, "I don't know whether I'll set it on fire. I don't know anything about the medium, but they've given me a job."[28] He went on to cowrite *Northern Pursuit, The Very Thought of You,* and *Smart Woman,* long confined to the studio slag heap.

While readily pocketing fat checks, some actors in or close to the Party also felt secretly ashamed of their craft. "I specialized in shit," said actor Jeff Corey, a reference to such films as *My Friend Flicka* and *Petticoat Politics.*[29] Sterling Hayden, of *Dr. Strangelove* fame, recalled one scene in which he was "tripping about like a queer with a burr in his pants." Such antics made him feel "like a frigging clown,"[30] a marked change from his previous career.

Born in Montclair, New Jersey, in 1916, Sterling Hayden had dropped out of high school and gone to sea at age fifteen, earning his master's license by the time he was twenty-one. He received his introduction to left-wing politics from Captain Warwick Tompkins, a seaman who was always carrying a load of Communist Party pamphlets and dealt secretly with the Soviets' Amtorg trading company, a front for their stateside spying. Purely by chance, Hayden met a Boston correspondent who knew a movie producer and got him set up for a screen test. Hayden thought it went badly, but the Paramount producers liked what they saw. Acting could be taught but appearance and presence could not. Hayden had both.

The former sailor found himself billed as "the most beautiful man in the movies" and "the beautiful blonde Viking god." He had scarcely been in Hollywood two weeks when he landed a role in the 1940 *Virginia* and shortly thereafter *Bahama Passage.* Despite his quick success, Hayden said he felt lost in the acting profession and sought out Captain Tompkins, who had moved his base of operations to San Francisco. Tompkins and his self-described class warriors encouraged Hayden on his leftward political voyage. When World War II broke out, Hayden wanted in on the action and changed his name to John Hamilton in order to distance himself from Hollywood.

Hayden had sailed with the son of Colonel Bill "Wild Bill" Donovan, founder of the Office of Strategic Services (OSS), a forerunner of the CIA. The temporary refugee from Hollywood trained in guerrilla warfare and found himself assigned to Bari, Italy, supplying Tito's communist partisans and using a fishing boat to rescue downed Allied pilots. By the time of his discharge in 1945 he had risen to the rank of captain and earned a Silver Star. After the war, Tomkins proposed writing a book about Hayden as the example of how a typical nonpolitical American youth could develop into a class-struggle warrior. Hayden gave his approval and expressed interest in Party membership.

When Hayden asked Tompkins whom to contact, the captain recommended V. J. Jerome. Ever the man of action, Hayden picked up the phone and called Party headquarters in New York, introducing himself as Captain John Hamilton of the Marine Corps and asking to speak to the foreign editor of the *Daily Worker*. Such direct approaches to the Party were unusual, and Hayden reported a considerable span of silence before anyone replied. Several days later, patrons of the Golden Eagle Cafe on West Twelfth Street witnessed a preview of *The Odd Couple* when the Viking god and most beautiful man in the movies sat down for lunch with the squat, owlish V. J. Jerome.

Hayden stunned Jerome again by asking the Party pedant if he knew of any guerrilla movements where Hayden's military experience might be of service. Jerome remained wary, suspecting that the eager wannabe might be a government agent. Even during its heyday, the Communist Party of the United States carefully screened those seeking membership. This time the cultural commissar opted for caution. "The captain might as well have been a banker from Boothbay, Maine," Hayden later explained.[31] But the most beautiful man in the movies would find his way into Party ranks by a more conventional route.

Once Hayden resumed his screen career, his political mentor put him in touch with Bea Winters, a secretary in the office of Hayden's agent. One day Winters said to him, "Why don't you stop talking and join the Communist Party?" and offered him a paper to sign, which he did.[32]

Shortly after he joined, Bea Winters set up a meeting at Victor's Restaurant on Sunset Boulevard with John Stapp, a Party official in charge of labor organizing, who served as liaison with the Hollywood unit. Hayden explained why he had joined the Party: "It seems to me the people in the Party not only know what's going on in the world but they have the guts to determine a course of action. . . . In Yugoslavia . . . when the going got rough and it was time to be counted, it was the Communists who stood up and fought." The apparently unimpressed Stapp asked if Hayden had a militant trade-union background, and Hayden said he did not. Stapp thought he should acquire one.[33]

The actor attended a meeting at the home of Abraham Lincoln Polonsky, who had attended City College of New York and also served in the OSS. Polonsky, who wrote *Body and Soul*, assigned Hayden to a group of back-lot workers, one of the links between their above-the-line and below-the-line offensive. In the years ahead, these two offensives—the above-the-line workers and the below-the-line workers—would provide a kind of pincer movement, meeting at key junctures.

"I was put in touch with a group of actors and actresses trying to swing the Screen Actors Guild in line with a strike, then in progress," Hayden explained. "The whole focal point of the activity of this group of actors and actresses was to swing the Screen Actors Guild in favor of Sorrell's CSU [Conference of Studio Unions]."[34]

Like Mafiosi who suspect a wiretap, Party members used aliases in phone conversations and would refer to meetings as the "poker game." One upscale member went so far as to rig a panel behind his bar to swing out with the push of a button, revealing a well-stocked Marxist library.[35] Such measures appealed to the romantic nature of many in Hollywood, but the secrecy was all business. "We weren't keeping secrets from the enemy," confessed Dorothy Healey, a Communist Party functionary in Los Angeles. "It meant you were keeping your political beliefs from the people you wanted to influence."[36]

The people they wanted to influence were Hollywood's legions of wealthy and well-meaning liberals, the Party's greatest asset for financial and strategic reasons. These wealthy liberals could only be manipulated to serve the Party's ends, while those doing the manipulating remained under cover. Exposure meant the loss of strategic assets, hence the mania with security and secrecy.

Betsy Blair, who acted in *The Snake Pit* and *A Double Life* and later gained fame in Paddy Chayevsky's *Marty*, wanted to join the Hollywood section of the Party, but the Communist leaders turned her down on the grounds that her membership might endanger the stature of her husband, actor–hoofer Gene Kelly. Born in 1912, Kelly had studied at his mother's dance school in Pittsburgh and took his trade to New York where he caught notice in the 1940 Broadway musical *Pal Joey*. The nimble hoofer easily jumped from the boards to the screen, moving to Hollywood and appearing with Judy Garland in the 1942 *For Me and My Gal*, the film that launched his career. Politically Kelly was a liberal and friendly to progressive causes. The Party wanted to maintain that perception, and Blair's membership might risk it.

Actor Lloyd Gough, one of the more orthodox Communists, broke the news to Blair on a drive in the Hollywood Hills, telling the actress that "the Party has decided" that she would be more useful on the outside.[37] Since the Party had decided, the decision was final, and Blair held no option but to stay on the outside as a kind of fellow traveler.

Leaders of Party squads, or "fractions," had to memorize the lists of their members and keep no written memoranda. In communications with other Party members, some used a code based on a key sentence containing all the letters of the alphabet, assigning each letter a number.[38] Members of the Hollywood studio section did not carry conventional Party identification cards; for security reasons, Party members from other local branches could not attend their meetings. The Hollywood section believed, correctly, that the Los Angeles Party had been heavily infiltrated by the FBI and local police.

Party man John Weber had become a Marxist while attending high school in New York and joined the Communist Party at age eighteen. After attending the Party's training school he was assigned to labor organizing, first among textile workers, and then to Hollywood. He considered that John Howard Lawson and Lester Cole, while doing a good job, lacked a thorough knowledge of Marxism. A longtime movie fan, Weber organized the Screen Story Analysts Guild, a group that read incoming scripts.

Weber married his common-law partner, likely on Party orders, in order to look respectable in Hollywood. The Party, which while fomenting strikes did not follow prevailing wage scales, had been paying Weber five dollars a week. But the organizer was able to augment his Party stipend when he became the head of the literary department at the William Morris agency, then the most powerful in town. There he represented Communist writers and directors such as Ben Barzman, Bernard Gordon, Ring Lardner Jr., Joe Losey, Jean Butler, Bernard Vorhaus, John Wexley, Ned Young, and Lewis Milestone. This strategic position gave Weber considerable advantages, among them clout regarding who worked and who didn't. As in New York, Party orthodoxy counted.

When not negotiating deals, Weber taught at a secret Marxist school for key writers, producers, directors, actors, and technicians. Unlike more public projects such as the People's Educational Center, which openly advertised, this operation remained secret, without an official name and meeting in people's homes, an "obviously protective" arrangement," as the instructor put it.[39]

The protective arrangements included keeping members of the Hollywood Party from the drudgery that was the lot of rank-and-file members in Los Angeles. Ordinary Party members were required to sell Party newspapers, march in parades, and even donate "Red Sundays" to the cause. The members had to supply themselves with copies of Party literature and then go door to door in an assigned neighborhood. Members who attempted to opt out could face discipline.[40] Hollywood members not only escaped such tasks but also avoided the payment of dues, another strict Party practice. Communist Party dues could be as high as 4 percent of one's income, double the assessment gangster Willie Bioff had slapped on back-lot workers.

Director Ed Dmytryk said he never paid any dues, and Lee J. Cobb, one of the wealthiest actors of the time, admitted that during one eight-month stretch, he chipped in no more than five or ten dollars.[41] At fund-raisers for Party-backed causes, wealthy members would pledge thousands of dollars, challenging others to match the amount, and then pay nothing at all.

Roy Erwin, a sound man, actor, and writer who had been assigned to a Party group with radio workers, said that those in the elite, talent-guild groups thought of themselves as the "commissioned officers" of the revolution,[42] a status other comrades resented. But even though they were given special treatment, the studio comrades had work of their own and did it well, particularly in the guilds.

A minority even in the Screen Writers Guild where they were strongest, the Party managed to wield considerable influence. Party writers capitalized on the lethargy and apathy that kept many away from meetings. Those who worked all day, sometimes under ferocious deadlines on the set, were seldom eager to attend union gatherings that could drag on until midnight or later. But the Party writers followed strict orders. Disciplined and militant to a man, they came in force and dominated, exploiting a Guild rule that required only 10 percent of the membership for a quorum. That enabled the Communists to control the agenda by bringing out all their members and sometimes even Party people who were not members of the Guild. They sometimes dragged out meetings until 5 A.M., and, when a matter came up that the Party disfavored, the Communist writers left the room, leaving the Guild without a quorum and unable to vote.

Party members would wait until their industry colleagues had grown tired and gone home before bringing up matters important to their agenda. They would use their second- and third-string speakers, such as Eddie Huebsch and Michael Wilson, to wear out the opposition in the early hours of the meeting. They would withhold their important items for late in the evening, when they would bring out the big guns, those Party members others knew as the "first team": John Howard Lawson, Lester Cole, Albert Maltz, and Dalton Trumbo, all eloquent and persuasive speakers and veterans of tough Party infighting.[43] The Party capitalized on proxy voting and used the "diamond formation" tactic to great effect. In this maneuver, the Communist core would not sit on one side of the hall but spread themselves out in a diamond formation, making it sound as if twice as many people were booing, hissing, or cheering as the occasion demanded.

As Guild officials noted at the time, the Communist writers were also careful not to espouse causes easily identifiable with the Party, or even overtly political. One of their causes was a request for $10,000 to support Herb Sorrell's Conference of Studio Unions, which was forming another link between branches of the Party's two-pronged offensive—one with the talent groups, the other on the back lots.

The Communists also controlled *The Screen Writer* which, under Dalton Trumbo's care, became a kind of supplement to the *People's Daily World*. When Alvah Bessie attacked Fred Niblo, a studio veteran who had directed the silent version of *Ben Hur*, the publication refused to allow Niblo a response and rejected letters by other prominent non-Communist writers.

Though less powerful in the Screen Actors Guild, the Party also wielded influence there. When George L. Murphy, who later became a senator, got on the Guild's board, he started receiving the *Daily Worker* even though he had not ordered it.[44]

In the talent guilds and technical unions alike, Hollywood Communists deployed such tactics with great success, wielding influence that far outstripped their numbers and largely without being recognized. The front group proved the ideal vehicle for influencing the wider Hollywood community on issues of international importance. These front groups, sometimes started by the Party, sometimes not, centered around noble causes on which Hollywood people agreed. The leadership and the vast majority of members were usually led by non-Communists, the kind of ventriloquist arrangement the Party preferred. As Communist screenwriter Walter Bernstein explained it, "We had our own sly arithmetic; we could find fronts and make two become one."[45]

At fund-raisers for causes like Spanish relief, Communists leveraged large amounts out of industry notables. Sometimes Party activists made direct appeals that proved unpredictable.

Joan LaCour, wife of producer and Communist Party member Adrian Scott, was charged with calling high-profile actors and requesting donations. Some stars found their own way of handling such appeals. When Scott called Groucho Marx, for example, he would pretend to be his own Japanese houseboy and evidently gave a rather convincing performance. But according to Scott, Groucho did make contributions.[46]

Most of the money did not go to Spanish relief or to help refugees from Nazi Germany. It found its way into Party coffers. Communist screenwriter Lester Cole noted that a "growing unity between Communists and left-liberals developed rapidly between 1936 and 1939,"[47] largely on issues such as opposition to General Franco in Spain. But this unity was not a partnership of equals.

"All over town the industrious Communist tail wagged the lazy liberal dog,"[48] wrote Philip Dunne, a professorial-looking writer and director whose screenwriting credits include *Count of Monte Cristo, Last of the Mohicans, How Green Was My Valley,* and

Pinky and who directed *Three Brave Men, In Love and War,* and *Wild in the Country.* Dunne, a liberal and active Democrat, had been in Hollywood since the early thirties and with increasing dismay watched the Party come to dominate political activity.

Local fascist organizations included the Hollywood Hussars and Light Horse Cavalry, but they claimed only a fringe following, and no branch of any fascist or pro-Nazi organization ever gained so much as a toehold anywhere within the motion picture industry. The industry's few conservatives usually found themselves outgunned, without the kind of far-flung support network the Communists enjoyed. Socialists, anarchists, and others on the Left fared little better.

"There was never any organized, articulate, and effective liberal or left-wing opposition to the Communists in Hollywood," noted John Cogley in his study of Hollywood.[49] As mogul's son Budd Schulberg put it, the Communist Party was "the only game in town."[50]

Much of the action centered on the Hollywood Anti-Nazi League, a group founded in 1936 by the ever-active V. J. Jerome, who had as his first chairman the versatile Donald Ogden Stewart, Ella Winter's second husband. The League capitalized on the Hollywood axiom that good villains make for good drama.

6

"Communazis"

THE HOLLYWOOD ANTI-NAZI LEAGUE, the front group that V. J. Jerome founded, grew to such esteem that its sponsors included the Most Reverend John J. Cantwell, archbishop of Los Angeles; the League never lacked illustrious figureheads or associations. When the League hosted a reception at the Wilshire Ebell Theatre for German Catholic exiles Prince Hubertus and Princess Marie Loewenstein, the group gained instant respectability, to the point that some people thought that the prince and princess operated the League. The account books of actor Frederic March, a non-Communist liberal, showed a contribution to "Prince Loewenstein's Anti-Nazi League."[1] The League's first anniversary, in 1937, drew a host of film notables, and the membership quickly shot to more than 4,000 people. Money flowed in, with studio mogul Harry Warner donating several thousand dollars.[2]

The League went on to sponsor a radio serial, which Donald Ogden Stewart wrote, and to support an anti-lynching bill in Congress. When Benito Mussolini's son, Vittorio, who headed a movie company, announced a visit to Hollywood, the League mounted a campaign against him in its weekly publication, *Hollywood Now*, blasting the young Mussolini as a "friend of Hitler and an enemy of democracy." Pressure from the Anti-Nazi League also succeeded in blacklisting German filmmaker Leni Riefenstahl. When MGM signed German actress Louisa Ulrich in 1937, *Hollywood Now* warned that she was "a close friend of Propaganda Minister Joseph Goebbels."[3]

When the German American Bund, the major supporter of the Nazis, held a convention in Los Angeles, the Hollywood Anti-Nazi League rushed to the barricades with pickets. The action inspired thousands of others to join them, from such groups as the American Legion, Veterans of Foreign Wars, the American Federation of Labor, and the California Christian Church Council. The League also led a boycott of Japanese goods and marked the fifth anniversary of Hitler's rise to power with a mass meeting addressed by Montana congressman Jerry O'Connell. Such was the League's prestige that when Texas Democrat Martin Dies attacked it as a Communist front, his colleagues in Congress bitterly attacked him. The League's star power, meanwhile, kept pace with its budget and political clout.

Edward G. Robinson was one of those stars. Born Emmanuel Goldenberg in Romania, Robinson came to the United States at the age of ten, a date he considered his true birthday. His role as gangster Rico Bandello in the 1930 *Little Caesar* launched his career as a movie tough-guy, an image that belied a genial personality. The actor loved to speak at events such as the "I Am an American" days held by local newspapers. Robinson's alarm at the rise of Nazism prompted him to join any group that purported to oppose it, as well as donating vast sums of money. The Communist Party used his home, known for its collection of modern art, for meetings, often when he was away on a shoot. It was at Robinson's home that, in 1938, the Hollywood Anti-Nazi League launched its "Committee of 56" to lobby the president for pressure against Germany.

The illustrious committee included Ben Hecht, Claude Rains, Spencer Tracy, Burgess Meredith, Lucille Ball, Don Ameche, John Ford, Joan Crawford, Rosalind Russell, James Cagney, Henry

Fonda, Jack Warner, Groucho Marx, James Cagney, and Melvyn Douglas. This committee of celebrities sent a declaration of "democratic independence" to President Roosevelt and to Congress, requesting them to "bring such economic pressure to bear against Germany as would force her to reconsider her aggressive attitude toward other nations."[4] All Hollywood people of goodwill could readily agree with such sentiments.

"May I express my whole-hearted ability to cooperate to the utmost of my ability with the Hollywood Anti-Nazi League," said director John Ford of *Stagecoach* and *Grapes of Wrath* fame. "If this be Communism, count me in."[5] But in spite of the Hollywood Anti-Nazi League's great success, more than a few were uneasy with the group, wondering why it limited its activism to opposing fascism.

"Given the depth of our alienation from the failing capitalism of the time, it would have been intolerable to see the clear parallels between the social institutions of the fascist and Nazi regimes and those of the Soviet Union," wrote playwright and screenwriter Arthur Miller, who was close to the Party for many years. "Captive trade unions, mass youth organizations, secret police, informers in the workplace and the home, masses of political prisoners, and at the center of it all idolatry of the state and its leader—all of these had originated in the Soviet system."[6]

Despite a growing body of literature about the achievements of the Soviet Union from writers such as Ella Winter, Anna Louise Strong, Maurice Hindus, Walter Duranty, and others, stories of massive atrocities in the Soviet Union had begun to emerge. Even the tightly controlled Soviet society could not completely seal up news of Stalin's planned famine in Ukraine, part of his brutal campaign against the independent farmers known as *kulaks*. While attempting to conceal some of his crimes, Stalin openly staged others.

In 1936 Stalin held public trials of former revolutionary colleagues Grigory Zinoviev, Nikolai Bukarin, Karl Radek, Mikail

Tomsk, Lev Kamenev, Aleksei Rykov, and others. They had all been threatened and tortured to the point that they confessed to fantastic crimes of treason and espionage. Most were executed, along with their families.

Following orders from the Comintern, the Communist Party of the United States defended the confessions as genuine, the punishment just, and the proceedings a model of justice. Comintern records even show that Party boss Earl Browder, who became general secretary of the Communist Party USA in 1954, was ordered to provide sufficient column space in the *Daily Worker* to cover the confessions.[7] But the Party did not stand alone it its position. Joseph Davies, President Roosevelt's ambassador to the Soviet Union, also saw the Moscow trials as genuine, and the diplomat's views helped sway many in the media and government. Led by educator and philosopher John Dewey, those liberals who condemned the trials as a sham found themselves attacked in Party publications.

At one meeting of the Hollywood Anti-Nazi League, MGM story editor Sam Marx made the statement that "Communism was the same as fascism." Using the same tactic they deployed in the talent guilds, the Party faithful drowned out Marx's statement with hisses and boos.[8]

Asked if he wanted to serve on the Hollywood Anti-Nazi League's publicity committee, conservative screenwriter and producer James McGuinness replied he would be delighted to do so, if only they would state somewhere in their principles that they were "equally opposed to Communism." McGuinness was told that such a thing was impossible.[9] David Selznick offered to donate a million dollars to the League on one condition: that the leaders would change its name to the Hollywood Anti-Nazi and Anti-Communist League. The League duly rejected the proposal[10] but continued to move from triumph to triumph, gaining star power by the day.

Meanwhile, rumors began to circulate of a pending alliance between the USSR and Nazi Germany, the very regime the

Communist Party, then at the height of its power, had been opposing with all its resources. By the middle of 1939 the Party boasted some 60,000 members (they claimed 100,000) and enjoyed the support of probably ten times as many sympathizers.

The *Daily Worker* blasted the "filthy falsehood that the Soviet Union was considering an agreement with the bestial Nazi regime." These were nothing but "whispered lies" by the "Munichmen of fascism."[11] Party leaders scrambled to dispel the rumor.

Party boss Earl Browder, who had a folksy side, coined the slogan "Communism Is Twentieth-Century Americanism," but he knew who was in charge. He dropped the slogan on direct orders from the Comintern, likely based on an order from Stalin himself. "We are indeed Stalinists, and we hope to become ever more worthy of such a glorious name," Browder wrote. "Truly it is a proud name, Stalinist, and we must bear it with all modesty, for it carries with it a tremendous responsibility."[12]

Born in 1891, Earl Browder had alternately supported and rejected a labor party, separate Communist Party unions, and Communist Party–dominated unions in the American Federation of Labor. In 1932 he denounced Roosevelt and the New Deal as fascist, but after a trip to Moscow he championed both. He attacked Republicans as fascist and charged that their party was under Nazi domination, but after that same trip to Moscow he declared that the Communist Party must work with Republicans as well. Browder's fidelity to direction from Moscow prompted Party pioneer Ben Gitlow to quip that "given the opportunity, Browder may yet endorse the Nazi regime in Germany, should his Moscow masters require it of him."[13] As it turned out, they did.

Browder told an audience in Charlottesville, Virginia, that there was as much chance of a Nazi–Communist pact as there was of "Earl Browder being elected president of the Chamber of Commerce."[14] Here he enjoyed considerable support. On August 14, 1939, some four hundred important Americans issued an open letter branding as "fascists" and "reactionaries" those who dared suggest "the fantastic falsehood that the USSR and the totalitarian states are basically alike." The letter also blasted John Dewey's Committee for Cultural Freedom for even including the Soviet Union in the ranks of the totalitarian nations. Signers of the letter included black novelist Richard Wright, left-wing journalist I. F. Stone, novelist James Thurber, the Reverend Harry Ward, and several names now familiar on the Hollywood scene: John Howard Lawson, Donald Ogden Stewart, Ella Winter, Lionel Stander, Ernest Hemingway, Clifford Odets, and novelist Dashiell Hammett, the longtime companion of Lillian Hellman who had used his experience as a private detective to write crime novels such as the 1930 *Maltese Falcon,* later made into a popular film.

Nine days later, on August 23, 1939, Hitler and Stalin signed the Nazi-Soviet Pact, which ceded the Baltic states to the USSR and divided Poland between the USSR and Hitler's National Socialist regime. One day after the signing, Browder told the *New York Times* that the new pact was "a wonderful contribution to peace."[15] But this pact between the totalitarian powers would effectively start World War II.

While Hitler invaded Poland from the west, Stalin invaded from the east. The deal placed the American Communist Party in the position of having to approve what had previously been condemned and condemning what had previously been approved.

"One may accept or reject the ideology of Hitlerism as well as any other ideological system, that is a matter of taste," proclaimed Soviet foreign minister Vyacheslav Molotov in the Supreme Soviet on October 31, 1939. "It is, therefore, not only senseless, but criminal to wage such a war for the destruction of Hitler, camouflaged as a fight for democracy."[16]

While Stalin supplied Hitler with war matériel, the American Party made common cause with the German American Bund and other pro-Axis groups, with whom they shared slogans such as "The Yanks Are Not Coming." The Comintern demanded that American Communists agitate for a U.S. policy of neutrality and oppose both the shipments of arms and the granting of credits and loans. Moscow also pressured American writers such as Anna Louise Strong to write pamphlets supporting the Nazi-Soviet Pact. Those who advocated intervention against Nazi imperialism were now blasted as warmongers trying to get American boys killed in a foreign war.

Screenwriter Roy Huggins recalled that in August 1939, when the Nazi-Soviet Pact was being signed, Party members in Berkeley had been handing out pamphlets calling for a third term for Roosevelt. When they got word of the Pact, Huggins said, they went door to door trying to get the pamphlets back again.[17] Down in Hollywood, things were every bit as frantic.

Bright and early on the morning of August 24, 1939, according to staffer Bonnie Clair Smith, the phones of the Hollywood Anti-Nazi League started ringing off the hook and a tide of telegrams blanketed their offices from members angrily withdrawing from the League.[18]

"The known Reds were in hiding," said Charles Glenn, who covered Hollywood for the *People's Daily World,* "afraid to stick their heads out of doors because the old country Jews, the ones who had fled Hitler, would have torn them apart."[19]

Literally overnight, the Hollywood Anti-Nazi League became the Hollywood League for Democratic Action. Gone in an instant was the contention that collective defense and "concerted action" were the only effective measure against "fascist aggression."[20] What had previously been an anti-fascist holy war now became an imperialist dogfight and intrigue of Wall Street, to be avoided by all peace-loving people.

Gone were protests of German American Bund meetings. Gone were Communist denunciations of men such as Charles Lindbergh and Senator Burton Wheeler, who had charged that foreign-born warmongers in Hollywood were trying to drag American boys into a European conflict. This pair suddenly became heroes to the Communists, who were now using slogans such as "Let's Skip the

Next War." Author and scenarist Guy Endore contributed another creative slogan: "No War for the USA but a House and Lot for Everyone!"

The organizational work of the Anti-Nazi League was taken over by the American Peace Mobilization (APM), one of the groups dominated by the suddenly peace-loving Communist Party, along with the American League for Peace and Democracy, the Keep America Out of War Committee, and the Hollywood Peace Forum. Screenwriter Herbert Biberman was on the National Council of the APM and was honorary chairman of its Los Angeles branch.[21] Beyond the speechmaking, lobbying, and demonstrations, the APM's line carried over into the Party's cultural offensive.

One person directly affected by the new Party line was Lillian Hellman. Born in New Orleans in 1905 and educated at New York University and Columbia University, Hellman had gained fame for her 1934 play, *The Children's Hour,* about accusations of lesbianism against two schoolteachers. Though hardly of proletarian background, the talented, chain-smoking Hellman became part of the Party's New York theater milieu and, according to Elia Kazan, gained the status of a member-at-large, a level reserved for the famous. While a brilliant writer and a superb dramatist by any standard, Hellman was capable of forsaking art for art's sake and deploying art as a weapon.

After scoring another stage success with *The Little Foxes,* she wrote *Watch on the Rhine,* in which an American anti-Nazi leader kills an Axis agent. The play won the New York Drama Critics Circle Award for 1941, but during the Pact, Party writers attacked the anti-Nazi work as not politically correct. Suddenly, the content of others' works changed.

The musical revue *Meet the People* ran for a year in Los Angeles and in its original form included a song called, "Mr. Roosevelt, Won't You Please Run Again?" By the time the show opened, the Nazi-Soviet Pact had been signed, and Communists with the Hollywood Theatre Alliance, which was then working on the show, cut the song and added anti-Roosevelt sketches ridiculing the president's support for Finnish refugees.

The show also included a scene of Hitler and Stalin dancing together, with Hitler holding a knife to Stalin's back. When someone suggested that both dictators should be holding knives at each others' backs, the Communists rejected the idea, and the scene was dropped. Former Party member Danny Dare, a producer and director who worked on the show, said that Party members in the Hollywood Theatre Alliance used the revue "to propagandize and expound the theories that at that time were the Communist Party line."[22]

Those covering Hollywood were used to writing about wild antics and scandals of personalities from Fatty Arbuckle to Errol Flynn. But they had never seen anything quite like the screeching reversals prompted by the Nazi-Soviet Pact. "Nothing since the advent of the talkies struck Hollywood quite so hard as the news of the Soviet-Nazi pact," wrote William Bledsoe, former editor of *Screen Guild Magazine.* "Certain glamour boys and girls, famous writers and directors, were on their knees at the shrine of the crossed hammer and sickle when the bombshell fell. It hit them like a dropped option. They were still staggering when the Red invasion of Poland exploded around their ears, and the panic was completed by Russia's assault on Finland. Only in the breasts of the most devout can traces of the Stalinist faith still linger."[23]

In Hollywood and across the nation, many Jews who had joined the Party largely because of its militant opposition to Nazism dropped out, never to return. Overall Party membership dropped from 60,000 in 1939 to 55,000 in January 1940 and to 50,000 in 1941, with many sympathizers abandoning ship. The League of American Writers, the Party's flagship front group, lost so many members that the organization was forced to discard its letterhead.

For many, the call to support an alliance with a genocidal regime led by Adolf Hitler finally confirmed that the charge that the Communist Party USA (CPUSA) was not a political party like any other but an instrument of Soviet foreign policy. The Pact prompted educator and author Granville Hicks, once one of the CPUSA's leading intellectuals, to quit the Party in disgust.

Actor Melvyn Douglas had been one of Hollywood's most ardent anti-Nazis, and the Pact convinced him that Party members were capable of anything, including remaining in a party that was allied with Hitler. Philip Dunne, Douglas's friend and colleague, disagreed and bet the actor that there wouldn't be more than a dozen Communists left in all Hollywood. Douglas merely smiled. "Write out your check now, so I don't have to remind you tomorrow," he said.[24] Douglas collected. Violent lurches of the Party line would send some tumbling off the train, but many stayed firmly onboard.

The notion that the Party was the only alternative to capitalism and fascism kept many in the ranks, to the point that, as Abbott and Costello writer Robert Lees put it, "I bought everything."[25] For Party underboss Lester Cole, the Pact was a purely tactical move, a question of Moscow biding time to build its defenses.[26] Elia Kazan, though not in the Communist Party at the time, said he still thought like a Communist and retained protective feelings about Russia, the first land of socialism, as a legacy of his Party days. He too considered the Nazi-Soviet Pact a defensive action.[27]

When the Pact filled Party members with doubt, it fell to writer Samuel Ornitz, who had been dubbed "the great explainer," to clarify the nuances of the Party line. For Ornitz, capitalism caused anti-Semitism, which could not, therefore, exist under socialism in the Soviet Union. Known for his devotion to Stalin, Ornitz had signed an open letter criticizing the American Committee for the Defense of Trotsky and denounced demands for investigation of the Russian purge trials as political interference in Soviet affairs.

Impressed by Communist Party organizing in the Screen Writers Guild, writer Robert Rossen had been led into the Party in 1937 by fellow writer Michael Uris, whose motto was "Socialism by Next Tuesday."[28] During the Pact, Rossen recalled that if a Party member had doubts about the alliance with the Nazis, the problem was not with the Party line but with the member himself. Those who had doubts were told that it was because they weren't good Marxists. If the doubters had really understood Marxism–Leninism, they would have understood the need for a pact with Germany. It was also explained, Rossen said, that the Pact "saved a million Jews from Hitler."[29] Robert Rossen wrote such films as *Edge of Darkness* and *The Roaring Twenties*, directed *Body and Soul*, and produced *All the King's Men* and *The Brave Bulls*.

Some Party members even claimed that the Pact was necessary to prevent President Roosevelt from leading the nation into war on Hitler's side. Philip Dunne, who encountered what he called that "malicious idiocy,"[30] along with other Party offensives during the Pact, discovered the Party's power firsthand.

During the Pact, Dashiell Hammett was living at the Beverly Hills hotel and conducting a long-distance relationship with Lillian Hellman in New York while he served as president of the Motion Picture Democratic Committee (MPDC), the group Jeff Kibre had called the most potent force in the 1938 elections. When Hammett became ill, Philip Dunne became the MPDC's acting president.

Stalin's invasion of Finland in late 1939 prompted the League of Nations to expel the USSR. Shortly after the invasion, Philip Dunne and Melvyn Douglas submitted to the MPDC a resolution that supported FDR's collective security policy against the Axis powers, praised the president for his condemnation of Stalin's aggression in Finland, and disagreed with Communist Party support of Stalin's invasion. The resolution went down to defeat at the hands of an executive board that included Sidney Buchman, writer of *Here Comes Mr. Jordan* and *Jolson Sings Again;* Frank Tuttle, director of *This Gun for Hire* and a number of vehicles for Bing Crosby; union boss Herbert K. Sorrell; and a back-lot man named Norval Crutcher, a member of the IA. Dunne then took the resolution to the MPDC membership, where it lost by an overwhelming vote, prompting the screenwriter to remark, "I couldn't believe that more than one hundred of them followed the Party line."[31] Following the defeat, Dunne and Douglas resigned from the MPDC, which would eventually become the Hollywood Democratic Committee, with Herb Sorrell serving on the board.

During the Nazi-Soviet Pact the Communist Party was determined to prevent the United States from arming itself or its allies, and it spearheaded strikes at defense industries, including Allis-Chalmers in Milwaukee, the Aluminum Company of America in Cleveland, and Vultee Aircraft and North American Aviation in Los Angeles, which was then producing bombers for both Britain and the United States. One of those involved in the action at North American Aviation was Jeff Kibre, then out of the studios but still active. President Roosevelt declared the North American Aviation strike a political action and called in troops to reopen the plant. The League of American Writers sent a protest telegram to the president, signed by, among others, Donald Ogden Stewart and John Howard Lawson.

Writers Sam Ornitz and Guy Endore, both known as Marxist theoreticians, began a series of peace lectures at the First Unitarian Church in downtown Los Angeles, under the auspices of the Hollywood Peace Forum.[32] Screenwriters Herb Biberman and Dalton Trumbo, director Frank Tuttle, and other Communists blasted Roosevelt as a "warmonger" at an April MPDC meeting titled "America Declares Peace," held at the Olympic Auditorium. That same month studio union leader Herb Sorrell spoke at a "Yanks Are Not Coming" demonstration at UCLA to urge a "peace strike" in cooperation with the American Student Union, another Communist Party front. Sorrell also supported the Ellis Patterson slate of candidates for state office backing the Party line toward Europe. The slogans of the anti-FDR Democrats included "No Men, No Arms, No Loans to Foreign Powers. Stop Intrigue Leading Us into War" and "No Arms, No Aid, to Britain and France. Down with Imperialist War."[33]

BY THE TIME OF THE NAZI-SOVIET PACT IN 1939, Stalin had elimi-
nated virtually all his rivals, but the one he loathed most of all,
Leon Trotsky, was still on the move. The Mexican government had
granted Trotsky asylum to the protests of many, among them a
Communist labor leader named Vincente Lombardo Toledano.
Painter David Alfaro Siqueiros unsuccessfully led a machine-gun
attack on Trotsky's home, where he was working on a book about
Stalin. There was talk of bringing Trotsky to testify before the
House Committee on Un-American Activities on the OGPU (forerunner of the KGB), which was believed to control the national
Communist parties, but the State Department would not grant a
visa. Arrangements were made to have J. B. Matthews, a former
investigator for the Committee, go to Mexico and take a deposi-
tion from Trotsky. But on August 20, 1940, Soviet agent Ramon
Mercader ended that possibility by smashing Trotsky's skull with a
mountain-climbing ax.

In Europe, Winston Churchill announced that Britain's purpose
was to wage war, to fight the Nazi menace in the air, on the sea, and
on land, until they had rid the Earth of its shadow. While the Royal
Air Force dueled with the Luftwaffe, the Communist Party propaganda was blaring "peace" and the Nazi juggernaut was sweeping
across Europe, aided by logistical and intelligence support from
the Soviet Union and the various national Communist parties,
especially the French. While American Communists claimed the
Pact saved a million Jewish lives, the Soviets were rounding up
German Jewish Communists who had fled to Moscow and handing
them over to the Geheim Stats Polizei, the Nazis' secret police,
more commonly known as the Gestapo.

By June 1940 the Nazis had conquered Poland, Denmark,
Norway, Luxembourg, Holland, and Belgium and were moving into
France. In America, the Communist Party kept to its isolationist
line, prompting some to label Party members as "Communazis."[34]
Liberals distanced themselves from Party members, and producers
became reluctant to give them assignments. Ring Lardner Jr. said

he had trouble finding work during the Pact, and the producers' negotiating team requested that Donald Ogden Stewart and John Howard Lawson, two of the most vociferous guardians of the Party line, be removed from the bargaining table.[35] Few would join a Party in open alliance with the Nazis, but in Hollywood some were up to the task.

Born in Montrose, Colorado, in 1905, Dalton Trumbo had in his early days nagged his father for nineteen dollars so that he could join the Ku Klux Klan; the young Trumbo was apparently attracted by the military nature of the organization.[36] He worked as a reporter for the *Grand Junction Sentinel* and spent one year at the University of Colorado. Trumbo then moved to Los Angeles and got a job at the Davis Perfection Bakery, moonlighting at his uncle's Harley Davidson dealership. He quit the bakery and soon found work at the *Hollywood Spectator*, where he made contacts with people in the film world. Warner Brothers hired him as a reader in 1934 and the following year inked him as a screenwriter, a job Trumbo saw as a way he could make money while he worked on his novels. But Trumbo possessed a gift for translating the ideas that were in a producer's head into a working script and quickly rose in the ranks to become the highest-paid writer in Hollywood, earning $4,000 a week. He had a clause in his contract that required producers to come to his home for story conferences. He also adapted well to the Hollywood lifestyle.

Trumbo preferred to sleep during the day and work nights in a bathtub rigged with a board to hold his typewriter. He could also be found parading around with a parrot perched on his shoulder. Colleagues described him as an aggressive and instinctive capitalist by nature, even though he thought of himself as a proletarian wage slave and told anybody who would listen that screenwriters were industrial workers toiling under monopoly capitalism.

Trumbo had been close to the Party before the Nazi-Soviet Pact. Local Communist Dorothy Healey said that Trumbo was one of those who would do "whatever they were asked."[37] Trumbo has claimed that he joined the Party in 1943, but fellow writer Paul Jarrico said he recruited Trumbo during the Nazi-Soviet Pact.[38] The Communist Party serialized Trumbo's antiwar novel, *Johnny Got His Gun*, in the *Daily Worker*.

In 1940, Trumbo wrote a novel called *The Remarkable Andrew*, in which he argues that the United States should *not* help the powers resisting Nazi invasion on the rather strange grounds that the ghost of Andrew Jackson would not approve of such actions. The question is raised as to who the British have been defending the Americans from. Andrew Long, the book's main character, answers:

> "The militarist powers of Europe who want to take over the Western Hemisphere."
>
> "Hm-m-m," murmured the General; and then, "Any of them ever attack us?"
>
> Andrew shook his head.
>
> "Well then," demanded the old Warrior, "how in tarnation can the British Fleet have been defending us when nobody ever made us any trouble?"[39]

Later General Jackson has another revelation:

> "You don't mean that the British and the Hessians are *at* each other?"
>
> Andrew nodded.
>
> "Well, God Almighty!" exulted General Andrew Jackson, his leathery old face wreathed in smiles. "Your hand, sir—and may they blast each other from the face of the earth!"[40]

As for an American alliance with Great Britain, then besieged by the Nazis and fighting for its very existence, General Jackson growls: "There's no point in cooking up an alliance with a country that's already licked."[41]

Clearly, unlike Budd Schulberg, who rejected Party interference on his novel *What Makes Sammy Run?*, Trumbo had welcomed the Party's plan for his story, which bears the stamp of a Party hack job from start to finish. Paramount optioned the book and it was eventually released in 1942, starring William Holden. But by then the Party line had changed again.

FOR STALIN, the Nazi-Soviet Pact had not been tactical but strategic. He had hoped that the combination of German technology and Russian raw materials would enable the two dictators to crush the capitalist democracies they both hated and rule the world. Stalin said that Hitler's rule represented "the organized state power standing above the nation,"[42] and the Comintern had praised National Socialism for "destroying all the democratic illusions of the masses" and preparing them for revolution.[43]

Stalin had dismissed intelligence reports that the Nazis were poised to attack the USSR, and the Nazi invasion of the USSR in June 1941 left him so distraught that it fell to Soviet foreign minister Molotov to call the nation to war several days later. Far from using the Nazi-Soviet Pact to prepare for a Nazi invasion, as Lester Cole had urged, the Soviet Union had stood virtually unguarded, while the Nazis advanced faster in Russia than they had in Poland.

Lillian Hellman, stylishly attired in white, got word of the attack on the USSR at the Bel Air mansion of Sidney Buchman. "The motherland has been invaded!" she cried.[44]

Others greeted the event more cautiously. As Soviet archives now confirm, even after Hitler invaded the Soviet Union, the Communist Party of the United States awaited a direct order from the Comintern before discarding the Party's isolationist line and supporting aid to Britain.[45]

Less than six months later, the Japanese attacked Pearl Harbor, bringing the United States into the first truly global conflict in history. Hollywood was ready to do its part, and the Communist Party was eager to pursue another of its goals—influencing the content of movies.

7

War Party

BY OCTOBER 1942 SOME 2,700 HOLLYWOOD PEOPLE—12 percent of all people employed in movies—had joined the American armed forces. Instead of lounging on the set, learning lines, or signing autographs, Clark Gable and James Stewart found themselves flying bombing missions over Europe. On the home front, the film industry strove to keep pace. At the Hollywood Canteen, actors and actresses kept up morale by mingling with GIs and even serving meals. They also marshaled their star power to keep the American war machine rolling. Screen siren Lana Turner thrilled admirers with a kiss in return for $50,000 in war bond purchases and Hedy Lamarr racked up bond sales of $17 million in a single day.[1] One of the few to turn down duty at the canteen was Charlie Chaplin, the first man to become an international film star.

Born in London in 1889, Charlie Chaplin toured the United States with a pantomime troupe in 1910 and decided to stay, making his film debut in the 1914 *Kid Auto Races at Venice* from the Keystone Film Company. He went on to play his tramp character in countless silent movies and in 1919 helped to found United Artists with Mary Pickford, Douglas Fairbanks, and D. W. Griffith.

While the silent film star's notoriety revolved around a fondness for girls many years his junior, Chaplin showed a gift for outrageous political statements that would later become a trend in Hollywood. The veteran of *Modern Times* (1936) and *The Great Dictator* (1940) charged that the Nazis had made inroads into American institutions and organizations and that this continued even after the United States entered the war.[2] Though not a conventional Party member, Chaplin's support for the Soviet Union never lagged. "Thank God for Communism," he told the *Daily Worker*. "They say Communism may spread all over the world. I say so what?"[3] He wrote a long tribute to Communist leader Art Young.[4] Chaplin passed on a picture about Napoleon because he "didn't like dictators." Asked if Stalin was a dictator, he responded that "it hasn't been settled what that word means."[5]

On the international stage, Stalin, Roosevelt, and Winston Churchill were now on the same side fighting fascist Germany. The Communist Party welcomed the studios' war solidarity as a way to erase memories of the Party's pro-Axis collaboration during the Nazi-Soviet Pact. The line had now been reversed, and the Party was easily the most jingoistic organization in the country, particularly after the United States entered the war in December 1941. Hitler was again the enemy.

Where the Party had previously called strikes within defense industries to cripple Allied defenses, they now called for a no-strike pledge, urged aid to the victims of Axis aggression, and took a hard line on domestic subversion. The draconian wartime move to relocate American citizens of Japanese descent on the West Coast met with full Party approval. At the same time, the Party toned down its harsh class rhetoric.

Party leaders dropped "comrades" in favor of the more bourgeois "ladies and gentlemen" in public discourse. The Party even recast itself as the Communist Political Association, the Comintern became the Cominform, and the Young Communist League became American Youth for Democracy, all moves that helped the Party regain popularity and recruit many new members.

One of the new members was Edward Dmytryk, born in 1908 to Ruthinian Ukrainian parents in Grand Forks, British Columbia, a few miles north of the American border. Dmytryk's parents had slipped into the United States to avoid a World War I internment for immigrants who had been citizens of the Austro-Hungarian empire. Once in America, the family headed south, settling near Hollywood, where Edward worked at the Famous Players Studio at Sunset and Vine, making six dollars a week in the lab as a messenger boy and projectionist. A bright student, Dmytryk gained admission to Cal Tech in Pasadena to study physics and mathematics, but the call of the entertainment business proved too strong. He quit school to work again as a projectionist. The advent of sound expanded the number of jobs, and Ed Dmytryk moved up to the position of film cutter, then a director of B movies.

The young, pipe-smoking director began to meet veterans of the New York theater scene—Clifford Odets and Harold Clurman—with whom his Marxist ideas found a favorable reception. Dmytryk came to believe that neither the Democrats nor the Republicans were doing enough to mobilize the nation's youth. The Communists, on the other hand, seemed to be doing the job. At a meeting of some twenty people at the home of director Frank Tuttle, writer Alvah Bessie, by then a celebrity in Hollywood political circles, made a strong pitch for the Party. It hit home with Dmytryk, who was also impressed with the preamble to the Party constitution, which by then included Stalin in the pantheon.

> The Communist Party of the United Sates of America is a working class political party carrying forward today the traditions of Jefferson, Paine, Jackson, and Lincoln, and of the Declaration of Independence; it upholds the achievements of democracy, the right of "life, liberty, and the pursuit of happiness," and defends the United States Constitution against its reactionary enemies who would destroy democracy and all popular liberties; it is devoted to the defense of the immediate interests of workers, farmers, and all toilers against capitalist exploitation, and to preparation of the working class for its historic mission to unite and lead the American people to

extend these democratic principles to their necessary and logical conclusions.

By establishing common ownership of the national economy, through a government of the people, by the people, and
for the people; the abolition of class divisions in society; that is,
by the establishment of socialism according to the scientific
principles enunciated by the greatest teachers of mankind,
Marx, Engels, Lenin, and Stalin, and the free cooperation of
the American people with those of other lands, striving toward
a world without oppression and war, a world brotherhood
of man.

Seeing himself as a legitimate heir of Jefferson, Paine, Jackson,
and Lincoln, Dmytryk duly joined the Party on May 6, 1944, using
the name of Michael Edwards and paying an initiation fee of fifty
cents. When the Communist Party changed its name to the
Communist Political Association, he enrolled again in his own
name. By this time memories of the Nazi-Soviet Pact had faded,
the Western Allies and the USSR were on the same side, and the
adulation of the USSR exceeded even that during the halcyon days
of the 1930s, soaring to millenarian heights.

"This feeling that the Soviet Union is the salvation of the world
is growing. I want it to grow more," said the Reverend Hewlett
Johnson, Dean of Canterbury Cathedral, in a message he told mass
audiences everywhere. "Communism," the clergyman explained,
"has recovered the essential form of a real belief in God which
organized Christianity just now has largely lost."[6] The Soviets
rewarded the hugely influential clergyman with an entry in the
Great Soviet Encyclopedia longer than the one for Jesus Christ
and eventually awarded him a Stalin Peace Prize.

In England, fourteen publishers rejected George Orwell's Animal Farm because they perceived that the satire of the Soviet
Union was particularly unkind to Stalin. In America, Bennett Cerf
of Random House proposed that the American publishing industry
withdraw from sale all books critical of the Soviet Union.[7]

The Red Army Chorus sang to packed houses in New York, and in August 1943 the first official Soviet Jewish delegation arrived in the United States, assuring Americans that tales of anti-Semitism in Russia were no more than malicious rumors. Screenwriter Samuel Ornitz, who believed that capitalism caused anti-Semitism, organized a reception for Soviet actor–director Solomon Mikoels and writer Itzak Feffer. The same pair had also been befriended by Paul Robeson on his trips to Moscow.

Born in Princeton, New Jersey, in 1898, Robeson became the nation's first black All-American football player at Rutgers, where he also excelled in the classroom. Robeson completed law school at Columbia but encountered prejudice in his first law firm, where a secretary refused to take dictation from him. He abandoned law for the stage.

A gifted singer with a rich bass-baritone, Robeson appeared in Eugene O'Neill's *All God's Chillun Got Wings* and *The Emperor Jones* and drew rave reviews for *Othello*. His eleven movies included the 1936 *Showboat,* in which his version of "Old Man River" set a standard perhaps never equaled. Robeson and his wife, Eslanda, lived in Europe from 1928 until 1938 and emerged from that sojourn as two of the Soviet Union's most outspoken friends.

Ambassador Joseph Davies, the diplomat who marveled at the fairness of Stalin's show-trials, wrote *Mission to Moscow,* an instant bestseller that was promptly serialized in *Reader's Digest.* With pressure from the Roosevelt administration, Hollywood came knocking, producing a film version of *Mission to Moscow,* starring Walter Huston as Davies. The picture was so flattering to Stalin and the Soviet regime that some dubbed it "Submission to Moscow," the first Soviet production to appear from a major studio. *Mission to Moscow* did indeed go more than the second mile beyond the American lend-lease policy of aid to the USSR; the film supported Stalin's charge that Zinoviev, Kamenev, and all the old Bolsheviks he executed were fascist agents, it ignored the Nazi-Soviet Pact, and it justified Stalin's invasion of Finland.

In Hollywood, the Communist Party hailed the film, while Max Eastman, James T. Farrell, Sidney Hook, Edmund Wilson, and other intellectuals protested. The screenplay of *Mission to Moscow* had been written by Howard Koch, cowriter of *Casablanca,* who was not a Communist but was close to a Party that remained determined to influence the content of films. In Hollywood this remained a tricky business.

Party leaders like William Z. Foster, author of *Toward a Soviet America,* knew it would not be possible to produce a blatantly propagandistic picture in the commercial cinema. In any case, that was not the product that Party bosses sought. "We are less interested in a film that has Communist content, where a few hundred people will come and see it," Party boss Earl Browder used to tell Party writers on trips to Hollywood. "We are more interested in an ordinary John and Mary picture, in which there is only a drop of progressive thought."[8]

Paul Jarrico bragged that the Party smuggled its ideology into all sorts of movies, claiming that the line he gave Burgess Meredith in *Tom, Dick, and Harry,* "I don't believe in every man for himself. I get lonesome," became the battle cry of the Chinese Red Army.[9] Lester Cole took the line "I would rather die on my feet than live on my knees" from Spanish Communist Dolores Ibarurri, La Pasionaria, and in a screenplay gave the line to a coach at a school.[10] "Every screen writer worth his salt wages the battle in his own way—a kind of literary guerrilla warfare," wrote Dalton Trumbo, who had forgotten his isolationist tract, *The Remarkable Andrew,* and had joined the ranks of the militant.[11]

Elia Kazan, Albert Maltz's friend and fellow veteran of the radical stage, had acted in the films *City for Conquest* and *Blues in the Night* and in 1945 began directing features. *A Tree Grows in Brooklyn* confirmed that his directorial skills translated well to the screen. As Kazan explained it, the Communist writers down at Stanley Rose's bookstore used to brag about what "good

things" they had slipped into their work, which the studio over-
seers were "too stupid and too unpolitical to notice."[12] Some of
these scribes learned their methods in the Communist Party
Writers' Clinic.[13]

Screenwriter and Communism teacher John Howard Lawson
told his students not to try to write an entire Communist picture
but to get in five minutes of the Communist doctrine or the Party
line in every script. He urged them to stick that five minutes into
an expensive scene with expensive stars, so that if someone in the
front office caught a whiff of it, he would find it hard to justify cutting the scene on a cost basis. When possible, the writers should
make someone like Gary Cooper or some other important star
actually say the message, so that if the scene had to be reshot, great
expense would be involved and it would be more likely that the
propaganda would stay in.[14]

When producer William Alland would show scripts to Party
officials such as Lawson, Dalton Trumbo, and John Stapp, they
would order changes. One strict taboo was that a businessman
could not be shown in a good light.[15] Anything with a psychological
angle, in the style of Alfred Hitchcock, was also forbidden, even
though some Communist writers wanted to pursue it, because, as
the *People's Daily World* put it, the psychological approach sent
the message that "the illness is not in the social system; it is within
you."[16] Party members themselves described the Party line as vio-
lently anti-Freud, even though some found the need for analysis
themselves.[17] When William Alland let it be known that he saw a
therapist, he was told he could not attend Party meetings.[18]

While they could not influence content as strategically as could
writers, actors also had a role to play. Lawson told them it was the
actors' duty to further the class struggle by their performances. Even
if the actors were only extras, wearing white flannels on a country
club verandah, they were to do their best to appear decadent, create
class antagonism, and look like victims of existing society.[19]

Lawson held up Lionel Stander, whose films included *A Star Is Born* and *Gentleman Joe Palace,* as an actor who plied his trade in accordance with Party policy. While waiting for an elevator in *No Time to Marry,* written by Party member Paul Jarrico, Stander whistled some bars from the "International," the anthem of the Left. He thought it would be cut but later explained that "they were so apolitical in Hollywood at that time that nobody recognized the tune, and they left it in the film."[20]

Howard Da Silva, another stage veteran, became a Party sub-commissar and hatchet man among the actors, a role that corresponded with his film career. The somewhat ornery, suspicious-looking actor gained roles in *Abe Lincoln* and *Sea Wolf* and became typecast as a maritime disciplinarian. He may be seen looking on grimly but approvingly, arms folded, as William Bendix flogs Alan Ladd in *Two Years Before the Mast.* Da Silva became an important figure in the Actor's Lab on Laurel Street, whose other personnel included Lee J. Cobb, Ruth Nelson, Jules Dassin, Rose Hobart, Henry Morgan, and Lloyd Gough. The Actor's Lab had links to the old Group Theatre, and newcomers were exposed to much Stalinist evangelism.

While the Party was limited in how it might include its propaganda in Hollywood films, it enjoyed greater success in blocking anti-Communist and anti-Soviet sentiment. Dalton Trumbo felt compelled to crow about it:

> We have produced a few fine films in Hollywood, a great many of which were vulgar and opportunistic and a few downright vicious. If you tell me Hollywood, in contract with the novel and the theatre, has produced nothing so provocative or so progressive as *Freedom Road* or *Deep Are the Roots,* I will grant you the point, but I may also add that neither has Hollywood produced anything so untrue or so reactionary as *The Yogi and the Commissar, Out of the Night, Report on the Russians, There Shall Be No Night,* or *Adventures of a Young Man.* Nor does Hollywood's forthcoming schedule include

such tempting items as James T. Farrell's *Bernard Clare,* Victor Kravchenko's *I Chose Freedom,* or the so-called biography of Stalin by Leon Trotsky.[21]

Story analysts, who had been organized by Party member John Weber, read incoming scripts and were strategically positioned to reject anti-Communist material. Communist agents sabotaged the careers of their own clients if they happened to be anti-Communists, or even leftists who for whatever reason displeased the Party's A team. For nineteen months Party agent George Willner withheld Martin Berkeley's material from those who could buy it.[22] Other pressures proved less subtle.

A producer asked Rupert Hughes to write a comedy script that would indirectly ridicule the Communists. They pitched the idea to a group that included Jack Warner and Al Jolson and eventually paid Hughes $15,000 to write it up. But when business manager Hal Wallis, producer of *Casablanca,* returned from vacation, he said that they were crazy even to attempt an anti-Communist picture because the Party would put stink bombs in every theater that tried to show it. The threats from the Communists were effective, and they never made the picture.[23]

In cases where a project got the go-ahead, insiders were able to pass advance copies of scripts to V. J. Jerome and the Party brass in New York. The advance warning gave the Party time to launch an opposition campaign. Jerome got hold of the script for a Paramount picture called *Our Leading Citizen* and told Howard Rushmore that it was one of the most anti-Communist movies in years. Jerome organized a boycott, beginning on opening day, through a Party-controlled public-relations outfit called Film Audiences for Democracy, which was so well camouflaged that it was able to get church groups to write letters demanding that the picture be halted.[24]

Pro-Party groups also used films such as *Blockade* (1938), produced by Walter Wanger, written by John Howard Lawson, and starring Henry Fonda. The film disclaimed any partisanship in the

Spanish conflict but features a villain that looks suspiciously like Trotsky. The Party exploited a rumor that Francisco Franco's government was trying to suppress the film when in fact they had neither seen nor heard of it. Party groups then turned to obstructionist protest when it was reported that Twentieth Century Fox was planning to make *The Siege of Alcazar,* telling the other side of the controversial war in Spain.[25]

In Hollywood proper, the Party's inside machinery also proved valuable in blacklisting non-Communists, even those on the Left who were not deemed helpful. Party writers would circulate rumors that certain actors, such as Adolphe Menjou, were sympathetic to Hitler, an effective smear with Jewish producers, who would quickly put out the word to other producers. Such actors found themselves out of favor but never knew what hit them.[26]

The Nazi smear held a certain irony, coming as it did from people who had remained faithful during the Nazi-Soviet Pact and who had found it difficult to work at that time. Many of Hollywood's most orthodox Communists suddenly found themselves working three shifts during the war when, as James McGuinness quipped, they had been given leave of absence to be patriotic. Under McGuinness's direct supervision, Trumbo wrote what McGuinness called "two magnificently patriotic scripts" for the films—*A Guy Named Joe* and *Thirty Seconds over Tokyo.*[27] During the war Trumbo readily complied with a request from the FBI to give evidence on certain writers who might be "anti-war." In the course of an interview, the FBI asked Trumbo to provide his own views on major political issues. Trumbo said he found the request "odd" but added "I hasten to comply."[28] Party members showed themselves willing to cooperate with the government against labor gangsterism and those opposing the war effort.

Other Party members who kept busy during the war included Party boss John Howard Lawson, who wrote *Action in the North Atlantic* and *Sahara,* both with Humphrey Bogart, one of the most bankable stars of the time, and *Counterattack,* with Roman Bohnen of the Actor's Lab and a young actor named Larry Parks.

In *Action in the North Atlantic,* a Liberty ship is unloading war matériel at Murmansk when a pretty Russian woman says, "*Tovarich! Tovarich!*" An American sailor explains to his buddy, "That means, comrades. That's good."

Though he had written nothing in the action or combat genre, Albert Maltz penned *Pride of the Marines* and *Destination Tokyo.* Alvah Bessie wrote *Hotel Berlin* and contributed the story of *Objective Burma,* which placed American troops where they had never actually fought, prompting audiences in Britain, whose troops were the ones involved, to pelt the screen with garbage. Lester Cole, who scripted *Objective Burma,* also wrote *Pacific Blackout.* Lillian Hellman contributed *Watch on the Rhine*— whose anti-Nazi point of view was now acceptable to the Party, which praised its publications. Hellman also scripted *North Star,* which presented a ridiculously laudatory portrait of the Soviet Union. So did *Song of Russia,* written by Paul Jarrico and Richard Collins.

Samuel Ornitz wrote *They Live in Fear* and Ring Lardner Jr. wrote *Tomorrow the World,* with Frederic March and Agnes Moorhead. Herb Biberman wrote *Action in Arabia* and directed *The Master Race.* Edward Dmytryk directed *Back to Bataan, Counter-Espionage, Hitler's Children,* and *Tender Comrades,* scripted by Trumbo. The film stereotypes of the subhuman, buck-toothed "Jap" and robotlike "Kraut," which lived on in ensuing decades to the chagrin of liberals, owe their origin in large part to Communist writers who were eager to make up in militancy for their lapses during the Pact. As later studies showed, the Communist writers were the busiest in Hollywood at this time, and they were not limited to war movies.

During the war Ring Lardner Jr. won an Oscar for *Woman of the Year* (1943), with Katharine Hepburn. Albert Maltz wrote *This Gun for Hire,* Lester Cole *The Men in Her Diary,* Dalton Trumbo *Our Vines Have Tender Grapes,* Alvah Bessie *The Very Thought of You,* and Samuel Ornitz *Circumstantial Evidence.* Adrian Scott produced *Deadline at Dawn* and *Murder My Sweet,* directed by his frequent partner Edward Dmytryk, who also directed *The Blonde from Singapore*.

According to Leopold Atlas, a member who had been critical of the Party, the more orthodox Communists tried to claim credit for work they had not done. Atlas, a New York playwright and Yale graduate, had come to Hollywood as a screenwriter in 1942. He wrote such films as *Raw Deal, Her Kind of Man*, and *The Story of G.I. Joe*, based on the books of war correspondent Ernie Pyle and for which Robert Mitchum was nominated for an Academy Award. Atlas worked harder on *The Story of G.I. Joe* (1945) than on any of his previous films, contributing some 90 percent of the script. But when it came time to hand out the credits, Party stalwarts Guy Endore and Phil Stevenson demanded equal share.[29] The arbitration committee, which included Party whip Richard Collins, slanted the decision to Endore and Stevenson.

Writer Waldo Salt and a number of his comrades worked in the Office of War Information,[30] and Party scribes came to control the Hollywood Writer's Mobilization, which included the Screen Writers Guild, the Radio Writers Guild, the Screen Publicists Guild, the Screen Cartoonists Guild, the Story Analysts Guild, and the Los Angeles branch of the American Newspaper Guild. The organization became a kind of clearinghouse for scripts and supplier of materials for speeches and various troop shows. Howard Koch served a term as chairman, and John Howard Lawson was one of the editors of its publication, *Hollywood Quarterly*, and also did his best to promote the Party publications, which praised the movies Party writers had scripted.

"John Howard Lawson, Herbert Sorrell Praise Our Hollywood Coverage," said the July 24, 1944, *People's Daily World*, which had been given full press accreditation and privileges during the war. Lawson and Sorrell, respective heads of the Party's above-the-line and below-the-line offensive, supported a $75,000 expansion of the paper. The U.S. presidential election campaign was then gearing up, and Party organs were fully in accord with many of the stars on their choice of a candidate.

On an election-eve Hollywood radio broadcast in 1944, staged by Norman Corwin, stars such as Bette Davis, Olivia de Havilland, Paulette Goddard, Tallulah Bankhead, Judy Garland, and others spoke out for Roosevelt. The biggest name of them all, Humphrey Bogart, said, "I'm voting for Franklin D. Roosevelt because I believe he is one of the world's greatest humanitarians, because he's leading our fight against the enemies of the free world." In a chorus rumbling with the rhythm of a locomotive, Bogie added, "I'm on the train for Roosevelt. All aboard for the Roosevelt special." The broadcast swung an estimated one million votes to the Democrats.[31]

Roosevelt's election to a fourth term maintained the alliance with the Soviets that was favored by the Party. Roosevelt's openly stated policy was to give Stalin everything he wanted, without asking anything in return, in the hope that, by some mysterious means, Stalin would somehow become an amiable democrat. It was said of Roosevelt's emissary Harry Hopkins, the Iowa-born social worker who was in charge of lend-lease, that Hopkins would have given the Russians the key to the White House if he could have sent it. While Hopkins did plenty of damage, Soviet agents such as Harry Dexter White and others were also funneling information to Moscow. Soviet moles in the Manhattan Project were giving Stalin the secrets to the atomic bomb. A New Englander named Alger Hiss moved from the Justice Department to State. With Roosevelt in ill health, Hiss and his associates drafted some of the policies of the Yalta Conference, which practically deeded Eastern Europe to Stalin.

Meanwhile, in early 1945, when the Allies had prevailed in the Battle of the Bulge and began to close in on Berlin, the Party was in a triumphal and evangelical mood. Leaders like Earl Browder prophesied continued Soviet–American cooperation. In Hollywood, the Communist Party was having its way in the studios as never before, moving from strength to strength practically unopposed. That reality was about to change.

Part 2

Stars and Strikes

Hollywood Communism's showdown battle opened on March 12, 1945, the Red dawn of what must forever be called "The Great Studio Strike." . . . It is not a simple story. Complex, devious, and sinister, it wouldn't make a very glamorous movie script, though it involves some of filmdom's brightest names.
—James Bassett, *Communism in Hollywood*

8

Taking It to the Streets

WHILE SCREENWRITERS John Howard Lawson, Dalton Trumbo, and other Party members in the above-the-line studio section enjoyed the best of times during the war, the below-the-line groups also grew in strength and contributed to the cause. Union organizer Herb Sorrell had towed the Party line during the Nazi-Soviet Pact, and his Conference of Studio Unions (CSU) had thrown its weight behind all Communist Party initiatives, from the release of Earl Browder to Stalin's demand for a second front in Europe. Far from shunning Party publicity, Herb Sorrell basked in it, on the front page of the *People's Daily World*, with talent commissar John Howard Lawson.

Sorrell used the CSU both as a tool for the Party and as a vehicle for his own ambition to become the undisputed boss of studio labor, the Harry Bridges of Hollywood. To gain supreme status as a labor leader, Sorrell would need to prevail in turf battles with the International Alliance of Theatrical Stage Employees (IA), the biggest player in Hollywood labor despite past difficulties. The quarrels between Herb Sorrell and the IA would soon deploy legions of back-lot workers as foot soldiers in Hollywood's larger wars.

A group of set decorators had formed their own union, called the Society of Motion Picture Interior Decorators, and had negotiated a deal with the studios in 1937. The agreement was renewed in 1942, but the Decorators' position as a bargaining unit was never certified by the National Labor Relations Board (NLRB). In 1939, the IA tried to negotiate for its own set decorators of Local 44, but the producers refused, claiming they already had an agreement. In 1943 the Society of Motion Picture Interior Decorators joined Herb Sorrell's Painters' Union and became part of the Conference of Studio Unions, but when Herb Sorrell tried to negotiate with the studios for them in 1944, studio negotiators first demanded NLRB certification. The IA claimed that 10 percent of the set decorators were members of their own local. Sorrell then demanded immediate recognition for his group of set decorators and called a strike when the demand was turned down.

An arbitrator with the War Labor Board, a federal agency overseeing wartime labor affairs, ruled that producers should deal with Sorrell's group until the NLRB handed down a ruling. The producers asked for an election in February 1945. A preliminary hearing was held on March 7, while the whole town was buzzing in anticipation of Oscar week. *Double Indemnity, Gaslight, Since You Went Away,* and *The Bells of St. Mary's* tussled for best picture. Bing Crosby, Cary Grant, Barry Fitzgerald, and Charles Boyer vied for best actor, while Ingrid Bergman, Claudette Colbert, Bette Davis, Greer Garson, and Barbara Stanwyck had been nominated for best actress. While fans picked their favorites, the studio dispute was vying for press coverage.

On March 12, 1945, Sorrell's painters and affiliated groups walked out with support from the AFL craft unions. That same day, the new representative of the International Alliance of Theatrical Stage Employees hit town.

Roy Brewer was a balding, bespectacled, and rather pudgy thirty-three-year-old from Hall County, Nebraska. Although an outsider to Hollywood proper, the soft-spoken Brewer was part of what was even then called "the industry." When he was fourteen, Brewer had been hired as a projectionist at the Empress theater in Sutherland, Nebraska.

Projectionists were the first group in the movies to unionize, joining the American Federation of Labor in 1908. Brewer joined the IA in 1926, at age seventeen, at a time when employers could, and did, fire those employees who joined unions. Brewer became an IA business agent, then, at age twenty-three, the nation's youngest head of a state federation of labor. With Brewer in that role in Nebraska, local labor conferences for the first time included blacks.

A New Dealer with socialist leanings, Brewer was convinced that the Depression meant the end of America's capitalist system and called for a new arrangement. He made radio broadcasts in favor of New Deal agencies such as the Works Progress Administration and National Recovery Act, defending them from attacks by conservatives. When he ran for city council of Grand Island, Nebraska, opponents tagged him a dangerous radical and a Communist, and he lost the election.

Brewer wanted to serve in the military, but he was a "tweener," too young for WWI and too old for combat in World War II. He found a place on the home front with the federal government, resolving labor disputes that might have affected the war effort. The work brought him a reputation as a fair and honest negotiator, traits he would need in his own union.

After the 1941 Browne–Bioff racketeering scandal in Hollywood, IA vice president Richard Walsh was appointed successor to Browne and elected in a landslide at the following convention. Cooperating with a probe of the union by the Department of Justice, Walsh removed corrupt union officials and held elections to replace them. Brewer, Walsh's assistant, supervised the proceedings, bringing in voting machines from out of state and bonding assistants to ensure an honest count. When Brewer's wartime service ended, in early 1945, Richard Walsh appointed him IA international representative for Nebraska, and when the dispute with the CSU heated up, Walsh sent him to Hollywood.

Brewer anticipated that settling the CSU/IA dispute would take at most thirty days, after which he would return to his wife, Alyce, and two children, Roy Jr. and Ramona, in Nebraska. But as a movie enthusiast since his days as a projectionist, the union man was glad to be in Hollywood. He checked in at the Hollywood Roosevelt Hotel, site of the first Academy Awards ceremony in 1929. The Wednesday after he checked in, Bob Hope hosted the national radio broadcast of the Academy Awards from Grauman's Theatre, where *Going My Way* won the award for best picture and its director, Leo McCarey, won best director. Gary Cooper, Oscar winner for the 1941 *Sergeant York*, handed out the best actor award to Bing Crosby, the star of *Going My Way*. Ingrid Bergman, whose role in *Casablanca* had lost to Jennifer Jones's performance in *The Song of Bernadette* the previous year, took best actress for *Gaslight*. The show gave no clue about the trouble in the industry, and the walkout continued to build.

Roy Brewer, who was knowledgeable about the American labor movement and skilled at negotiating jurisdictional disputes, questioned the credentials of Herb Sorrell's Conference of Studio Unions, which actually held no charter and no international division. Herb Sorrell not only showed no interest in negotiating with the IA's new representative, but openly scorned the Nebraskan as a "carpetbagger." When Brewer's efforts to persuade rank-and-file members in the various local unions brought little success, he turned to local labor organizations.

The Los Angeles Central Labor Council, Brewer reasoned, would reflect whatever conflicts were taking place in the studios. The president of that council was Tommy Ranford of the Painters' Union, a partisan of the CSU. Norval Crutcher, a member of IA Local 683, which represented lab technicians, held another council post. Before long, a vote came up within the Labor Council about the CSU/IA dispute.

To Brewer's astonishment, the painter, Tommy Ranford, willingly took a position against the walkout, while Norval Crutcher, the IA man, denounced Brewer and championed the rival Conference of Studio Unions, a shift roughly equivalent to a baseball player praising an umpire's call that had gone against his own team. The more he looked at his own union, the more Brewer found fault lines underlining the conflict.

IA Local 44, the Allied Property Craftsmen, which represented skilled mechanics, was one of Brewer's most important groups. But Brewer soon found that an entire group within that local opposed the IA position against the walkout and supported the CSU's strike. The leader of this group, which called themselves the "Rank and File Committee," was Irving Hentschel, the old comrade of Jeff Kibre, who had failed in his first organizing efforts and now seemed eager to make up for past lapses. Hentschel (also known as Henschel and Henshel) badmouthed Brewer and the IA, his own union, at every opportunity. An open and evangelical Communist, Hentschel lectured to the IA membership, handing out Communist literature and recruiting members into the Party itself.

Brewer had seen the Industrial Workers of the World, the IWW or Wobblies, try to organize Nebraska farm workers and had encountered Communist labor recruiters while working with New Deal agencies such as the National Recovery Administration. None of that experience had prepared him for the Communist militancy he was to find in Hollywood.

Hentschel and his group showed unshakable faith in the Party organization and told anybody who would listen that sooner or later the Communists would take over the movie industry and the country. When they did, Hentschel told Brewer, the Party's opponents would "see the error of their ways."

The Nebraskan began to feel like someone arriving late for a movie, entering a dark theater well into the first reel, after the titles had run, the main characters had been introduced, and the problem had been set up. While groping for some solid background,

Brewer got a tip and was told to see someone at the Lido Hotel on Santa Monica Boulevard. There, in a room packed with Party literature, he found Harvey Wolf, a studio craftsman who had organized back-lot workers for the Communist Party. Brewer at first found it difficult to believe what Wolf and other veterans of the Party told him. But soon the "back story" of Party involvement began to emerge.

Brewer called IA president Richard Walsh in New York and told him that the Hollywood conflict was not a simple jurisdictional dispute; there was evidence that the Communist Party was involved. Walsh was skeptical. He told Brewer to go ahead but warned the new IA representative that Brewer would be held responsible for his actions. That did not prove much of a mandate, and Brewer quickly discovered that the situation was even more complicated than it looked.

Though in 1945 things were going well for the Allies in Europe, it was still wartime, and American labor had taken a no-strike pledge, a stance the producers heralded but the strikers ignored. On Wednesday, March 14, 1945, the American Federation of Labor's president William Green disavowed any support for the CSU strike that had begun on March 12. Sorrell said the CSU men would return to work if the government took over the studios. On March 19, the CSU extended the strike to all the studios, even the vulnerable independents on what was then called "poverty row." Every day the conflict escalated, on all fronts.

The CSU put out a regular publication called *The Picket Line,* which noted that the IBEW, the union of electricians, would refuse to cross the CSU lines. IBEW Local 40 had its own enforcer in the mold of Irving Hentschel, a radical named Helmar Bergman. Some of the electricians would apply for unemployment insurance, *The Picket Line* said on March 27, because "possible endangerment of life and limb cannot be required by law except in armed service and public calamity."

Despite a career spent negotiating labor disputes, Brewer had no direct experience with the kind of violence prophesied in *The*

Picket Line. Based on what he had learned from Harvey Wolf and other former Party men, he thought the best strategy would be to go on the attack himself. The next day Brewer issued bulletins attacking the CSU and the "progressive" IA groups that supported the walkout. These had little effect, and Brewer soon received another setback.

The Carpenters, a craft union, had been rivals of the IA since the early days of organized labor, when both groups would squabble over which one would build and move sets. William "Big Bill" Hutcheson, leader of the Carpenters' Union, struck a deal with Sorrell, and Hutcheson's Carpenters walked off the sets. If someone else did not build the sets, the studios would close. If the studios closed, both Sorrell and the Carpenters' Union would have a chance to force through jurisdictional concessions, just as Harry Bridges had forced through concessions on the San Francisco waterfront.

Brewer took an action that was risky and went against some of his labor instincts but was his only true recourse at the time. Some of those now in the CSU had entered the industry by taking the jobs of IA men during the 1933 strike. And since the current dispute was not economic but jurisdictional, Brewer volunteered IA personnel as replacements for the striking Carpenters. To do that required the services of the 1,600 skilled craftsmen of IA Local 44, but at a March 29 meeting, Irving Hentschel, leader of the renegade "Rank and File" group within Local 44, presented a motion that would forbid his men to change their jurisdiction. Only two hundred IA members were present at the meeting, but Hentschel showed the effectiveness of the "diamond formation" and other Party tactics and got the motion passed.

Brewer moved swiftly to take over Local 44, which touched off more disputes and even legal action. He got a break when the studios canceled the contracts of those walking out, and on April 5, Brewer claimed jurisdiction over all the work under dispute. This put Sorrell, who had started his union career smashing cameras, in a foul mood.

On April 7, the CSU distributed a bulletin warning that if the producers brought in replacements it "looks like we'll have to forget we are gentlemen and give the picket line the '37 spirit." In that year Herb Sorrell and his CSU men had piled up cars in the streets, completely blocking off Paramount studios, and busted up an IA hiring hall. It took nineteen ambulance loads to haul away the wounded. No such action took place in 1945, but another attack proved just as harmful.

An April 10 article in *Variety,* the flagship trade paper of the entertainment industry, claimed that IA president Richard Walsh had received thousands of dollars in racket money, raising the specter of IA men George Browne and Willie Bioff, both of whom were now in prison, having been convicted on racketeering charges. Brewer had been chosen for the Hollywood post precisely because he had nothing to do with that group and had even helped clean up their mess. But despite Brewer's clean record, Sorrell continually tagged him with a gangster smear.

National events, meanwhile, would come into play. On April 12, 1945, President Roosevelt died at Warm Springs, Georgia, and Americans mourned the man who had been president for more than twelve years and who had led the nation through two of its major crises, the Great Depression and World War II. Harry S. Truman was sworn in as thirty-third President of the United States. The studios shut down, and the pickets disappeared as Hollywood mourned, joined by others around the world.

When the studios went back to work, the walkout continued, with 8,000 workers marching the picket lines with a swagger in their step. Their leader, Herb Sorrell, was hinting that his men might start throwing stink bombs in theaters, a tactic that had worked in the past but now ran the risk of alienating the public, which loved its movies. Brewer's IA faced the same two-edged sword whenever their projectionists walked out. But Brewer was now forced to try new tactics.

Convinced that he was dealing with a secretive, underground movement, Brewer employed secret, underground countermeasures, infiltrating the CSU and IA's rebel locals, and even to a degree the Communist Party. One of Brewer's agents, Jay Keelan, whose real name was Gene Hagberg, was able to attend many Communist meetings. With Keelan's reports, Brewer could identify key players and sometimes stay one step ahead of the action.

He kept the diplomatic channels open, meeting regularly with those in the rebel locals, where one of his most strident opponents was Ted Ellsworth, a Communist. Based on inside reports from Ellsworth's spies, Brewer told a meeting of IA business agents everything Ellsworth was going to say. Ellsworth duly appeared and fulfilled Brewer's prophecy, prompting the others to burst out laughing.

Anti-Communists in the Screen Actors Guild set up "cells" of their own and passed information to Brewer. A SAG publicist attended Communist meetings and kept Brewer posted about the traffic between Sorrell and Harry Bridges. The Los Angeles branch of the Communist Party was heavily infiltrated by anti-Communists, and Brewer got valuable information from these channels. Other methods proved more in line with the IA's craft.

Motion picture sound men knew how to simulate every sound from a bomb blast to a pin drop. They also knew how to hide microphones, and Brewer took full advantage of their skill, bugging CSU meetings and rallies and sometimes getting advance notice of Sorrell's plans. If the CSU leader ever found out, it was long after the fact. Through these channels Brewer learned that the CSU was planning to lay charges against him with the Central Labor Council. After one hearing nothing came of the charge.

Herb Sorrell commanded a union espionage network of his own and, just as important, still held a strategic advantage in the public relations battle. While it charged the IA with corruption, *Variety* proclaimed Sorrell to be the type of representative of which all labor could be proud.

While Sorrell gained folk-hero status, Brewer was acquiring new enemies. The CSU, CIO, local and national Communist parties and all their various fronts and organs blasted Brewer at every opportunity. Now *Variety,* major sectors of the labor organizations, talent guilds, and more than a few local politicians also opposed him. Since the conflict involved various craft unions, the AFL could not provide solid backing for Brewer, who also faced opposition from studio management. The anti-Brewer forces in the IA scourged him through an unsigned sheet called *The Watchman,* which grew more bellicose as the conflict unfolded.

The powerful Catholic Archdiocese of Los Angeles also favored the Conference of Studio Unions, not only criticizing Brewer, but going over his head to pressure his boss, Richard Walsh. Though a Catholic, Walsh told the Church officials in colorful terms that the dispute was none of their business. But the CSU also deployed a local chaplain, who proved to be a strategic weapon.

Father George Dunne, a cousin of writer–director Philip Dunne, taught at Loyola Marymount University near Santa Monica and took up the Hollywood strikes as a kind of holy cause with Sorrell as its patron saint. Dunne once testified that he had come to know Sorrell "quite intimately,"[1] and at public meetings the priest announced that the rough-hewn, violence-prone Sorrell, an eloquent swearer, was the most Christ-like man he had ever known. For Father Dunne, Sorrell was "a man of entire honesty and unimpeachable integrity... not a saint, least of all a plaster saint.... His powerful and rough-hewn exterior and his direct and homely manner of speech, actually a rare kind of eloquence, cannot conceal a first-rate and sometimes powerful intelligence. To watch Sorrell thinking something through is a fascinating spectacle. It is like watching the powerful gears of a bulldozer slowly meshing, laboriously gathering strength, painfully struggling with the obstacle and relentlessly thrusting forward to the goal."[2]

The CSU rewarded the favor by publishing Dunne's *Hollywood Labor Dispute: A Study in Immorality,* a forty-four-page booklet that gave the impression that God was on Sorrell's side. The Reverend Sam Crawford, who published a newsletter called "CLUV," meaning "Charitable, Lasting, Unselfish, and Vital," described the

CSU leader as a "generalissimo" but added, "We need more Herb Sorrells."[3]

Brewer was also attacked by 57th District state assemblyman Albert Dekker, an eccentric left-wing Democrat and actor whose credits include *Dr. Cyclops, Slave Girl,* and *Among the Living,* in which he appeared with Frances Farmer. Party men in the CSU circulated false rumors that Brewer had been run out of Nebraska. Murray Kempton, then a labor writer, noted that the pro-Communists smeared Brewer as "an anti-Semite, a fascist, a tool of Wall Street, a mobster, a one-man plot against the people." The mud stuck, Kempton added, "because Brewer had no means of competing with the Stalinist propaganda apparatus."[4] Brewer began to search for allies and found them in, for him, unusual quarters.

The Motion Picture Alliance for the Preservation of American Ideals (MPA) had been formed by conservative writers such as Jim McGuinness, Rupert Hughes, and John Lee Mahin as a bulwark against Communist insurgency in the guilds. A writer for the *New Yorker's* "Talk of the Town," McGuinness had been working as a writer and producer in Hollywood since 1927. Rupert Hughes, who had been in Hollywood since the early days, had been an early sponsor of the Hollywood Anti-Nazi League. Both McGuinness and Hughes were veterans of the wars between their Screen Playwrights and the Screen Writers Guild during the early 1930s.

Clark Gable, the erstwhile Rhett Butler of *Gone with the Wind,* was an MPA member from the beginning, as were Charles Coburn, Gary Cooper, Adolphe Menjou, Sidney Blackmer, John Wayne, who came to be one of the MPA's more outspoken members, and Ward Bond, a former football player at the University of Southern California who appeared in *The Grapes of Wrath* and Dalton Trumbo's *A Guy Named Joe.* Though the group was criticized as antilabor, early MPA members included Ralph Clare and Joe Touhy of the Teamsters and Lew Helm and Ben Martinez of the Plasterers' Union. All segments of the industry jostled in the

MPA, but the group held no consensus outside of their opposition to Communism.

The intellectual force of the MPA was perhaps the only person on either side of the Communism/anti-Communism dispute who had actually lived under Communism. Unlike most of the others, Ayn Rand had made a political decision to live in the United States.

Born in St. Petersburg in 1905, Rand had come to the United States in 1926. She published *We the Living* in 1936 and *Anthem* in 1938 and in 1943 was working as a scriptwriter in Hollywood when her novel *The Fountainhead* was released. Rand was the opposite of Party boss John Howard Lawson, not just because she dealt with Communism on a theoretical level, but because she also took a leadership role. Startled to find that the same brand of Communism that oppressed the land of her birth was becoming increasingly popular in her adopted country, America, she took it upon herself to write the MPA's *Screen Guide for Americans*. The booklet showed that she was familiar with what Communism meant in practice. And it seemed as if Rand had been sitting in on John Howard Lawson's art-is-a-weapon classes—with instructions about smuggling in bits of Marxist doctrine and the Party line—and was now responding from the other side. The influence of Communists in Hollywood, she wrote, "is due, not to their own power but to the unthinking carelessness of those who profess to oppose them. Red propaganda has been put over in some films produced by innocent men, often by loyal Americans who deplore the spread of Communism throughout the world and wonder why it is spreading."

The purpose of the Communists in Hollywood, Rand wrote, "is *not* the production of political movies openly advocating Communism. Their purpose is to *corrupt our moral premises by corrupting non-political movies*—by introducing small, casual bits of propaganda into innocent stories—thus making people absorb the basic premises of Collectivism by *indirection and implication*" (original emphasis). If moviemakers wanted to employ "Reds," she said, they should learn how to recognize propaganda when they see it and not foolishly assume that the Communists would somehow remain neutral.

"*Don't* let yourself be fooled when Reds tell you that what they want to destroy are men like Hitler or Mussolini," she wrote. "What they want to destroy are men like Shakespeare, Chopin, and Edison." It was wrong to describe people living in Russia as the same as those in any other country because "the Russian people live in constant terror under a bloody, monstrous dictatorship." Movie people, she said, should not be tricked into thinking that being anti-Communist, as the Party maintained, meant that someone was pro-fascist.

"Only savages and Communists get rich by force," Rand wrote. The Communists, in her view, had every right to state their case and work in the movies, but "let us put an end to their use of our pictures, our studios and our money for the purpose of preaching our expropriation, enslavement, and destruction. Freedom of speech does not imply that it is our duty to provide a knife for the murderer who wants to cut our throat."

Rand told filmmakers not to slander businessmen, the American political system, the Free Enterprise System (capitalization hers), wealth, and the profit motive. She urged her film colleagues to uphold the individual over the collective and not to glorify the "common man" above others. "Don't tell people that man is a helpless, twisted, drooling, sniveling neurotic weakling," she wrote. "Show the world an *American* kind of man, for a change."

Rand's booklet contained much of what would emerge as her "objectivist" philosophy, with its disdain for public works. Despite her anti-totalitarianism, Rand shared the atheism of the Communist founders—she did not tell filmmakers not to slander religious leaders—something Brewer, who spent a semester at a Baptist college, could not understand.

In her thick Russian accent, Rand would lecture the New Deal types in the MPA about the evils of government, her version of the devil. She found particularly horrifying Roy Brewer's concept of a public monopoly for utilities. He asked her if there was any place for the government in managing the streets, or was each citizen obliged to build a private road in front of his house or wherever he wanted to go? At the next meeting Rand confessed that maybe there was a role for the state in this regard, but she never became comfortable with the representatives of labor.

The MPA was the only specifically anti-Communist group that combined both above-the-line actors and directors and below-the-line back-lot workers. Despite the presence in the MPA of Jewish writers such as Morrie Ryskind, the Communist press denounced the group as pro-fascist and anti-Semitic, a sure sign that the MPA had touched a raw nerve. Rarely was the group called anti-Communist, the cause that had united its wildly disparate members.

Just how disparate Brewer discovered when he picked up a few tabs at the Brown Derby, a favorite Hollywood haunt, with Ward Bond and John Wayne, whose incessant swearing shocked Brewer's wife, Alyce. Though he was not part of the glamour crowd and didn't want to be, Brewer's dealings with the MPA taught him not to be in awe of the movie people, something that was to serve him well in the days ahead.

THE MOGULS WERE PERHAPS THE CLOSEST THING to absolute rulers ever seen in America, and to speak with them was tantamount to requesting an audience with royalty. They were used to having their way and did not appreciate interruptions in their work. But they now realized that if they wanted to get their movies made and keep their cash flowing, they would have to deal with a rustic union man from Nebraska named Roy Brewer, whose phone began to ring. One day David Selznick was on the line.

Selznick had poured some $7 million into *Duel in the Sun*, thinking he could get another *Gone with the Wind*. He had spent a million in advertising alone and at one point even released thousands of *Duel in the Sun* matchbooks. With so much invested, David Selznick naturally didn't want any unskilled substitutes botching the job.

When Brewer went to see Selznick, he found the mogul accompanied by actors Joseph Cotten, Barbara Stanwyck, and Gregory Peck, who were nervous about their own prospects for work in light of the strike. Brewer told Selznick that his men were not scabs but legitimate replacements. When Brewer assured him that his people could do the job, Selznick asked him to supply the workers. Brewer did, and the picture was completed, prompting other moguls and producers to seek Brewer out.

As Brewer kept the studios going as best he could, Sorrell escalated the struggle by demanding immediate settlement of all jurisdictional issues as a condition of ending the strike. When nothing came of this, and Sorrell saw that he could not stop film production, he changed tactics, calling for a boycott on fifty-five films made during the strike, including *They Were Expendable*, which featured Sorrell adversary Robert Montgomery and MPA man John Wayne, *Early to Wed, Stork Club, Bells of St. Mary's, The Bandit of Sherwood Forest, Abbott and Costello in Hollywood,* and *The Blue Dahlia,* whose cast included Howard Da Silva.

When few went along, the CSU struck a more menacing pose, as demonstrated in the May 3, 1945, issue of *The Picket Line:* "Any more volunteers for the Technicolor picket line, fellows? That's where the excitement is these days, if that's what you're after. Many fellows on the picket line want some action; would even welcome some rough stuff. It's part of the producer's war on nerves. Everything kept legal so far *but,* men, if anybody steps out of line like [Teamsters leader] Joe Tuohy's goons, grab yourself a fist-full of action."

The NLRB ordered an election of the rank and file, prompting hopes that a vote would end the trouble and that the studios would return to normal. But the May 12 vote solved nothing, with the IA, the CSU, and the NLRB challenging the outcome. The picketing grew to mass proportions, and changes on the international scene escalated the conflict.

As of May 8, 1945, the war in Europe was officially over, though the conflict in the Pacific continued. This increased confusion in Hollywood over the Communist Party's no-strike policy and Party leader Earl Browder's policy of accommodation with capitalist America. Both, as it turned out, became victims of the new Party line through its French connection.

In the April 1945 *Cahiers du communisme,* the theoretical journal of the French Communist Party, Jacques Duclos, an official of the French Communist Party, wrote an article called "On the Dissolution of the American Communist Party." The frontal attack on the American comrades blasted Earl Browder's belief in post-war Soviet–American cooperation as "erroneous conclusions in no wise flowing from a Marxist analysis of the situation" and a "notorious revision of Marxism." Duclos also quoted a secret anti-Browder letter Party rivals sent only to Moscow, and the American Party concluded that the charge was a message to them direct from Stalin. They were right.

The Party line from Moscow now was that the American comrades should stop their cooperation with the forces of capitalism and get on with the business of class struggle and revolution. While America had been a gallant ally in the fight against Hitler, she was now *glavy vrag,* the main enemy. This shift marked the true origin of the Cold War, nearly a year before Churchill's famous Iron Curtain speech in early March of 1946. Earl Browder himself called the article "the first public declaration of the Cold War."[5] In May the Duclos article appeared in the *Daily Worker* and the Scripps–Howard paper the *World Telegram.* Thereafter it was widely reproduced and publicized. As former Party member Bella Dodd wrote, the new lurch of the Party line threw the Party into "immediate confusion and hysteria."[6]

The Party's National Committee, on which Dodd served, then met for three days, and the lines quickly began forming. Some comrades stood with Browder, but Party stalwarts such as William Z. Foster and even his old flame, Mother Bloor, opposed him. According to Bella Dodd, a string of Communist officials scourged Browder as a bourgeois satan. It was the nearest thing to a purge trial, she had ever seen. An emergency convention was held at the end of June and was attended by some fifty delegates. When Earl Browder appeared, come of the comrades screamed that their former leader be *hanged,* while others cheered the demand. Browder was out, expelled from the Party, and William Z. Foster was in.[7] In Hollywood the change proved nearly as wrenching as the Nazi-Soviet Pact.

Browder had been a hero to many Hollywood Communists, particularly those who had joined during the heyday of American–Soviet cooperation, which they thought would outlast the war and bring in a happy ending. When Browder was ousted, some Party members wept. For others it was the signal that, as Silvia Richards, writer of *Secret Beyond the Door* and other films, put it, "the honeymoon was over."[8]

FOR SOME OF THOSE CRITICAL OF THE PARTY, the shift provided further evidence that the Communist Party was not like other political parties on the American scene, but that it was controlled from abroad. How else, reasoned many, could Jacques Duclos have such influence on a party in another country? Director Frank Tuttle, who had made a film for Browder, began thinking of leaving the Party. Any divergence from the new line, however, was branded "internal renegacy,"[9] and the Stalinist hard core carried on.

In one argument over the Duclos letter, Dalton Trumbo said: "It comes down to this, if Lenin was right, then Browder was wrong—and vice versa. I prefer to believe that Lenin was right."[10]

When Party leader William Z. Foster came to Hollywood, the locals threw a party for him at Trumbo's mansion on Rodeo Drive in Beverly Hills. The elite of the studio section had been expecting some enlightenment from the new Party boss, who, it turned out, was a great fan of cowboy movies and was hoping to meet some western stars at the Trumbo gala. He was disappointed to find that none showed up.[11]

The host, who never slandered wealth in his personal life, found himself taking a more active role under the new Party line. Trumbo said that films such as *Sahara* and *Action in the North Atlantic* were examples of films that "went over to the offensive," as opposed to simply keeping anti-Communist material out. In 1946 Trumbo wrote that these "offensive" films had occurred "under the impact of *one historical phase of the war against fascism*" and "there is no reason to believe that it cannot develop and deepen *in the succeeding phase of the same war*" (emphases added).[12] Thus, the United States, in the Communist mind-set, was a fascist regime and the successor to Nazi Germany. About this time the creative Trumbo had pulled duty outside of Hollywood.

When the United Nations was being formed, Stalin's foreign minister, Andrei Gromyko, suggested Alger Hiss as the organization's first Secretary General, the first and only time a Soviet official has suggested an American for an international post. French intelligence had warned the United States of Hiss's Communist ties, and he had even been fingered by a Czech official.[13] Secretary of State Edward Stettinius, who had been under the wing of Alger Hiss and Harry Hopkins, delivered a speech to the U.N. written by Dalton Trumbo. It has been reported that Hiss was responsible for bringing Trumbo to the opening U.N. conference in May and June of 1945.[14] Trumbo admitted that he "ghosted" Stettinius's speech, and on October 26, 1959, he explained to leftist historian Carey McWilliams that during the course of the events, he had stayed at the Fairmont Hotel "unregistered on the blotter" in a room between those of Harold Stassen and Foster Dulles. Not only did he write the speech for Stettinius, but he said he "worked most closely with Thomas Finletter,"[15] Truman's secretary of the air force and later an ambassador to NATO.

Interestingly, when Trumbo's biographer, Bruce Cook, interviewed Finletter during the 1970s, he refused to talk about Trumbo. In fact, Finletter acted as if he had never met the famous writer, which was clearly false.[16] Cook was baffled by the silence and was certain that Finletter was being deliberately evasive. As for Stettinius, he was so pleased with Trumbo's script that he presented the writer with an autographed picture of himself. But later Stettinius also denied that he had ever known Trumbo.[17]

In Hollywood, Trumbo started to work with others trying to throw the full weight of the talent guilds behind the Conference of Studio Unions' strike, the true front line of the conflict. The lurches of the Party line made that task difficult for those of independent mind. Writer and Party official Richard Collins tried to get the Screen Writers Guild to support the secretaries and painters, but many people could not understand why it was all right for them to walk through picket lines in February but not in June and refused to go along. But Sorrell's forces could count on other allies, including one actor who had served in the army's motion picture unit—Ronald Reagan.

9

Fronts, Feuds, and Blacklists

RONALD WILSON REAGAN was born in Tampico, Illinois, in 1911 and served as student body president and swim team captain at Eureka College, where he had won a scholarship. His father, Johnny Reagan, had worked as a traveling shoe salesman during the Depression and credited the Works Progress Administration of the New Deal with saving him from the scourge of unemployment. Reagan found an entree to show business as a radio announcer for WHO in Des Moines, Iowa, in 1937, and he moved the following year to Hollywood. After World War II, the actor returned to Hollywood a self-described "near-hopeless hemophiliac liberal," joining every organization he could find that would guarantee to save the world from the rising tide of what he called "neo-fascism."[1]

Reagan joined the American Veterans Committee (AVC), a group he perceived to be more tolerant than other veterans' groups on questions of color and creed. The eager actor also served on the board of the Hollywood Independent Citizens Council of the Arts, Sciences and Professions (HICCASP), formerly the Motion Picture Democratic Committee. The name change came about in June of 1945, after the Jacques Duclos article was published, and despite its awkward acronym, HICCASP held enormous prestige. For example, wildly popular crooner Frank Sinatra performed at HICCASP's 1946 Labor Day event at the Hollywood Bowl. The singer had showcased his acting talent in the 1941 *Las Vegas Nights*, followed by *Ship Ahoy, Higher and Higher*, and *Step Lively*. On the set of the 1945 *Anchors Aweigh* he sat in a director's chair labeled "The Voice," and it was that voice that accompanied the sailors and soldiers overseas, the signature sound of the time along with the big-band sound of Glenn Miller, Benny Goodman, and Artie Shaw.

HICCASP openly backed Herb Sorrell's CSU, with some of the more vocal supporters including the Reverend Clayton Russell, Linus Pauling, Ira Gershwin, Frank Tuttle, and Edward Dmytryk. Such an all-star lineup carried considerable clout, prompting Roy Brewer to write a letter to each member of the group's board, sent through E. Y. "Yip" Harburg, then HICCASP's secretary, who had written songs for *The Wizard of Oz*.

In the letter, Brewer asked each member whether they subscribed to HICCASP's pro-CSU position and said that if he got no reply, he would conclude that they did. The only reply came from George Jessel, the former vaudeville singer who later became known as the nation's "toastmaster in chief" and who claimed he didn't know anything about the issues because he had been traveling.

The CSU and its allies openly blacklisted actors and actresses, no matter how famous, who crossed picket lines to work. The fifty-one performers who crossed the picket lines included Rosalind Russell, Lee Bowman, Robert Montgomery, John Wayne, Lucille Ball, Van Johnson, Clark Gable, Greer Garson, Leo Carillo, Maureen O'Hara, Alice Faye, Gene Tierney, Bette Davis, Jack Carlson, Humphrey Bogart, and Barbara Stanwyck, a collection of front-line talent. The CSU-allied unions told their members nationwide to boycott films in which these stars appeared.[2]

Ronald Reagan had been on the Screen Actors Guild (SAG) board in 1938, where he had championed the union as a noble organization demonstrating the brotherhood of show business. As proof, he cited Eddie Cantor, Edward Arnold, Robert Montgomery, James Cagney, Walter Pidgeon, George Murphy, Harpo Marx, Cary Grant, Charles Boyer, Dick Powell, and other stars who used their personal power to better the lot of their fellow actors. On his return to Hollywood after the war, Reagan had been reappointed to the SAG board and went on to head the Guild, which remained suspicious of the studios.

It was known that the studios sometimes had hired detectives to tail Robert Montgomery and other SAG leaders, who were forced to meet in secret. Herb Sorrell played to fears of studio chicanery by charging that the IA was a company union with designs on the actors. Gene Kelly, who was prominent in the Guild, was a friend of Herb Sorrell. Kelly's Screen Actors Guild colleague Ronald Reagan also favored the Conference of Studio Unions' boss and rejected Roy Brewer's charges of Communist influence. But the actor was willing to let Brewer make his case.

Brewer argued that the IA had helped the actors organize back in 1919. More recently, he reminded Reagan, while Reagan was away Brewer had successfully worked with Robert Montgomery on the issue of union representation for movie extras. Brewer had argued that extras were part of the acting profession and did not belong in the IA. Brewer further encouraged the extras to form their own independent union, which eventually became the Screen Extras Guild.

In view of all that, Brewer argued to Reagan, how could the actors support the upstart Conference of Studio Unions, a position running contrary to their own professional interests? Support for the CSU, after all, meant that actors would lose work. The argument made some headway with Reagan, who was getting a postwar political education of his own.

Ronald Reagan, eager to fight neo-fascism, became the new star of the American Veterans Committee (AVC), which showcased him on the speaking circuit, a task he welcomed since he had been away from the screen for so long. But over time Reagan began to notice that neither his speaking material nor his audiences were of his own choosing, that he was being, as he put it, "steered more than a little bit." At one gathering he was applauded loudly until he denounced Communism, when the silence became deafening.

The AVC provided other clues to its true agenda. They held one of their meetings at the Cartoonists' hall, which could hold only about seventy-five people. When he got there, Reagan found the place so packed that he and others had to wait outside while the AVC pushed through, with only 73 votes out of a membership of 1,300, a vote to support and participate in the picketing of a studio. Such moves eventually convinced Reagan that the AVC was in fact a Communist front. Similar arrangements, which the Party preferred, prevailed at the Committee for Motion-Picture Strikers, Film Audiences for Democracy, Associated Film Audiences, People's Education Center, the Mooney Defense Committee, Hollywood Unit, and other groups.

Reagan experienced similar disillusionment with HICCASP. The organization's executive secretary, George Pepper, was a Party member, and other Communist members included Eleanor Abowitz and press agent Ray Torr, a former staffer of the *Daily Worker.* At one HICCASP meeting, when Reagan disagreed with a musician who claimed that, in a war, he would choose the USSR over the USA, he found himself consigned to a lower order of mankind. With John Howard Lawson and Dalton Trumbo leading the attack, waving a finger in Reagan's face, Party members called the actor a fascist, a piece of capitalist scum, and an enemy of the proletariat.

Olivia De Havilland began to suspect something amiss in HICCASP after she was told to give a speech Dalton Trumbo had written about the studio dispute. The good-hearted but dim Melanie she had played in *Gone with the Wind* did not represent De Havilland's true character. Having made her mark in that blockbuster she began to demand more challenging roles. Warner Brothers responded by suspending her for six months and then claiming that the suspension extended her contract. De Havilland hit back with a lawsuit that eventually shook the studio system to its foundations. While so embattled, she also won an Oscar for *To Each His Own* in 1946.

Displeased with the lines Trumbo had written, De Havilland tossed the speech and had Ernest Pascal write another one that included criticisms of Communism. Dalton Trumbo was furious, but the move surprised Reagan, who had previously thought De Havilland was one of "them." As it turned out, she had thought the same about him. The two joined with Dore Schary, then head of MGM, Jimmy Roosevelt, and "Body and Soul" composer Johnny Green in a plan to smoke out the Communists. They drafted a statement that affirmed free enterprise and repudiated Communism "as desirable for the United States." When they read their statement at a HICCASP meeting, John Howard Lawson angrily countered that "this organization will never adopt a statement which endorses free enterprise and repudiates Communism!" Reagan and the others resigned that night.[3]

One who stayed in the Hollywood Independent Citizens Council of the Arts, Sciences and Professions was bandleader Artie Shaw. The Communists had tried to recruit the clarinet virtuoso as early as 1941, and after he served in the navy through 1944, Shaw loaned his name to groups and events the Party controlled. During the Hollywood studio disputes, Shaw took part in radio broadcasts against Brewer and the IA.

While Shaw allowed his name to be used, his experience with the Communist Party struck some dissonant chords. When HICCASP held a meeting about its position on international policy, Shaw found that his input was not welcome. "What they were saying to me was, nobody in these things was allowed to talk," he said, recalling the debate over HICCASP and Communism as a "pretty hot issue."[4]

In 1945 Shaw wrote a screenplay for Frank Sinatra with Hy Kraft, a Communist writer whom Elia Kazan remembered as having the thinnest talent of any dramatist he had worked with.[5] Shaw says Kraft tried to use the collaboration with a marquee name to advance his own foundering career, by no means the first time such a maneuver had been attempted then or since. "I did most of the actual writing on the screenplay but he refused to let me have any screen credit," Shaw testified.[6] A dispute of this type also affected HICCASP member Edward Dmytryk, whose career, like that of other Communists, was then on a roll.

In the summer of 1945, director Dmytryk and his frequent partner, producer Adrian Scott, were walking across the lot at RKO studios when Dmytryk mentioned that he was reading an interesting book, *Darkness at Noon.* The producer stopped in his tracks, took Dmytryk aside, and spoke in hushed tones. Party members were not allowed to read *Darkness at Noon,* Scott explained, or anything else by Arthur Koestler.

Born in Budapest in 1905 and radicalized as a youth, Koestler was recruited by what he called the SSS, the Silent Soviet Services: idealism, naiveté, and the unscrupulousness of Party workers. A gifted writer, he used his cover as a journalist to work for the Comintern and quickly became one of the Party's international stars. He planned a worshipful book on the USSR, but what he saw there disturbed him, particularly the swollen bodies of children during the Ukraine famine. Some people he knew had vanished into labor camps or were shot as spies. When Stalin signed his pact with Hitler, Koestler abandoned Communism and turned his literary gifts against Stalin, whom he referred to by his real name of Dzhugashvili. He dubbed the Party's slogan-strewn political jargon as "Dzhugashvilese." Party organs worldwide smeared Koestler as a corrupt liar and banned his books.

As for Dmytryk and Scott, they were soon to receive a more severe lesson in Party discipline than that for violating the approved reading list. They had been working together on the film *Cornered*, about a Canadian pilot whose French bride had been murdered by the SS. Scott's choice for screenwriter had been fellow Communist Party man John Wexley, whose credits include *The Last Mile, Footsteps in the Dark*, and *The Long Night* and whose Party group included director Joe Losey, Richard Collins, Waldo Salt, Leo Townsend, and John Weber.[7]

Wexley had freighted his script with long anti-Nazi speeches, which, Dmytryk said, "went to extremes in following the Party line on the nose."[8] Scott and Dmytryk thought that the speechmaking, though politically correct in content, blunted the dramatic effect of the story. They hired John Paxton, a non-Communist who had worked with them before and who now produced a script that contained a strong anti-fascist viewpoint without resorting to speeches. John Wexley lost the credit arbitration, but the issue did not die there.

Wexley called for a meeting at Dmytryk's home and brought along Richard Collins and Paul Trivers, who joined the aggrieved writer's attacks. Dmytryk and Scott held their ground, but Wexley pushed for another meeting and this time brought Party boss John Howard Lawson, whose word was final.

Lawson charged that Wexley's work had been so altered that *Cornered* not only ceased to be an anti-fascist movie but was now effectively a pro-fascist picture. Lawson wanted Dmytryk and Scott to reshoot the film and to insert the propaganda scenes, an impossibility at that stage since prints of *Cornered*, starring Dick Powell with Luther Adler and Walter Slezak, were already being made.

At still a third meeting Scott brought in Albert Maltz, one of the more talented Communist Party literati, a veteran of the Group Theatre. Try as he might, Maltz failed to sway the issue, and the meeting ended in a standoff. Some days later, Lawson summoned

Scott and Dmytryk to lunch at the Gotham Cafe in Hollywood and told them that since they could not accept discipline, they should leave the Communist Party.

PRESIDENT HARRY TRUMAN DROPPED AN ATOMIC BOMB on Hiroshima on August 6, 1945, and on Nagasaki three days later. Eight days later, on August 14, World War II officially ended, touching off wild celebrations and removing all Communist Party reluctance to support the Conference of Studio Unions walkout.

Roy Brewer had been living out of a suitcase until the summer of 1945, when it became clear that his latest assignment was not a typical jurisdictional dispute and that he was doing battle with the Communist Party. Brewer sold his house in Nebraska and moved his family to Los Angeles.

On August 10, Brewer and IA president Richard Walsh appeared before the American Federation of Labor's executive council in Chicago, where Brewer told Painters' Union boss Lawrence Lindelof that every local he had chartered in Hollywood was under the influence of the Communists. Lindelof agreed but explained that he was trying to get enough information on Herb Sorrell to boot him out. Brewer's presentation prompted the AFL to move for an investigation of the matter, but the study never took place.

Harvey Wolf, the studio craftsman who first tipped off Brewer at the Lido Hotel, and other ex-Communists helped Brewer show that the CSU had rigorously followed the line of the Communist Party. Brewer accused Herb Sorrell of Communist Party affiliation, and Sorrell counterattacked by suing Brewer for libel, demanding $150,000 in damages. The CSU boss had begun holding regular mass rallies at Legion Stadium, at which sympathetic writers and actors would appear and participate. Karen Morley, the actress and Party activist who had helped recruit Sterling Hayden, said that Dalton Trumbo had written key speeches for Sorrell,[9] who stepped up the pickets at all the major studios, outraging the moguls.

On September 21, Richard Walsh met with the AFL presidents in Chicago, but nothing came of it. During that month, the Hollywood pickets had been getting more vocal, more restless. In spite of support from the CIO and the Communist Party, many picketers were feeling the pinch. Party and CSU leaders tried to put the best face on the conflict and maintain high morale. The *Hollywood Atom,* a pro-CSU newspaper, offered new lyrics to "Accentuate the Positive," the Harold Arlen and Johnny Mercer tune Bing Crosby had sung that year in *Here Come the Waves:*

> *You've got to ac-cen-tuate the picket line*
> *E-lim-inate the scabby kind*
> *Latch on to that old picket sign*
> *Till those producers see the light.*

But behind the scenes, the CSU ranks were tense. Brewer learned through his intelligence network that Harry Bridges was telling Herb Sorrell that Sorrell had better start getting tough, otherwise the strike and the Conference of Studio Unions were finished. In his 1934 strike on the San Francisco waterfront, Bridges had enjoyed the support of the Teamsters, who in this standoff were supporting Brewer's IA. To help Sorrell's cause, Bridges had sent down about fifty of his toughest men, leading Brewer to expect a major escalation. Sorrell was ready to accentuate the positive in his own way.

On October 4, Sorrell gathered his men to a mass rally at Legion Stadium, took the podium, and whipped the troops into a frenzy. The next morning, as *The Picket Line* put it, they were ready to grab themselves a fist-full of action.

10

The Battle of Burbank

IN THE DEAD OF NIGHT, on October 5, 1945, while most of the city slept, hundreds of CSU men began to converge on the Warner Brothers studios in Burbank. Herb Sorrell knew that Burbank's small police force would be incapable of handling a mass disturbance, especially one that included the experienced professionals Harry Bridges had sent.

By five in the morning, at least 1,500 men and women had arrived on the scene, flipping over cars so that they blocked the street and forming lines across studio entrances. These moves alone frightened both bystanders and studio workers, and those who ventured near found themselves threatened and attacked. Sorrell led the troops in his usual way: by example, taking an active part in the violence.

Sorrell told Ed Basche, a Warner guard, that no one was going to get in and if anyone tried, "I won't be responsible for what happens."[1] The strikers entered the premises to attack Blaney Matthew, head of plant protection, and threw bottles and bolts at guard Lee Ryan when he tried to climb on the roof. Basche, who had been handed Communist Party pamphlets, then called Burbank chief of police Elmer Adams. When Adams arrived about nine, the pickets tried to overturn his car. The police chief read the riot act over the studio loudspeakers, but Sorrell's forces simply ignored him.

Not all those intending to work that day were intimidated. Soon the IA men had joined the battle, creating a mass brawl beyond anything the town had ever witnessed. Kirk Douglas recalled the scene: "Thousands of people fought in the middle of Barham Boulevard with knives, clubs, battery cables, brass knuckles, chains, and samps."[2]

Some of the CSU men carried short two-by-fours and had mastered a way of hitting a car door so that it would pop open. Then they would drag the driver and passengers out of the car and beat them. Other CSU members carried steel bars hidden inside rolled-up newspapers. Soon the debris, mostly bottles, had piled up everywhere, and blood flowed in the streets. The Burbank police tried tear gas and fire hoses, but the sheer numbers of the strikers rendered the move ineffective, and because of jurisdictional squabbles, the Los Angeles police could not provide assistance. Even when units from Glendale arrived, Sorrell's forces outnumbered the police approximately 1,500 to 122.

When choreographer LeRoy Prinz showed up at Warner Brothers, he said that he was not involved in the dispute and fully intended to go to work. Sorrell told him, "You or no other son of a bitch don't get in there today." Prinz, a veteran of World War I, told him: "Mr. Sorrell, you or no other son of a bitch is going to keep me out."[3] Prinz got in, but not before he was thoroughly beaten up by a group of CSU men. The police watched, but because they were so outnumbered, they did nothing. Prinz later testified that he saw Sorrell riding on the back of a police motorcycle.

The studio was able to get a local judge to issue a restraining order that was read over a loudspeaker. "To hell with the law," Sorrell yelled back. "We don't need the law and we are going to close this studio."[4]

Sorrell attacked Warner Brothers' paperhanger James Balash with brass knuckles, breaking the victim's jaw. Before Balash could get up, he was surrounded and kicked, suffering broken ribs. A police officer viewed the entire episode but did not intervene and did not offer to take Balash to the hospital.[5]

Paul M. McWilliams, superintendent of medical services at Warner Brothers, later testified that his staff treated eighty-nine Warner employees, three Burbank policemen, three Burbank firemen, one policeman, six pickets, and one IA representative. The mass pickets and violence continued through the week, both on and off location, and the homes of several IA members were firebombed. The strike halted work inside the Warner studio and got attention in the proper quarters. On October 12, the National Labor Relations Board ruled that the set decorators should be affiliated with the Painters, an apparent victory for the CSU. But Sorrell continued the mass picketing, and his men began flinging hot coffee into the faces of those trying to enter the studio. Jack Warner watched the battle from the roof of his studio, helpless to do anything about it. Some of his employees crawled through pipes to get in and remained inside for three weeks. Outside, Sorrell welcomed reinforcements from the talent guilds.

John Howard Lawson joined the pickets on the barricades, getting himself arrested. A few days later, Lawson, John Garfield, John Wexley, Sidney Buchman, Carey McWilliams, Frank Tuttle, Robert Rossen, William Pomerance, and others signed a telegram blaming Warner for the violence, which some of the signers had helped perpetrate and which continued through October. When Burbank chief of police Elmer Adams again tried to read the riot act at the scene, pickets pelted him with bolts, bricks, and bottles.

At CSU rallies, Father Dunne and Dalton Trumbo charged that Roy Brewer was linked to convicted racketeers George E. Browne and Willie Bioff, a smear campaign so extreme that labor writer Oliver Carlson called it the most vicious ever seen on the West Coast. The pro-CSU *Hollywood Atom* began to read like a cross between the *People's Daily World* and the *National Enquirer*. *Atom* headlines from October 10 to October 24 included:

GIRL AND VET TORTURED BY STUDIO GESTAPO
IS HITLER SAFE WITHIN WARNER'S WALL'S?
SHERIFF'S BROWNSHIRTS LAVISH WITH BRUTALITY
WARNER BROTHERS SET UP TORTURE CAMPS A LA NAZIS
RAMPANT FASCIST SCABS WIELD DEADLY CHAINS

In the *Atom,* Sorrell bragged that he could shut down any studio at will. He briefly extended the mass pickets from Warner to Republic, MGM, and Paramount, where Kirk Douglas was shooting *The Strange Love of Martha Ivers*. "We continued to shoot, but it meant that we were locked in at the studio," Douglas said. "If we went out, we couldn't get back in."[6]

Herb Sorrell kept the bulk of his forces on the front lines at Warner Brothers, where some days the number of pickets surged to 4,000, with fewer than a hundred police on hand. Local officials and citizens alike pleaded with California governor Earl Warren to call in the National Guard, but he refused to do so. Roy Brewer, meanwhile, was making moves of his own. He rented a small cottage near enough to the Warner studio to be a convenient base of operations, but one just removed from the front lines. Herb Sorrell could not always be on the scene, and most of the CSU leaders did not know Brewer by sight. Dressing in old work clothes, Brewer found that he could circulate in the area unrecognized.

In his quest to keep the studio open, Brewer enjoyed another advantage. One of the main groups on strike was the Painters, who practiced a craft that could be easily mastered by replacement workers. From his cottage base, Brewer got replacement workers into the studio in buses, which were too heavy for even a gang of strikers to overturn. The replacements kept the studio going, but not without cost. Brewer's men, drawing support from the Teamsters, still found themselves in pitched battles. Sorrell told Teamster Ralph Clare that he was going to beat him to death, and Clare believed him.

State officials only moved to investigate after the worst was over. While the CSU had supported state intervention into labor gangsterism and anti-war sentiment, this time the CSU marshaled its powers to block an investigation of the violence led by California assemblyman C. Don Field. Field's inquiry concluded that the Conference of Studio Unions had remained in complete control of the area around Warner Brothers from October 5 to October 28.

Although they did not achieve the total studio shutdown they had sought, the CSU's mass action captured national attention and prompted cries to put an end to the dispute, now more than half a year old.

The "Cincinnati Directive" came on October 25, 1945. In this ruling, the AFL's executive council called a halt to the walkout, ordered workers back to their jobs, demanded local negotiations for thirty days on jurisdictional questions, and appointed a three-man committee to rule on any issues not solved in the local negotiations. Brewer's displaced men were to be paid until a final settlement was reached, a directive he agreed to with some reluctance.

The three-man committee was composed of Felix H. Knight of the Brotherhood of Railway Carmen, William C. Doherty of the National Association of Letter Carriers, and William C. Birthright of the Journeymen Barbers and Hairdressers International Union. Each was an AFL international vice president. This improbable trio became known officially as the "Knight Committee" and unofficially as the "three wise men." They were each cast in their role for their supposed neutrality concerning Hollywood but in fact were completely ignorant of the movie industry and its complicated labor history.

On October 30, William Green of the AFL announced that all those who had been on call on March 12 should return to work immediately, to the positions they formerly occupied. For sixty days, management was to have the prerogative of assigning employees wherever it liked without interference from any union. The bad feelings and confusion fueled by the strike continued. Some of the CSU men refused to work beside those who had replaced them during the strike. On October 31, the replacement workers were removed from the studios. In some cases, the CSU people got there first and destroyed their personal property.

By December, the Knight Committee thought it had reached a decision, and the day after Christmas, it issued its directive. The IA lost its jurisdiction over the set decorators, a victory for the Conference of Studio Unions but not, as Brewer saw it, a major loss for the IA, which picked up the office workers in the deal. The three wise men gave the Carpenters' Union the outside work, permanent construction, and mill work. The IA got props, miniature sets, and the erection of sets on stages, an agreement that more or less conformed with the compromise, which recognized the "proscenium division" that the IA had made with the Carpenters in 1926. Everything on the stage was IA work, and the back-lot work went to the craft unions.

Overall, Brewer added three hundred jobs to the IA rolls, and though he was not entirely satisfied with the terms, he was prepared to live with them. William Hutcheson, of the Carpenters' Union, remained dissatisfied and asked for a clarification. In January 1946, CSU representatives traveled to an AFL executive meeting in Miami to ask to have the Knight Committee's directive set aside, but they were not successful. They kept up their pickets at the Warner Studio, joined by a number of sympathizers, including some actors and radical faculty and students from UCLA.

By the new year there had been some subtle shifts in power. The CSU violence shifted more support to Brewer's side, particularly from the producers and actors. Sorrell eventually withdrew his libel lawsuit against Brewer and blamed his lawyers for giving him bad advice. Within the AFL, there was still a reluctance to give serious consideration to the reality of Communist involvement in the union dispute.

Communist Party publications backed the CSU forces, and the Party's studio section, when not taking a place on the barricades, supplied logistical support and wrote fiery speeches for union leaders. While the conflict had been taken to the streets, it continued backstage, in high places, and even on the theoretical level.

The Communists perceived morale and unity to be all-important at this crucial moment in history and key juncture in the Party's campaign to gain control of the movie studios. During class warfare, dissension could not be tolerated. Party bosses soon faced a chance to show how they dealt with a rift within their own ranks.

Hollywood Inquisition

THOUGH NOT AS WEALTHY AS DALTON TRUMBO, Albert Maltz was a man on the rise inside and outside of the Communist Party. He followed up the O. Henry award he won in 1938 with a 1944 novel, *The Cross and the Arrow,* and his bank account bulged from the war movies he had written. He had also networked with one of the day's fastest rising stars and been honored at the 1945 Academy Awards.

Maltz had donated his writing for *The House I Live In,* a short film on the subject of tolerance. In the film, which was given to theaters free of charge, Frank Sinatra sang two songs and lectured young toughs about religious tolerance and brotherhood. Maltz added the Academy Award to his trophy case. But despite his commercial and critical success, the writer remained troubled.

His earlier intervention on the side of Ed Dmytryk and Adrian Scott in the *Cornered* affair had failed, and the Party doctrine of art-is-a-weapon, long a concern, now weighed heavily on his mind. Just how heavily became apparent in February 1946 when his article "What Shall We Ask of Writers?" appeared in *New Masses.*

"It has been my conclusion for some time that much of left-wing artistic activity—both creative and critical—has been restricted, narrowed, turned away from life, sometimes made sterile—because the atmosphere and thinking of the literary left wing has been based upon a shallow approach," wrote Maltz. "I have come to believe that the accepted understanding of art as a weapon is not a useful guide, but a straitjacket. I have felt this in my own works and viewed it in the works of others. In order to write at all, it has long since become necessary for me to repudiate it and abandon it."

Maltz blamed "wasted writing and bad art" on "the intellectual atmosphere of the left wing" and called the art-is-a-weapon approach vulgar and disastrous. "From it flow all of the constrictions and—we must be honest—stupidities too often found in the earnest but narrow thinking and practice of the literary left wing in these past years." As an example he cited Lillian Hellman's "magnificent play" *Watch on the Rhine*, which the *New Masses* critic had attacked when it was staged during the Nazi-Soviet Pact, but which the same publication had praised when it appeared as a film in 1942 after Hitler had attacked the USSR. The essence of the work had not changed, Maltz noted, only the politics.

"I know of at least a dozen plays and novels discarded in the process of writing because the political scene altered," Maltz complained. "I even know a historian who read Duclos and announced that he would have to revise completely the book he was engaged upon." Maltz meant John Howard Lawson, who was in the process of writing a book on U.S. history, no easy task for a Party member at any time but particularly tough in the 1940s. Lawson would no sooner finish a draft of his book than something would happen that would force him to rewrite part or all of it to conform to the new Party line.[1] The People's Educational Center's Hollywood Center listed Lawson, one of their prominent faculty members, as the author of "a work in progress: a book on American history."

Besides his dig at the Party line and at Hollywood Party boss Lawson, Maltz raised questions about the literary future of Howard Fast. Fast had joined the Communist Party in 1944, the same year his *Freedom Road* was praised by Eleanor Roosevelt and W. E. B. Du Bois. The Soviet Union heavily promoted Fast's works, such as *Citizen Tom Paine*.

Maltz saw no direct connection between the "correct" politics of a writer and his or her art. "Writers must be judged by their work and not by the committees they join," he wrote. Engels, he noted, had praised the works of Balzac, who was not only a royalist but a man "consistently and virulently antidemocratic, anti-Socialist, anti-Communist in his thinking as a citizen." Wealthy middle-class Englishman John Galsworthy wrote two plays, the *Silver Box* and *Justice*, which "no socially conscious, theoretically sagacious, left-wing writer of today has come within 200 miles of equaling." Dostoyevsky, Tolstoy, and Thomas Wolfe stood among those producing works of value despite what Maltz called "philosophic weaknesses." He culled other examples from contemporary writers, primarily James T. Farrell, "one of the outstanding authors in America," and praised Farrell's *Studs Lonigan*. Maltz closed his article with a caution: "Where art is a weapon, it is only so when it is art. Those artists who work within a vulgarized approach to art do so at a great peril to their own work and to the very purposes they seek to serve."

If Maltz had written those words with some trepidation, and he surely had, the first reviews of his *New Masses* article pleased him. He discovered he wasn't alone in his thinking. Ed Dmytryk, Adrian Scott, and others in the Hollywood section of the Party welcomed the article as a breath of fresh air, a veritable breakthrough. Screenwriter Leopold Atlas, also a Party member, congratulated him for taking an independent stance. Arnold Manoff, a writer Maltz had named in his piece, told the author he agreed with his position. But the response from higher circles in the Party proved different.

Soon Albert Maltz found himself the target of Mike Gold, the Party's literary enforcer, who shared V. J. Jerome's belief that Marxists were better writers because they understood the social forces that shaped human beings. Scholar Lucy Dawidowicz described

Gold as "the most gifted writer the Communists ever completely captured," and Lewis Mumford, with whom Gold grew up in New York, pronounced him, "one of the most promising literary talents that was ever sacrificed to the petrified dogmas of Russian Communism."[2] Gold's attack on Maltz lived up to those reviews.

"Albert Maltz, who wrote some powerful political and proletarian novels in the past, seems about ready to repudiate that past, and to be preparing for a retreat into the stale old ivory tower of the art-for-art-sakers," growled Gold in the *Daily Worker*. "The fact remains that for 15 years, while Maltz was in the Communist literary movement, he managed to escape with his talents and get his novels written." Further, "this Communist literary movement in the United States was a school that nurtured an Albert Maltz and gave him a philosophic basis. It gave him his only inspiration up to date." In a further jab, Gold said that this same Communist vision had inspired "the best American writers of the past 15 years."

What really got Gold racking rounds into his Luger was Maltz's praise of James T. Farrell, who, unlike Maltz, had turned down lucrative offers from Hollywood. The author of *Studs Lonigan* styled himself a political radical and had supported the Communist Party from 1932 to 1935. As Maltz pointed out, Farrell had even been held in esteem by the writers at the *New Masses*. But like his brawling characters, Farrell would not be held to any Party line nor bend his writing to any political purpose. He attended one meeting of the League of American Writers, one of the Party's more successful front groups, and promptly trashed it as the "League Against American Writing."[3] His unpardonable sin came in 1937, when he joined with other liberals and non-Communist leftists on committees to defend Trotsky, an unforgiveable action for the Stalinists even years after Soviet agent Ramon Mercader had buried an alpenstock in Trotsky's skull.

"It [Maltz's article] has the familiar smell," huffed Gold. "I remember hearing all this sort of artistic moralizing before. The criticism of James T. Farrell, Max Eastman, Granville Hicks, and other renegades always attacked the same literary 'sins of the Communists,' and even quoted Lenin, Engels, and Marx to profusion. . . .

Further, "Maltz's coy reference to the 'political committees' on which James Farrell serves is a bad sign. Farrell is no mere little committee server but a vicious, voluble Trotskyite with many years of activity. Maltz knows that Farrell has long been a colleague of Max Eastman, Eugene Lyons, and similar rats who have been campaigning with endless lies and slanders for war on the Soviet Union.

"It is a sign on Maltz's new personality that he hasn't the honesty to name Farrell's Trotskyism for what it is; but to pass it off as a mere peccadillo."

In the eyes of Gold, Maltz had been contaminated. "Let me express my sorrow that Albert Maltz seems to have let the luxury and phony atmosphere of Hollywood at last to poison him. It has to be constantly resisted or a writer loses his soul. Albert's soul was strong when it touched Mother Earth—the American working class. Now he is embracing abstractions that will lead him nowhere."

By themselves these sins would have been bad enough, according to Gold. But Maltz had committed them at the very worst of times. "We are entering the greatest crisis of American history," preached Gold. "The capitalists are plotting (and the big strikes are a first sample) to establish an American fascism as a prelude to American conquest of the world."

Maltz was not the first writer Gold had attacked. He had gone after Farrell, who replied back in kind. Thomas Wolfe, when told that he could learn something from Mike Gold, replied: "Why in hell doesn't Mike Gold write like me?"[4] Ernest Hemingway's writings on Spain had displeased the American Communist Party, and when the author of For Whom the Bell Tolls learned of Gold's disapproval, he shot back: "Tell Mike Gold that Ernest Hemingway says he should go fuck himself."[5] Such responses may well have occurred to Maltz, but as a Communist Party member, he did not have the luxury to indulge them, at least not with impunity.

In the *New Masses* and elsewhere, other writers tore into Maltz in similar style. Gold wrote that he would have more to say about Maltz at some other time. As it turned out, he would say it to Maltz's face, and he wouldn't be alone. Since Maltz was a writer of growing stature, honored at the Oscars and a key player in the important Hollywood section, the Communist Party decided that his sins were worthy of special treatment. Lest others should be tempted to lower agitprop standards, the Party would make an example of Maltz, using the same sort of inquisition that had forced Elia Kazan out of the Party.

"A week later the roof fell in, and that is a very mild way of putting it," said Leopold Atlas.[6] "The execution squad, shipped in from the East, came marching in. Some high muckamucks, whom I had never known . . . came striding on giant steps. This was the intellectual goon squad."

The squad included cultural commissar V. J. Jerome, Mike Gold, Party leader and trade-union boss William Z. Foster, *Daily Worker* columnist Samuel Sillen, novelist Howard Fast, and many of the California comrades, including Nemmy Sparks, a Party organizer in Los Angeles County. Sparks brought to the proceedings not merely a desire to punish Maltz but a scarcely disguised loathing for the entire studio section, whose commissioned officers had been given many privileges not enjoyed by the rank and file.

The squad called a general meeting of all the writers at the home of Abe Polonsky, one of the more orthodox of the Party's Hollywood scribes. Polonsky told comrades he didn't try to get Marxist ideas into pictures; rather, he wrote the way he did because he was a Marxist.[7]

Maltz's strategy suggested he had underestimated the gravity of his crime in Party eyes. As the meeting started, he tried to explain his thoughts on the article, but a chorus of howls stopped him cold and he clamed up. When one or two of the others tried to speak in

Maltz's favor, the Party squad shouted them down. There was no question of debate. Rather, Maltz and his defenders were not to be heard. Arnold Manoff, one of the first to congratulate Maltz on his article, said nothing. "The wolves were loose and you should have seen them," said Leopold Atlas. "It was a spectacle for all time."

For Howard Fast it was payback time. He blasted Maltz as a "reactionary," which, while falling short of "Trotskyite," remained one of the more serious accusations against anyone claiming progressive credentials.

Alvah Bessie rose from a corner and tore into Maltz with all the venom he could muster. When Bessie had finished, Herb Biberman stood up spouting, as Atlas described it, "elaborate mouthfuls of nothing, his every accent dripping with hatred."

Maltz's associates of long standing, his friends and comrades, joined in the kill with the greatest zeal. In their circles, Maltz had been known as a person of talent and integrity. Now none of that counted for anything. "They worked over him with every verbal fang and claw at their command," said Atlas, "every ax and bludgeon, and they had plenty. They evidently were past masters at this sort of intellectual cannibalism."

The meeting went on long into the night, with the battered Maltz weathering the storm as best he might. The squad reconvened the proceedings the next week at the same place. Atlas, who was there, was prepared to follow Maltz out of the Party if he stood up to them. But at the next meeting, he said, "they completely broke him. . . . The hyena attack—that is the only way I can describe it—continued with a rising snarl of triumph, and made him crawl and recant."

Though the inquisition had been grueling, Maltz's reeducation and purification had not yet run its course. He had crawled in person; now he would have to crawl in print. On April 7, 1946, "Moving Forward," by Albert Maltz, appeared *The Worker*.

"I published an article in the *New Masses* some weeks ago which was greeted by severe criticism," he wrote. "The sum total of this criticism was that my article was not a contribution to the development of the working cultural movement, but that its fundamental ideas, on the contrary, would lead to the paralysis and liquidation of left-wing culture." The charges, Maltz said, were serious.

"I consider now that my article—by what I have come to agree was a one-sided, nondialectical treatment of complex issues— could not, as I had hoped, contribute to the development of left-wing criticism and creative writing. I believe also that my critics were entirely correct in insisting that certain fundamental ideas in my article would, if pursued to their conclusion, result in the dissolution of the left-wing cultural movement."

Maltz confessed that he had omitted the "total truth" about the left wing and "presented a distorted view of the facts, history and contribution of the left-wing culture to American life. This was not my desire, but I accept it as the objective result. And, at the same time, by my one-sided zeal in attempting to correct errors, and so forth, I wrote an article that opened the way for the *New Leader* to seize upon my comments in order to 'support' its unprincipled slanders against the left."

"Of all that my article unwittingly achieved, this is the most difficult pill for me to swallow. Misstatements are now being offered up as fresh proof of the old lie: that the left puts artists in uniform. But it is a pill I have had to swallow and that I now want to dissolve."

It wasn't the Left, he wrote, that put artists in uniform. It was the dreadful social conditions in the West. "The left wing, by its insistence that artists must be free to speak the absolute truth about society, by the intellectual equipment it offers in Marxist scientific thought, is precisely the force that can help the artist strip himself of the many uniforms into which he has been stepping since birth."

Then there was the matter of James T. Farrell. "I agree now that my characterization of him was decidedly lax," Maltz wrote. "Farrell's history and work are the best example I know of the manner in which a poisoned ideology and increasingly sick soul can sap the talent and wreck the living fiber of a man's work." And the treatment Farrell received was now, in Maltz's view, entirely justified.

"The intense, ardent, and sharp discussion around my article, therefore, seems to me to have been a healthy and necessary one—and to have laid the foundation whereby a new clarity can be achieved, a new consciousness forged, and a struggle undertaken to return, deeply, to sound Marxist principles."

Before Maltz finished, he even attacked "Browderism," the softer line of the ousted Party leader, doubtless confirmation to his inquisitors that his absolution was complete. Despite the humiliating rigors that Maltz had endured, the Party had him scheduled for still more public flagellation.

On April 8, 1946, the day after his recantation appeared, Albert Maltz took part in "Art: Weapon of the People," a Hollywood forum event first announced in the *People's Daily World* on March 29 and chaired by screenwriter Waldo Salt. The lineup included Samuel Sillen, John Howard Lawson, Dalton Trumbo, and Carlton Moss, a black writer and filmmaker who had produced *The Negro Soldier* documentary with Frank Capra. Members of the public could pay fifty-five cents to hear Maltz, in effect, recite his recantation. Actress Carin Kinzel Burrows, who liked Maltz and had read his books, was there. "Mr. Maltz got up and made a speech and said how wrong he had been, and blamed himself for having fallen into such a grave error, and said art was a weapon and had to be used as a weapon," she said. "He publicly disgraced and humiliated himself. It was a terrible spectacle to see a man I had always respected behave in this way."[8]

The Maltz affair even landed on the pages of *Life* magazine, which noted that the writer had even castigated his sympathizers for objecting to the harshness of his inquisitors.[9] Closer to home, the anti-Communist Motion Picture Alliance, with members John Wayne, Ayn Rand, and Roy Brewer, took note with great glee of the events in a pamphlet titled "Albert Maltz Eats Red Crow."

The Party evidently thought Maltz had learned his lesson, because six months later the *People's Daily World* announced Maltz's appointment to the board of a new Marxist literary magazine, along with Howard Fast, Alvah Bessie, Mike Gold, V. J. Jerome, John Howard Lawson, Carlton Moss, and Dalton Trumbo.[10]

While the inquisition pushed some Party members to beef up their orthodoxy, many others were having second thoughts. It was one thing to join a Party that saw itself as part of the mainstream of American tradition, an heir to Jefferson and Lincoln, and on the front lines of the patriotic struggle against the dark forces of the Third Reich. It was another to be a member of a Party that portrayed one's own country as the fascist heir to the Third Reich and was increasingly coming under fire. To join a Party that supplied easy answers to tough questions, that provided an intellectual status symbol, a social support network, an inside track on jobs, access to stars like Frank Sinatra through front groups like HICCASP—all that had been easy, even a matter of fashion, for people like Edward Dmytryk and Leopold Atlas.

It was another thing entirely, they discovered, to be in a Party where the simple idea that art should be free of political constraints brought down the wrath of Party bosses and ended in a humiliating session of re-education. An increasing number of members wanted no part of it but hesitated to simply resign and walk away.

"After this I knew positively that I had to get out," said Leopold Atlas. "But how, I frankly didn't know. . . . They were placed in strategic positions throughout the industry. . . . Withdrawal from them would have meant professional and economic suicide."

Faced with that dilemma, many of those fighting it out in the talent guilds and on the streets decided to stick with the Party, a decision that entailed both duty and consequences. Party organs and events were reflecting the new anti-Western militancy and the same type of "peace" rhetoric aimed at weakening the West that was prevalent during the Nazi-Soviet Pact.

The Treaty of Beverly Hills

AS EUROPE CONTINUED TO DIG OUT OF THE RUBBLE, it was becoming more apparent that peace was not in the offing, despite the efforts of the new United Nations, now in its second year. East was East and West was West, and those who had been expecting post-war cooperation between the former allies were beginning to believe that never the twain would meet. On March 15, 1946, ten days after Churchill's speech about the "Iron Curtain" from the Baltic to the Adriatic, the *People's Daily World* ran a front-page story in which Hugh DeLacy, a popular-front politician from Washington State, blasted the British leader as an enemy of peace. In an inside interview in the same issue, Josef Stalin himself attacked his former wartime ally.

Four days later the Party journal touted Anna Louise Strong, Lincoln Steffens's mentor, as "one of the best informed living Americans on the Soviet Union," citing her book *I Change Worlds*, in which she said that Stalin was too important to be regarded as a mere god. Strong defended Stalin's control of Eastern Europe and said that "the Soviet people have a passion for peace greater than any other in the world, so the real answer depends on America."[1] The Party also defended the *Atlantic Monthly* for publishing two articles by Strong, a move that had been criticized by James T. Farrell and William Henry Chamberlain, a former correspondent in Moscow who complained that articles critical of Stalin and his policies had been rejected.[2]

On March 25, 1946, actor Paul Robeson, who was appearing in a highly political program at the Second Baptist Church with writer and Party leader John Howard Lawson and singer–actress Lena Horne, told an audience of 3,000 people to beware of "this nonsense about a Red scare." Robeson denied that there was anti-Semitism in the USSR; in that country, he said, people who spoke against the Jews were jailed. In the same vein, at a Conference of Studio Unions rally at Legion Stadium, Communist screenwriter Samuel Ornitz called anti-Semitism "the tool of reaction. Whenever an imperialistic power was threatened by progressivism, anti-Semitism was brought up as a scapegoat."[3]

"Imperialist" had become part of Party boilerplate, with *People's Daily World* columnist Joseph Starobin calling the United States "the greatest imperialist power on earth."[4] Even the Party's film critics did not miss an opportunity to attack the United States.

According to the *People's Daily World*, the movie *The Outlaw*, with Jane Russell, was "the most vicious attack on women in history. . . . It itself is an outlaw and should be attacked as the harbinger of a rotten spring." Producer Howard Hughes, the *Daily World* charged, had made "a picture which is the rottenest in the history of motion pictures." But the problems ran deeper than *The Outlaw*, according to the Communist journal. "The industry is mighty sick," it said. "It is sick with the deep sickness of our society. There is a pervading cultural degeneracy in this imperialist country."

In the postwar scene, the Moscow purge trials of the 1930s were again getting attention as evidence of Stalin's malevolent character and intentions. Party writers stayed busy giving the show trials a fresh coat of revisionist paint and warning of a Nazi resurgence.

People's Daily World writer Sender Garlin attacked the former Communists and anti-Stalinists who wrote about the trials and other Soviet atrocities, calling them part of a postwar Nazi conspiracy. The assumption that the people Stalin executed were innocent, he wrote, was simply a propaganda ploy. The book *I Choose Freedom*, by defector Victor Kravchenko, was being used as a weapon by reactionaries "who are encouraging the Nazi conspiracy for a return to power. . . ."[5]

While covering the fast-moving international scene, Party newspapers did not neglect the studio conflict.

IN APRIL 1946 HERB SORRELL and seven other CSU men were acquitted of rioting charges but found guilty of failure to disperse. The *People's Daily World* indulged no criticism of Sorrell, whose men had started the riot; the paper compared the Burbank police to Nazi stormtroopers.[6] Bolstered by the acquittal and support from the Party, Sorrell continued his rallies at Hollywood Legion Stadium. There he relied on familiar weapons.

On June 24, he charged that a conspiracy between gangsters and "misleaders of labor" had set out to destroy the democratic unions of Hollywood one at a time. "We do not want a strike," Sorrell said, "but if a strike becomes necessary, if that is what the studios want, we know how to give it to them."[7] But despite a return to a militant stance, Sorrell had lost some momentum.

When Brewer came to Hollywood in March of 1945, Josef Stalin and Franklin Roosevelt were allies against the Nazis, and the Communist Party was staunchly pro-American. Sorrell had taken the lead, and the embattled Brewer had responded as best he could. Now the war was over, and the Communists had swung back to a stance of anti-American class hatred. That convinced even some of Brewer's harshest critics that he had been right about the issue all along.

As scholars of the Hollywood disputes noted, while quick to charge that his colleagues were naive about Communism, Roy

Brewer was slow to charge anyone with actual Party membership.[8] Many of those he accused in the early days now played open roles in Party initiatives. Brewer was able to capture the momentum and now could force Sorrell to respond. Convinced that his opponents in the Party and the CSU could dish out but not take, Brewer attacked wherever he saw a chance of success.

During the original jurisdictional dispute in 1945, a group of machinists had joined the IA. According to the terms of the American Federation of Labor settlement, the IA had reluctantly agreed to remove the machinists from the studios. In the spring of 1946, however, Machinists' Union 1185, a CSU group, withdrew from the AFL after they had quarreled with the Carpenters. Brewer saw an opening through which he could get his IA machinists back to work; with help from the Teamsters, he succeeded in getting an AFL charter for Machinists Local 789, a group of about forty men, most from the old IAM (the International Association of Machinists). These were skilled technicians who could recalibrate cameras and work on props and in the film lab. The Los Angeles Central Labor Council supported the IA, as did the studio producers, who discharged all machinists who would not join the AFL affiliate. The CSU machinists tried to retaliate by refusing to handle work done by AFL groups, but the tactic proved ineffective.

An outraged Herb Sorrell launched a strike, but the National Labor Relations Board stepped in, and the walkout lasted only two days. Sorrell's agreeing to NLRB arbitration showed that he had lost some strength. He tried to recapture the initiative by shifting his emphasis from jurisdictional issues to wages and started demanding a 50 percent pay raise for his workers. He didn't have much of a case. The average hourly wage in Los Angeles in 1946 was $1.65, but in the movie business the average was $2.25, with generous fringe benefits.[9]

In search of a rallying cry, Sorrell appealed directly to IA members for support. When Brewer found out about it, he arranged a meeting and took up his rival's challenge. On July 2, 1946, Brewer and Sorrell met in the producers' luxurious "negotiation bungalow" at the Beverly Hills Hotel and hammered out with the studios an agreement for a 25 percent raise and other concessions for both the CSU and the IA. Both agreed that jurisdictional issues would be kept out of the deal. The agreement became known as the "Treaty of Beverly Hills" and stirred hopes for a lasting peace in the industry.

"Peace! It's Wonderful," proclaimed the *Hollywood Sun,* which duly crowned starlet Poni Adams as Miss Treaty of Beverly Hills. "Studio Unions Score Big Gains," headlined the *People's Daily World*. "25% Pay Hike, 36-Hour Week."[10] Later that month, when Richard Walsh was reelected head of the IA, the *People's Daily World* noted that a resolution to take steps against subversive, radical, and Communist groups had been passed only after heated debate.

Herb Sorrell wasn't entirely pleased with the deal struck in the treaty, but other troubles loomed for the CSU boss; later in July, the Los Angeles Central Labor Council brought charges against him for Communist affiliations.

On August 16, 1946, the Knight Committee, which in October 1945 had issued a preliminary settlement of the studio dispute, handed down its "clarification," which did more to confuse than to clarify. For the most part the new ruling kept everything in place, but the Carpenters claimed it gave back their jurisdiction over the erection of sets.

One version of the clarification, reportedly from the arbitration trio, was mimeographed and unsigned. The following year the Los Angeles Archdiocese assigned two scholars to investigate disputes. The two men recommended that the mimeographed, unsigned clarification, whose authenticity had always been in doubt, be rejected.[11] It was later discovered that this document came directly from Hutcheson's Carpenters' Union and was a fraud.[12]

STALIN, MEANWHILE, had set up the World Federation of Trade Unions (WFTU) as a kind of Comintern for his international postwar push in labor. The AFL's international representative, Robert Watt, denounced the WFTU as a front dominated by Moscow and called for a halt to appeasement of the USSR. But the CIO unions, dominated by Communists, approved of the WFTU and so did Herb Sorrell. "My organization desires to support the WFTU," he said.[13]

Support for Moscow's labor front hurt Sorrell in union ranks, but the CSU leader could still count on key allies for support. On September 11, Bill Hutcheson of the Carpenters' Union and Herb Sorrell told their people to refuse to work on "hot" sets, that is, sets that IA people had erected. On September 26, the studio producers responded to their move by firing those who had refused to work and bringing in IA replacements.

The CSU claimed that it had been locked out, and Sorrell added wage increases for his workers to his demands to the studios. The studios had recently approved a large pay increase, and they refused to allow another. The lines were clearly drawn. The studio producers, the IA, and the Teamsters were on one side, facing the CSU, the craft unions, and the Communist Party on the other. On September 27, Herb Sorrell told reporters that "there may be men hurt, there may be men killed before this is over, but we are in no mood to be pushed around any more."[14]

Soon the action thriller first staged at Warner Brothers in October 1945 was running at every major Hollywood studio.

13

Technicolor Violence

ON SEPTEMBER 27, 1946, the *Los Angeles Times* reported, in a piece headlined "Violence Opens Studio Strike": "Early in the morning several thousand pickets threw up human barriers at studio entrances."

That day, tens of thousands of workers got into the studios with only a jostling, but that would quickly change. The pickets themselves warned that the worst was yet to come. It was. The next day, at MGM in Culver City, CSU mobs threw bricks and bottles and ripped the wiring from cars that were trying to enter. In ongoing battles in the following days, "blood streaked from battlers' faces as the fighting spread over a long Culver Boulevard block in front of the studio's south and main gate," said an account. "The street was slippery with mud and in some spots with blood."

As at Warner Brothers the previous year, the local police were badly outnumbered. Deputy Dean Stafford got separated from his fellow officers by a gang of twelve strikers who downed him with a blow from a bottle to the side of his face and then kicked him unconscious, yelling, "Kill him! Kill him!"[1] A CSU picket captain at Paramount told a reporter, "We have a regular traveling mob for the rough stuff."[2]

Soon all-out war raged at every Hollywood studio. Even with his carefully cultivated intelligence network, Roy Brewer found it hard to keep up with Herb Sorrell's attacks. One day the CSU forces abandoned hundreds of their own cars in the street outside Columbia Studios, creating chaos and keeping people out. The tactics initially proved effective: work on all movie sets was shut down by the end of September, and the actors were thrown into a crisis. Writers could write during the strike, but actors could not act.

On September 16, Franchot Tone, an actor of left-wing inclinations, made a motion that members of the Screen Actors Guild be instructed to cross the CSU picket lines and live up to their contracts. The Guild voted for it by more than 98 percent.

On October 14, Robert Montgomery of the Screen Actors Guild contended that SAG believed that no jurisdictional dispute should be allowed to reach the stage of a work stoppage. Therefore, he said, "the Guild has instructed its members to pass through the picket lines and to live up to its contract with the producers."[3] Most actors, famous and otherwise, kept reporting for work, but crossing the lines proved no easy task. Sorrell now relied on threats and sabotage. His men scattered tacks in front of the stars' automobiles and threatened to throw acid in the face of Ronald Reagan.

Sorrell himself was then close to fifty, but he remained a man who liked to lead by example, and he could still mix it up with the best of them. The studios got a court injunction to keep him away from their property, but the CSU boss avoided it by moving to a place where he couldn't be reached. As the *Los Angeles Times* described it, "Sorrell shouted exhortations over a loud-speaker to pickets as he cruised overhead at MGM in his private airplane."[4] Sorrell once testified, "[Flying is] one of my ways of relaxing, and I hate to pay ten or fifteen dollars an hour to get to fly somebody else's old crate."[5] How he could afford an airplane on the salary of a painters' union business agent remains a matter of some mystery, perhaps traced to the time when Sorrell described himself as "a little bit filthy rich" and could travel the world at will.

Sorrell maintained his air patrol until the police got in their own planes and chased him. He would flee out to sea until, he said, "they thought I was going to China" and abandoned pursuit. Then Sorrell would return and land at a different airport. One time he touched down in a berry patch and wrecked his plane. He claimed that the craft had been sabotaged.[6]

Though this was a daring maneuver that inspired the CSU troops, the true risk of Sorrell's campaign lay in other areas. Even with some 9,000 men available for combat duty, it was difficult to maintain massive pickets at all the different studios, especially when the city police forces were both larger and better prepared than the Burbank police had been. In a brilliant strategic move, the CSU general concentrated his forces where they would wield the most devastating effect. To do this, Sorrell relied on longtime allies still within the IA.

Local 683 of the IA had long been dominated by Norval Crutcher, Russell McKnight, and John R. Martin, all Communist hard-liners. On October 13, 1946, Local 683 joined Sorrell's Conference of Studio Unions in a walkout, using low wages as their excuse. But Roy Brewer, who had just negotiated a pay raise for the local, knew that the reason lay elsewhere.

Local 683 operated a strategically important unit in the film industry—the Technicolor lab on Cahuenga Boulevard in Hollywood, which at that time was the only place in town where color film could be processed. If Sorrell could shut that lab down, he could stop the entire industry. With no processed film, there would be no new movies. Directors had to see the dailies before tearing down a set; with no lab there would be no dailies, so production would halt, too.

At the time of the walkout, some $20 million worth of negatives awaited processing. Sorrell marshaled 2,000 strikers at the lab; they kept workers out and brawled with the outmanned police in the worst of the rioting. There were thirty-eight arrests. "Clubs and fists swung in three waves of fighting during the tense moments of a two-hour period shortly after dawn," wrote the *Los Angeles Times*.[7]

The Technicolor campaign scored such successes for the CSU that the *People's Daily World* bragged about it, noting on October 31 that twenty-seven movies had been postponed because the studios had not been able to process film. On November 9, in a story headlined "Film Producers Find the Going Rough," the Communist daily said "things aren't going so well on the film production front, particularly since the key lab technicians hit the picket lines before major studios. . . ." *Sinbad the Sailor* was to be replaced in black and white and *Duel in the Sun* was now slated for the following spring. Within a month, Paramount stopped *Popeye* and *Little Lulu* cartoons, and *Up in Central Park*, with Deanna Durbin, was postponed. "Not even the promise of Roy Brewer . . . to furnish scabs is panning out at Technicolor and other studios," said the Communist Party paper. CSU morale continued to run high.

Brewer tried diplomatic channels, but when all negotiations failed, the IA placed the lab technicians' Local 683 under emergency status and suspended its officers. Brewer moved to establish successors, negotiate contracts, and put people back to work. Within thirty days, Technicolor was again processing film. Brewer took legal channels to get the IA's property returned, but the 683 radicals managed to hold on for a full year, after which they finally gave in and handed everything over voluntarily. By then they had trashed the place, but in the rubble of 683 headquarters Brewer found a set of minutes for the Conference of Studio Unions. These minutes provided more clues to the CSU's inner workings.

Back on the barricades, the pickets were pulling out all the stops, trying to regain the edge in the propaganda war. CSU men posed as suffering veterans who were being done in by reactionary police forces. *People's Daily World* headlines such as "Blood Flows as Cops Club Picketing Vets" also wrapped the strikers in the

American flag.[8] But the populace that was once inclined to take his side was disturbed by Herb Sorrell's violence. In comparison, as labor writer Victor Riesel pointed out, "not a single nose was bloodied" in the much larger strikes at General Motors and the coal and steel industries.[9] The *Los Angeles Times* gave ample coverage to CSU attacks on non-strikers, and the CSU responded with demonstrations at the *Times* headquarters, alienating journalists and editorial writers who might otherwise have been inclined to give Sorrell the benefit of the doubt.

The Communists also called for a boycott of films made by the major studios.[10] "Avoid them," said the *People's World*. "Tell your friends to do so. Tell the theatre manager in your neighborhood you won't go to see films made by these seven phony outfits. Until the strike is won, the *People's World* will not review any films of the above studios."[11]

In December 1946, Hugh DeLacy, the popular-front politician from Washington State, told a crowd at the Shrine Auditorium, "Your fight for peace begins on the CSU picket lines in Hollywood."[12] Paul Jarrico and other Communist writers sponsored a motion in the Screen Writers Guild to give $10,000 in support to the CSU, but the non-Communists, now familiar with their tactics, voted it down.[13]

JOHN WEXLEY, DALTON TRUMBO, RING LARDNER JR., Albert Maltz, and the whole Communist caucus in the Guild earned more in a week than most back-lot workers did in months. They earned even more than what the Party itself paid some of its hardest working organizers, which did not even amount to scab wages. Although they stood shoulder to shoulder on the lines, the Party rank and file still resented the revolution's designated commissioned officers.

Hollywood is a business community, not an artistic colony. Millions of Hollywood dollars were affected by the strike, and money was the primary reason for the number of attempts to settle the dispute. Stars and Screen Actors Guild officials were as much affected as the carpenters and painters. In December 1946, SAG sent Eddie Arnold, Gene Kelly, Robert Montgomery, George Murphy, Walter Pidgeon, Dick Powell, Ronald Reagan, Alexis Smith, Robert Taylor, and Jane Wyman to the American Federation of Labor convention in Chicago, hoping to leverage the AFL into action. Reagan, Montgomery, and others believed that Bill Hutcheson of the Carpenters' Union was flouting the December 26 directive, and the SAG representatives told AFL president William Green that if he didn't do something, SAG would fly actors to major cities and would show films of the violence that was taking place outside the studios. Green told Reagan that since the unions were independent, he was powerless to do anything.[14]

Hutcheson admitted to the SAG people what Brewer had known all along: the Carpenters' Union was using Sorrell and the Communist Party to break the IA, and Hutcheson planned to dump them afterward.[15] The Carpenters' boss proposed a deal. If the actors could get IA president Richard Walsh to give in on the August clarification, Hutcheson would "run Sorrell out of Hollywood and break up the CSU in five minutes." Just how he could run anybody out of town was not quite clear, but he added that he would "do the same to the Commies."

Sorrell was staying in the same hotel and had caught wind of all this. "It doesn't matter a damn what Hutcheson says," he told Reagan. "This thing is going on no matter what he does. When it ends up, there'll be only one man running labor in Hollywood, and that man will be me!"[16] Sorrell's statement showed evidence of Party pressure on him to be the movies' all-powerful labor boss.

When pressed as to responsibility for the bloody conflict in the studios, Sorrell said he didn't advocate violence, telling SAG leaders, "We can no more control our members than you can keep your actors from committing rape."[17]

Though the Chicago summit had failed, the SAG delegation pressed on with meetings at the Knickerbocker Hotel in

Hollywood, gatherings Edward Arnold said would go down in the annals of labor history.[18] The three wise men of the Knight Committee weren't there, but two of them, Felix Knight and William Birthright, made an attempt to clarify their clarification over the telephone. "All parties," they said, were right in their claims, and the clarification that had caused so much controversy was *not* the one they had written. But when they telegrammed the supposedly correct version, it was the same version that they denied writing. The clarification had failed to clarify.

By this time Sorrell had squandered the actors' support. "We discovered that the culprits in the thing were the CSU," John Garfield later testified. "They didn't want to settle the strike."[19]

At the Knickerbocker Hotel, Sorrell screamed at his erstwhile friend Gene Kelly, but the days when Sorrell could dish out and not take were over. At one point in the meeting Reagan turned to Sorrell. "Herb, as far as I am concerned," he said, "you have shown here tonight that you intend to welsh on your statement of two nights ago, and as far as I am concerned, you do not want peace in the motion picture industry."[20]

A rousing ovation followed Reagan's statement, confirming that a clear majority in the talent guilds and back lots *did* want peace in the motion picture industry. After this incident, Reagan took a leading role opposing the CSU and Communists. Though still a Democrat and not a member of the Motion Picture Alliance, Ronald Reagan became Roy Brewer's closest counterpart in the talent guilds.

Within the following year, Father George Dunne, the Hollywood Catholic diocese, and Joe Keenan of the American Federation of Labor, backed by SAG, all made attempts to arbitrate the dispute. None succeeded. In all cases, the Conference of Studio Unions' lawyers, most of them Communist Party members, raised new issues or refused to follow through on questions that had already been settled. CSU pickets continued, and their supporters became more vocal, spurred by changes on the national scene.

Communist Party screenwriter Dalton Trumbo scripted Katharine Hepburn's fiery speeches at Legion Stadium.

As stars of the 1940s learned, blacklisting did not begin during the 1950s nor with the House Committee on Un-American Activities.

Progressive Citizens of America lent star power to Communist Party initiatives.

Roy Brewer (standing), former Communist Howard Costigan (to the left of Brewer), and Ronald Reagan (to the right of Brewer) founded the League of Hollywood Voters to isolate movie industry Communists. Helen Gahagan Douglas sits to the right of Reagan.

CSU forces massed outside of MGM in Culver City in September 1946.

During the worst of the violence, CSU strikers torched a car outside of the MGM studios.

Ronald Reagan and Gene Kelly were initially on different sides of the conflict.

Communist-backed factions portrayed the struggle as patriotism versus fascism.

Entering a studio during CSU walkouts was a risky proposition, but Herb Sorrell's prediction that men might die went unfulfilled.

Star status carried no leverage with the CSU or its publication, *The Picket Line*.

The CSU film boycott included the work of actors friendly to its cause.

Rhetoric ran at a fever pitch throughout Hollywood's political wars.

Famed W. B. 'Citizenship' Proves Lacking

HOLLYWOOD ATOM

Published under sponsorship of the 15 local unions belonging to the Hollywood Studio Strike Strategy Committee

Vol. I, No. 33   Hollywood, Calif., Tuesday, Oct. 9, 1945   Price 5c

WARNERS HIRE THUGS

Fascism Runs Wild

Flag Raising Signal For Scab Attack

Hundreds Of Patriotic IA Craftsmen Refuse To Join In Unwarranted Onslaughts On Picketers By Gestapo

By JIM LUNTZEL

At ten minutes of six Monday morning the sun was beginning to show over the range of mountains east of Burbank. It was a quiet dawn.

Since 4 A.M. striking studio workers had been slowly walking the sidewalk in front of the auto entrance at Warner Bros. Studio.

Feeling of Tenseness

The gradually increasing light of day revealed tense looks on the workers' faces. They kept their eyes on the enlarging group of men across the street.

As they looked inside the studio gates they could see platoons of uniformed men being shuffled from one stand stage to another. Policemen glanced frequently at their watches and at intervals looked to the roof of the time office building.

Battle Looms

Picket captains exhorted the studio workers in low voices to "Keep your eyes open!"

Word flashed in an undertone up and down the line that the strike breakers probably would make their move at six o'clock.

The pickets closed up their ranks drew in deep breaths. They walked with heads up.

At five minutes of six two policemen inside the studio walked over to the main gate, released the catch and swung it inward.

(Continued on Page 3)

Two hundred Warner Bros. goons yesterday failed to break the Hollywood strike which has closed that studio since Friday morning.

When the noise of a pre-dawn battle had died away, 25 men and women were treated for bruises and lacerations.

Warner Bros. studio police, backed up by squads of uniformed "gestapo" sluggers from the Los Angeles County Sheriff's office, Pasadena, Glendale, Burbank and San Fernando police departments, opened a way through the picket line. Then Blayney Matthews, of Warners' "plant protection" invited all workers on call to come inside.

IA Workers Balk

A few did, but 75 or 100 workers aren't enough to maintain studio production. Hundreds of honest IATSE workers refused to cross the picket lines.

The goons were loaded into their truck and driven away, waving $50 bills they had received for their morning's work, and yelling "sucker" at the pickets.

Then the picket lines were reformed, and marched without molestation.

(Continued on Page 4)

Warner Bros. New Policy Is Tear Gas For Women

Questionable as may be Warner's title to their self-styled "First In Citizenship, First In Pictures," there's no dispute about their being the first movie company to turn tear gas on women.

"A car becomes a lethal weapon when its obvious purpose is to clear a path over the bodies of pedestrians. What can you do to defend yourself except turn it over?"—Dalton Trumbo.

The L.A. Times report that there were 4,000 persons at the Sunday night mass meeting came much closer to the fact than the Examiner's reported 800. Actually, close to 5,000 persons attended the meeting.

Many IA wives who learned the score for the first time when they drove their husbands to work on Monday, are urging their men to RESPECT the picket lines.

Great credit is due the girls from homes where they have heretofore been shielded from everything disagreeable. These (Continued on Page 4)

MASS MEETING

The film workers Strike Committee has called a mass meeting for Wednesday evening, October 10, at 8:00 P.M. at the American Legion Stadium in Hollywood. Everyone carrying a union card is urged to attend.

HOLLYWOOD ATOM

Small But Mighty

Bursting With Truth

Published under sponsorship of the 15 local unions belonging to the Hollywood Studio Strike Strategy Committee

Vol. I, No. 42   Hollywood, Calif., Wednesday, October 24, 1945   Price Five Cents

Republic Shut Down To Prevent Riot

FOUR STUDIOS CLOSED

Reluctant Actors Refuse To Pass Through Pickets Battered Aside By Police

Public opinion, as expressed through the activity of nearly a score of militant unions, kept production at an almost irreducible minimum in four Hollywood studios yesterday, while in other studios, technically open, production managers complained of "slowdowns" by sympathetic workmen.

Three studios, Warner Bros., Paramount and Republic were completely shut down, with production at a standstill.

At RKO, some technical workers were smuggled inside in motor trucks, at considerable expense, and others were escorted through picket lines by solid phalanxes of club-swinging policemen, also an expensive procedure—also to taxpayers.

No Actors

RKO heads, however, had forgotten to include actors in their scheme to break the picket smashing program, and a number of companies were all ready to shoot hot period principals.

"We thought the actors would crash the lines in their own cars!" one producer wailed in frustration.

Technicians Warned

Most of the actors had heeded (fairly broad hint) of the Screen Actors' Guild, which passed a resolution last week, extending the guild's protection in contractual disputes with studios should any actors decide "for any reason" that picket line busting would endanger health or reputation.

Meanwhile it was reported that (Continued on Page 3)

MASS PICKET LINES SET FOR LION'S DEN

More than 25,000 pickets will be thrown around Metro-Goldwyn-Mayer studio in Culver City Saturday to express the opinion of 160 labor unions and civic bodies that the producers are responsible for the current studio lockout, and should at once end it.

Call for this giant mass picket line, which is expected to include most of the 8,000 workers now locked out, was issued after a meeting of the United Labor and Citizens' Committee at the Royal Palms Hotel last night.

Present were delegates from a number of AFL, CIO and Railway Brotherhood unions, as well as representatives of numerous clubs, leagues, student bodies and religious organizations.

"Kidnaped"

HERB SORRELL ... Escorted to police station by cop who "found" new way to serve big bundle of injunction papers. (Story on Page 4).

Patterson Continues Americanism Fight

WASHINGTON, D. C. (Special to the ATOM)—Rep Ellis E. Patterson continued his two-handed his campaign against the un-American activities of the House Un-American Activities committee yesterday.

Leading the fight to abolish the Rankin group "has blanketed the committee, Patterson charged that its un-American activities of the main committee, calling them subversive.

JOIN THE PICKET LINES!

Yates Halts Production For Duration

Quick thinking and common sense on the part of Herbert J. Yates, majority stock holder of Republic Studio, prevented a clash between locked-out employes and replacement workers in the valley studio yesterday morning.

Yates drove his car between an advancing line of men determined to break the picket line and hired them to disperse and go home.

"You all will be paid for today's hour," he shouted, "I want no violence!"

Immediately Yates informed picket captains that he would close his studio and cease production until the strike was brought to a conclusion. A conference between Yates and Herbert K. Sorrell followed.

The decision to shut Republic came when the hard core of locked out workers set to appear showed up at Warner Bros. at 5 A.M. yesterday morning. Squads of pickets then were shifted to Republic where lines were thrown in front of the main administration entrance and the auto gate.

By 7 A.M. the core of Republic employe congregated across the street and grown to better than 300 while the picket forces totaled approximately 100, including women.

"If Yates had not moved in when he did," one picket captain declared, "There might have been a battle and bloodshed."

To force through concessions, Herb Sorrell needed to shut down the movie industry.

"I got in my airplane and rode around the studios a thousand feet high," testified CSU boss and former boxer Herb Sorrell, faithful to the Communist Party line through the Nazi-Soviet Pact.

"Generalissimo" Herb Sorrell (hatless, center) lost support when he backed Stalin's World Federation of Trade Unions.

Anti-Communist New Dealer Roy Brewer (left) entered the industry during the 1920s as a projectionist, the first branch of the movies to be unionized.

Outside Fox studios, leftist radio rabble-rouser Averill Berman deploys a megaphone for the CSU. Herb Sorrell is to the right of Berman and behind Sorrell stands Party member Frank Spector.

In the fall of 1946, the Republican Party gained control of both houses of Congress for the first time since 1928. The GOP numbered 246 to 188 in the House and 51 to 45 in the Senate, which now included a lawyer and former marine tailgunner from Wisconsin named Joseph McCarthy. These majorities wasted little time taking aim on the New Deal and its perceived ally, labor. While the election wasn't quite the reactionary victory that HICCASP had predicted, the Republican initiatives sharpened the class-war attitudes on the Left.

At a rally on January 19, 1947, CSU men distributed a pamphlet called "What Is the Role of Communists in the Hollywood Unions?" It was set up in question-and-answer style:

> Are there Communists in Hollywood unions?
>
> Yes. Communists are working people; Communism is a working class movement. So it is natural to find them in trade unions.
>
> Do Communists want to dominate the film industry for propaganda purposes?
>
> No. The producers try to evade the real issue of signed contracts for their workers by raising the phony issue of "Red Control." You know and we know film policy and content is determined by those who own the studios, not those who work in them. . . . The banks and their producer stooges continue their long tradition of "cheesecake" and "escapism," hoping to divert the attention of the common man from the real problems of housing, peace, health, jobs and high prices.
>
> What is a Communist?
>
> A Communist trade unionist understands it is not enough to be militant and progressive. He knows the working class must know where it is headed if it is to avoid blind alleys. The fight of the labor movement for its just demands, important as it is, can but partially solve the problems of the working class. The Marxist theory of Scientific Socialism provides the answer. . . . The Communist trade unionist accepts Socialism as the ultimate goal, while working to improve the living

conditions of the people and helping to raise the political consciousness of the working class.[21]

The pamphlet mentioned a special movie edition of the *People's
Daily World* that would appear on January 24. The special edition,
Hollywood—The True Story, showed on its cover actress Arlene
Dahl, decked out like a turkey and proudly displaying her tailfeath-
ers, to "capitalize on Thanksgiving." A second photo showed police
stopping CSU pickets, and a third captured Robert Taylor and
Katharine Hepburn in a love scene from *Undercurrent*. But the
special edition's editorial, titled "Monopoly Control—Can It Be
Defeated?," set the tone:

> Hollywood is often called the Land of Make-Believe, but
> there is nothing make-believe about the Battle of Hollywood
> being waged today. In the front lines of this battle, at the stu-
> dio gates, stand the thousands of locked out film workers; be-
> hind the studio gates sit the overlords of Hollywood, who
> refuse even to negotiate with the workers. . . .
>
> Behind the movie producers loom the shadows of their
> masters—the financiers who really own the industry, the same
> economic royalists who control the bulk of the nation's econ-
> omy. . . . The tycoons of Wall Street and the NAM [National
> Association of Manufacturers] want not only to crush labor in
> Hollywood. They want their union-busting scheme in Holly-
> wood to serve as a pattern for union-busting throughout the
> country. And the prize of victory for them means more than a
> servile labor movement. The prize would be complete control
> of the greatest medium of communication in history.
>
> Today the movies serve reaction subtly—by distorted
> values, by omission, by diverting the audience from its real
> problems. Tomorrow, if the men who control this industry
> have their way, the movies will be a naked weapon of Fascist
> propaganda.
>
> Can these men be fought?

They can be fought, they must be fought and they must be defeated. They can be fought by the 25,000 creative, technical, and back-lot workers who actually make the films. Without their hands and brains no script is written, no set is built, no camera rolls. . . . When the State Department fronts for the movie industry in taking over the screens of the entire world, its chief purpose is to use films as advance propaganda for U.S. imperialism. . . .

The moguls of Hollywood and Wall Street have been made bold by the Republican victory in the November elections. They have launched their offensive on many fronts—not only against progressive trade unionism in Hollywood, but other drives aimed at the seizure of control over every industry in the communications and cultural field, both at home and abroad.

These offensives of reaction are interconnected. But the counter-offensives of the people are interconnected too.

The special edition quoted Lenin's dictum "Of all the arts, the cinema is the most important," adding, "Monopoly capital knows and respects the truth behind Lenin's words. It recognizes that the optic nerve is the short-cut to the brain. Hence the ruthless drive of American Big Money to dominate world film markets."

Hollywood—The True Story outlined a history of Hollywood labor, blasting the IA, recalling Jeff Kibre's United Studio Technicians Guild, and praising the CSU as a "family" of unions. In this special issue, the Party indulged its own brand of film criticism: "Contrast between the 1946 crop and the better pictures of the war years: *Watch on the Rhine, Action in the North Atlantic, Pride of the Marines, G.I. Joe, Destination Tokyo, Tomorrow the World* —these and a number of other wartime movies, whatever their weaknesses, had something in common: a sense of reality, of warm humanity, a projection of situations and character in terms of the real needs and aspirations of our people. . . ." Those films, all written by Communists who had stayed with the Party during the

Nazi-Soviet Pact, were in the Party's view superior to the new product. "The trend toward unmotivated violence is marked in the bumper crop of so-called realistic, hard-boiled melodramas—*The Big Sleep, The Blue Dahlia, The Killers, The Postman Always Rings Twice*—to mention only a few" pictures guilty of "violence for violence's sake."

Hollywood—The True Story turned its guns on Hollywood's recent entry into the field of psychology, attacking *Spellbound, Love Letters, Somewhere in the Night:* "These pseudo-psychological films do serve a useful purpose for the men who financed them. Their message is: the illness in not in the social system; it is within you."

A third trend in recent Hollywood films, as identified in *Hollywood—The True Story,* was the "increased emphasis on mysticism, fantasy and religious themes. Apologetics for the Catholic church are so common in films."

Hollywood—The True Story praised *A Walk in the Sun* and *The Best Years of Our Lives* as "products of struggle between workers and creators of integrity and the forces of greed, cynicism and reaction." Other issues of the *People's Daily World* charged that the moguls were trying to quash pictures such as *The Grapes of Wrath* that showed the "seamy side" of American life. One issue charged that Disney's *Song of the South* "casts a golden glow over southern slave days." The movie "furthers the evil jim crow in a forum calculated to appeal to most moviegoers" and "fairly oozes with a sickening nostalgia for the old plantation."[22]

As it happened, *Song of the South* had been written by a Communist, Maurice Rapf, the son of a studio executive who had been radicalized on his trip to the USSR, and another leftist named Morton Grant. When the film was attacked by the NAACP, Rapf was supposed to defend it at the People's Education Center, but instead he attacked it. Rapf thought that Disney, whom he describes as a decent man and not an anti-Semite, had failed to make it clear that the story took place during Reconstruction.[23] The episode confirmed that the Party's left and far-left hands did not always coordinate.

While blasting Hollywood movies, the Party began to promote the movies they thought the American populace should see. The pictures centered on the victories and intrigues of one star, Josef Stalin. "Hollywood has its Academy Awards—the Soviet Union has its Stalin prize awards," said the *People's Daily World*. "Unlike Hollywood's awards, those made in the Soviet Union are not dictated by a handful of calculating major studio executives whose chief interest is box office 'take.' And unlike Hollywood, the USSR awards are as likely to be given to a technician, a script writer, or a set designer as they are to a 'star.'"[24]

The Vow, billed as "the epic film story of STALIN and the Soviet people, as seen through the eyes of a Russian mother" (capitalization original), was based on "the great historical vow which became Russia's program of action!" As the review explained: "the vow taken by Stalin at Lenin's grave 23 years ago—a vow that they would carry out with honor the will of the beloved leader and founder of the first Socialist state." The film showed the "building of the great tractor plant in the '20s when Russia's internal enemies were still alive, and of the amazement of a friendly American journalist who saw the Soviet people achieve impossible feats of engineering and production." Stalin, played by Mikhail Gelovani, inspects the plant as workers stand by in reverence.

The Vow shows the men and women "who had built up their beautiful city in the face of Trotskyite sabotage. . . . The Soviet Union is shown advancing on the road to socialism, advancing despite traitors like Bukarin and Kamenev" and the "Trotskyite fifth column." It was a movie "filled with revealing human episodes," and "a film to think about—a solid work with important things to say to Americans."[25]

At the Sunset Theatre, curious Americans could see the award-winning *Pageant of Russia*, which showcased marching legions of the Soviet youth, and which *People's Daily World* Los Angeles editor

Sidney Burke said "should be seen by every American imperialist who dreams of a world empire at the expense of the Soviet Union."[26]

Theaters also showed the Soviet documentary *Guerrilla Brigade*, narrated by Norman Corwin.[27] Actor–singer Paul Robeson received heavy promotion, as did banjoist Pete Seeger, a stalwart for the Party even during the Nazi-Soviet Pact, and writer Howard Fast, described by Samuel Sillen as "an ever-maturing talent that has already proved itself to be one of the most fertile and forthright in our country today."[28]

Communist allies showed support for the Conference of Studio Unions at the same time that its pro-Soviet stand alienated sympathetic liberals. In early February of 1947 the CSU brought in Vincente Lombardo Toledano, the Stalinist who had protested the presence of Trotsky in Mexico and who supported the World Federation of Trade Unions. Soviet intelligence traffic, intercepted by the United States and published in the 1990s, revealed Toledano to be a Soviet agent. At the time he contacted Gabriel Figueroa, a powerful figure in the Mexican film industry, and pressured him not to process any film from Hollywood as a show of sympathy for the CSU.[29] Appearing on the platform with Toledano was Father George Dunne, who said he felt humbled to be in the presence of such a great man.[30] Father Dunne, a frequent public speaker and radio broadcaster, defended Sorrell and blasted all opponents of the CSU, especially the IA and SAG. And the CSU enjoyed other champions on the airwaves, including Averill Berman, who broadcast on KXLA radio. On one of his broadcasts, Berman attacked Roy Brewer directly and compared the studio producers to Nazis. "Herman Goering would have smiled at the scene at MGM," Berman said.

IN MARCH, HERB SORRELL WAS ABDUCTED by three men who posed as police. The trio drove the CSU boss ninety miles north of Bakersfield, where they beat him and left him for dead. Sorrell said he survived by feigning unconsciousness. Investigations never revealed who had perpetrated the kidnapping, but the Communist Party claimed to know the very next day.

"Outraged movie unionists today charged that a conspiracy between producers and racketeer 'labor leaders' was responsible for last night's attempt to kill Herbert K. Sorrell," ran the *People's Daily World*'s lead story, in which Carl Head, CSU treasurer, said, "This violence of last night is a thing to be laid directly at the door of the conspiracy between the producers and the racketeer labor leaders in Hollywood." Russell McKnight, who was then running for city council of Los Angeles, said the act was "obviously perpetrated by hardened criminals of the most vicious type."[31]

On March 10, a bandaged and bruised but triumphant Sorrell appeared before 7,000 cheering supporters at the Olympic Auditorium. He was accompanied by Phil Connelly from the CIO, Dalton Trumbo, and Father Dunne, who said, "Neither the Screen Actors Guild nor any other honest union in Hollywood can be a party to that conspiracy and continue to cross the picket lines."[32]

SAG continued to hold meetings about the strike; at one such meeting Katharine Hepburn read a speech that Ronald Reagan recognized as a word-for-word copy of a CSU strike bulletin that had been distributed several weeks before.[33] Hepburn's longtime lover, Spencer Tracy, used to say, "Remember who shot Lincoln," as sufficient reason for actors to stay out of politics.[34] It was advice ignored by Hepburn, who had experienced a "rather leftist upbringing" under a mother openly sympathetic with Marxism and the USSR, but whose commitments to the downtrodden did not prevent the pursuit of personal affluence.

Hepburn went through a much ballyhooed romance with Howard Hughes and lived for a time with husband Leland Hayward in a home owned by Fred Niblo above Benedict Canyon. Her house guests included Donald Ogden Stewart and his new wife, Ella Winter, who doubtless helped fan her leftist tendencies into flame. But even the star power of Hepburn and others could not carry the day for Herb Sorrell, who would need to shut down the studios in order to force the concessions that would benefit him and the Party.

When pickets failed to obey court injunctions, they were arrested en masse and their trials upheld, despite fierce opposition from the Communist Party press and threats of worldwide boycotts through Moscow's World Federation of Trade Unions. Most of Sorrell's striking men were not Communists, and they were no longer willing to sacrifice themselves and the good of their families for the goals of their leader and his Party allies. In October, Sorrell's own union voted in a measure that allowed CSU members to cross the picket lines and work if they were suffering financially, which most, if not all, were after two years of struggle.

With the studios still operating and its own men crossing the lines, the Conference of Studio Unions began to weaken. But even though it seemed to be losing the battle of the back lots, the Party organization in Hollywood remained strong in the talent guilds. The war would soon shift to that front, as the Cold War heated up and Washington entered the fray.

Part 3

A New Kind of Talky

The hearings opened with all the glitter of a premier.
—*People's Daily World*, October 21, 1947

14

The "Reds in Movieland" Show

THE RISE OF NAZISM IN EUROPE and the appearance of pro-Nazi groups in the United States alarmed Samuel Dickstein, a U.S. representative whose constituency during the 1930s was a largely Jewish district in New York. Dickstein sought to strike at the Nazi danger not with the legislative function of Congress but with its investigative arm.[1] During the 1920s and 1930s, Congress had held investigations on the munitions industry and the Teapot Dome Scandal, along with railroads, banks, strikes, and the stock market. The big-money interests who were under investigation often attacked the proceedings as a roving star chamber, while liberals defended the investigations as upholding the American people's right to know.

Dickstein proposed a standing committee of the House of Representatives known as the Committee on Un-American Activities, which would watch "every subversive group in this country."[2] The resolution that established what would become the House Committee on Un-American Activities passed, in 1938, by a 191 to 41 margin. Texas Democrat Martin Dies was named chairman of the new committee.

In 1938, its first year, the Committee exposed the pro-Nazi German American Bund's propaganda apparatus, and in 1939, it helped convict Fritz Kuhn, the leader of the Bund, of larceny. In 1940, during the Nazi-Soviet Pact, the Committee published a massive 414-page report on Nazi activities in the United States; the report was later cited by President Roosevelt when he shut down the German consulates in the United States.[3] The Committee was clearly hitting where it hurt: at hearings in New York, several hundred German-Americans packed the place and chanted "Down with Dickstein" and "Heil Hitler!"[4] The Committee next turned its attention to the Communists.

"The agents of Russian Communism have been at work in the United States three times as long as the agents of German Nazism,"[5] said Committee chairman Dies. Dies had discovered that fifty-five National Labor Relations Board attorneys were members of the National Lawyers Guild, a Party-controlled group.

The first witness to testify against Communism before the Committee was John Frey of the American Federation of Labor. The Committee became interested in Communist activities in Hollywood when movie actors' names started to appear in Party publications. Committee investigator J. B. Matthews cited the French Communist newspaper *Le Soir,* which had recently featured hearty greetings from Clark Cable, Robert Taylor, James Cagney, and even Shirley Temple.[6] That prompted Jack Tenney, a left-wing musician from Los Angeles and composer of "Mexicali Rose," to quip that Dies would soon discover the Communist Party card of Donald Duck. Tenney and future Los Angeles mayor Sam Yorty had joined in welcoming the *People's Daily World* when it made its debut.

The Committee took testimony from Hollywood screenwriters, including John Howard Lawson, who testified under oath that they were not Communists. The Committee chairman also talked to Frederic March, James Cagney, Humphrey Bogart, and writer–director Philip Dunne.

"Dies decided to prospect for golden headlines in the Hollywood Hills," wrote Dunne, "and thereby awarded me the honor of becoming the first motion-picture personality to be investigated for un-American activities by the Congress of the United States."[7] When Dunne learned that Committee chairman Dies planned to hold hearings, complete with newsreel cameras, he tracked down the Texas Democrat at the Fairmont Hotel in San Francisco, told him the rumors were false and even showed him anti-Communist articles that Dunne had written. Dunne had fought the Party during the Nazi-Soviet Pact, and knew the Hollywood community well both from his work and his service on the Motion Picture Democratic Committee. Impressed with the presentation, Dies issued a statement that Dunne, along with Frederic March, James Cagney, and Humphrey Bogart, who had also met with him, were fine Americans.

Dunne had not forgotten his experiences with the Party during the Nazi-Soviet Pact and had watched Party writers and directors dominate the town during the war. After the Party's shift back to the anti-American line following the Duclos article, Dunne took appropriate precautions. He helped found Americans for Democratic Action, a group that he hoped would enlighten his fellow liberals to the realities of Soviet power and "which cordially invited the Communists *not* to join us."[8]

Momentarily abashed, the Committee followed other leads, which would find their way to Hollywood through a different route and with a different cast. The Dies Committee lasted until 1944, when New Jersey Republican Parnell Thomas took over as chairman. In 1946, Congress renewed the Committee by a vote of 240 to 81. That year Louis Budenz, Party insider and former managing editor of the *Daily Worker,* testified before the Committee that a major leader of American Communism was Gerhart Eisler, the Comintern agent who had given orders to Morris Childs, a key Soviet agent in the United States. Eisler had also been recognized by William Nowell, a black former Communist courier from Detroit, who met Eisler in Moscow in 1933 when Eisler was traveling under a false name. After the former Party man identified Eisler in Washington, local Communists threatened to kill Nowell, and he took refuge in the home of a Washington detective.

According to Ruth Fisher, Gerhart's sister, Gerhart Eisler was a major Communist agent in America, directing Party affairs on behalf of the Kremlin. Party insider Howard Rushmore testified that even Party cultural commissar V. J. Jerome took orders from Eisler,[9] who sometimes used the name Samuel Liptzin.

When a State Department official dug out a passport application in that name, he found a photo of Gerhart Eisler. Eisler was charged with passport fraud and contempt of Congress, with only Vito Marcantonio of the American Labor Party, a staunch friend of the Communists, voting against the citation. The Communist Party itself, including the Hollywood branch, mounted a furious campaign in support of Eisler, complete with "Free Gerhart Eisler" rallies.

The *People's Daily World* blasted Ruth Fisher as a "German Trotskyite," and Louis Budenz as a "fifth-rate turncoat" spinning "fairy tales." For Party columnist Joseph Starobin, Eisler was a "fighting anti-Fascist," and he said that his good friend reminded him of Kurt Muller, Lillian Hellman's "unforgettable character" from *Watch on the Rhine*. As for the charges, Starobin wrote, "this 'foreign agent' stuff is a double insult. . . . his only purpose was to escape from the Gestapo."[10]

Eisler himself wrote that "before Hollywood makes the picture 'The Song of Budenz,' they should make sure about him. Because he isn't a saint, and he lies like the devil." Eisler denied he was an agent of the Comintern, adding that "the choice of Moscow did not make the Communist International an instrument of the Soviet State. . . . A Communist party is not a conspiracy, it acts in the open, and does not make any secret of its adherence to an international organization of the workers."[11]

Both Eisler and Party secretary Eugene Dennis charged that it was Adolf Hitler who had said that the Communists were agents of a foreign power, so therefore the claim wasn't true. When some in Congress proposed banning the Communist Party, a move opposed by liberals and conservatives alike, Communist screenwriter Samuel Ornitz said that "such a proposal is in keeping with Hitler's Reichstag fire tactics, which at first was made to seem a plan merely to outlaw the Communists but moved to take all the people's liberties away." CSU champion Averill Berman said, "This is exactly what happened in Nazi Germany where first the Communist party was outlawed in March 1933, the trade unions in April 1933." Carlton Moss, producer of *The Negro Soldier*, predicted, "If this proposal goes through, my people are next."[12]

In March 1947, fifty prominent Americans, including John Howard Lawson, Dashiell Hammett, Dorothy Parker, and Ellis Patterson, signed a statement decrying the "shameful persecution" of Gerhart Eisler.[13]

While the proceedings against Eisler continued, a State Department official suggested that the Committee look into the passport escapades of Gerhart's brother Hanns, who was also identified by Ruth Fisher as a Communist. Hanns Eisler, a musician, had been championed as a "revolutionary composer" by the Communist press. His works included the "Comintern March."

Oh you who are missing,
Oh, comrades in dungeons,
You're with us, you're with us,
This day of our vengeance.
No Fascist can daunt us,
No terror can halt;
All lands will take flame
With Fire of revolt.

The Comintern calls you,
Raise high Soviet banner,
In steeled ranks to battle
Raise sickle and hammer.

Our answer: Red Legions
We raise in our might
Our answer: Red Storm Troops
We lunge to the fight

From Russia Victorious
The Worker's October
Comes storming reaction's
Regime the world over
We're coming with Lenin
For Bolshevik work
From London, Havana,
Berlin, and New York

Rise up fields and workshops
Come out workers, farmers,
To battle march onward,
March on, world stormers
Eyes sharp on your guns,
Red banners unfurled
Advance, Proletarians
To conquer the world.[14]

Hanns had been taken to Moscow to reorganize its International Music Bureau. In America he had received a $20,000 Rockefeller Foundation Grant and been a professor at New School of Social Research in New York. In the spring of 1947, Hanns Eisler was in Hollywood composing film scores for Dore Schary at RKO. The Committee's Robert Stripling found Eisler sitting in a deck chair in front of his beach-front Malibu home, placidly sunning himself. Stripling disturbed the scene by handing the composer a subpoena, hot-pink in color. "I've been expecting you," Eisler snapped. "Now get out of here."[15]

Eisler went on record with the Committee saying that the woman who accused him of being a Communist was his "former sister," adding, "I admire Gerhart Eisler, my brother, a great fighter against fascism and reaction."[16] In a short executive session with Committee member Robert Stripling and investigator Louis Russell, Eisler proved evasive, leading the investigators to begin calling in other Hollywood people to hear their accounts. There were plenty of stories, many based on the treatment film workers had received from Communists during the Nazi-Soviet Pact, the war, and the ongoing labor disputes. The two investigators obtained enough preliminary testimony, in their view, to justify a public hearing.[17] Once again, as Philip Dunne put it, the Committee could prospect for golden headlines.

In a letter to Committee chairman Parnell Thomas, film industry representative Eric Johnston said he welcomed the hearings as a chance to meet the rumors of Communist domination head-on. But privately the movie moguls were circling the wagons. "No half-ass congressman is going to tell MGM how to run its business,"[18] bragged studio boss Eddie Mannix. But business at that time was not booming.

The ongoing labor dispute had slowed film production, cost millions of dollars in lost revenue, and brought bad publicity. Attendance at the movies was down from 80 million per week in 1946 to 67 million by 1948.[19] The studios also faced the loss of their theater chains under antitrust legislation, and the shakeup of their contract system, which was being challenged by Olivia De Havilland and other actors.

For years, many Americans had seen Hollywood as a morally corrupting influence. Democrat representative John Rankin of Mississippi longed for a chance to castigate an industry dominated by the Jews he viewed as a corrupting influence in Christian America, and the film industry continued to receive bad press from religious groups. In 1947 Archbishop Cantwell, a political liberal who had supported the Conference of Studio Unions, said that no Catholic could in good conscience see *Duel in the Sun*. And the film industry was beginning to feel competition from a new medium called television.

In 1947 the House Committee, including the anti-Semitic Rankin, had raised the specter of Communism within the movie business. Some studio moguls reportedly feared that in its public hearing the Committee would ask them about the moguls' personal lives as the newsreel cameras rolled. The whole idea of the Committee hearings provoked a backlash in the industry against friendly and unfriendly witnesses alike, both of whom were perceived as bringing a plague on the Hollywood house. Worse, the hearings would be held not on studio turf, but in Washington, D.C.

The Communist Party called the House investigators the "Rankin Committee" and used the widely reviled Mississippian as a symbol for the proceedings. In a *People's Daily World* piece headlined "Un-Americans Setting the Stage for 'Reds in Movieland' Show," Travis Hedrick wrote that "insiders here say the word has gone down to put the quietus on the publicity-hunting stooges who have indicated a willingness to rat to the House committee." Industry representative Eric Johnston was expected to put up a "united front," a common theme in days ahead. The Committee, the Party journal said, "will use the publicity from the Hollywood probe to build up the stature of men with little minds and moronic intellect—a stature that neither Chairman Thomas nor Rep. John Rankin could hope to attain in the normal course of congressional procedure."[20]

Political groups controlled by the Party chimed in. One group was the Progressive Citizens of America (PCA), an amalgam of various leftist groups headed by sculptor Jo Davidson, whose bust of President Roosevelt had been personally presented to Josef Stalin by Averell Harriman, U.S. ambassador to the Soviet Union. The indefatigable Paul Robeson, still Moscow's favorite American performer, served on the group's executive committee. Attorney Bartley Crum, a liberal Republican who had worked for Wendell Wilkie in 1940 but backed Roosevelt in 1944, and one of the founders of the PCA, maintained that the PCA should not exclude Communists. Philip Dunne of the Americans for Democratic

Action (ADA), which did exclude Communists, criticized Crum as a *naif* for refusing to believe that the Communist Party was in fact controlling the PCA.

A *People's Daily World* election special from January 31, 1947, featured a lament from Crum, who feared that progressive voters had "no place to go." Crum was critical of the Americans for Democratic Action for not cooperating with the Communists. Although not a Communist himself, Crum said, "I can't understand a political organization refusing to admit persons because of economic or political belief." That statement struck a chord with Hollywood liberals.

Director John Huston, son of *Mission to Moscow* star Walter Huston, had worked as an artist, reporter, and boxer before turning to the family business. He made his directorial debut with the film version of Dashiell Hammett's *The Maltese Falcon*, starring Humphrey Bogart and nominated for an Academy Award in 1941. During the war, Huston made three documentaries for the army, winning the Legion of Merit and a promotion to the rank of major. Huston allowed his name to be used on the PCA letterhead because he believed PCA's intentions were good.[21]

The organization, which boasted a membership of 75,000 in 125 city and state chapters, would become a backer of Henry Wallace. Born in 1888, Wallace had served as secretary of agriculture from 1933 to 1940, then as vice president to FDR from 1941 to 1944 and as secretary of commerce in the final FDR administration. Critics of Wallace charged that he confused the common man with the Comintern, and when he announced in 1946 that he had accepted a Soviet sphere of influence in Europe, President Truman promptly fired him. That move cast Wallace in the role of underdog, a favorite with Hollywood liberals.

Katharine Hepburn was the opening speaker at a Progressive Party rally in Hollywood Legion Stadium on May 19, 1947, clad in a flaming red dress and reading a speech written by Dalton Trumbo.[22] Her appearance scored lavish coverage in the *CSU*

News and the *People's Daily World*, which printed the full text of both Hepburn's and Wallace's speeches.[23]

For its part, PCA took its strategy directly from the Party play book. "Hysteria is the biggest bill of goods Hitler ever sold us," said the PCA's national chairman, sculptor Jo Davidson. "Our efforts are nothing until you're called Communist. When you're called a Communist, then you know you're doing something."[24]

Like other Party fronts, PCA could command some star power. In a *People's Daily World* article published in September 1947, party organizer Harold Salemson noted that political lines were being drawn among the Hollywood elite. He cited the "top Republicans" such as Ginger Rogers, Robert Montgomery, Adolphe Menjou, George Murphy, Walt Disney, writer Morrie Ryskind, and producer–director Leo McCarey. On the other hand, the Progressive Citizens of America enjoyed the backing of John Garfield, Lena Horne, Edward G. Robinson, Anne Revere, George Coulouris, Richard Conte, Gene Kelly, Paul Henreid, Larry Parks, Betty Garrett, Katharine Hepburn, Paul Draper, Larry Adler, Howard Da Silva, Lee J. Cobb, Morris Carnovsky, Gregory Peck, and all others who "are in there pitching on the side of the common man."[25]

The House Committee on Un-American Activities, meanwhile, selected for testimony some forty-five film-industry people of various political profiles, including many familiar Party heavyweights from the talent guilds, such as John Howard Lawson and Dalton Trumbo. Of the forty-five selected, nineteen witnesses declared that they would not cooperate: Alvah Bessie, Herbert Biberman, Bertolt Brecht, Lester Cole, Richard Collins, Edward Dmytryk, Gordon Kahn, Howard Koch, Ring Lardner Jr., John Howard Lawson, Albert Maltz, Lewis Milestone, Samuel Ornitz, Larry Parks, Irving Pichel, Robert Rossen, Waldo Salt, Adrian Scott, and Dalton Trumbo. They became known as the "unfriendly nineteen." Billy Wilder, the refugee from Hitler's Germany who cowrote *Ninotchka* and directed *Double Indemnity*, famously quipped that only a few in this group were talented; the rest were just unfriendly.

Paul Jarrico, Abe Polonsky, and Michael Wilson among others could have been included by the Committee, but the Committee's selection represented many familiar Party heavyweights from the talent guilds, especially Lawson and Trumbo. Others on the Left who were called to testify longed for a showdown with the hated Committee, a phenomenon Norman Mailer dubbed "subpoena envy."

On the other side of the political spectrum stood Frances Farmer. She had come to hate those she called the "card-carriers," whom she said "lied through their teeth. If she had been called to testify, Farmer wrote, "I would no doubt have provided the rope to hang many of the industry's luminaries." She was in an asylum at the time, driven there largely by harassment from a Party whose line she refused to obey, and did not emerge until March of 1950.[26]

One of Farmer's former directors, Elia Kazan, was still a man of leftist inclinations who gave work to Communist actors such as Zero Mostel. Kazan could have provided much information but also was not called to testify. During the hearings he directed *Gentleman's Agreement*, which he won an Oscar for, beating out George Cukor, David Lean, and Edward Dmytryk, whose film *Crossfire* featured Robert Ryan as a crazed soldier who murders a Jew.

When the unfriendlies were about to depart for Washington, Louis B. Mayer squared off with screenwriter Lester Cole. As Cole explained it, the mogul said that he and Trumbo were among his best writers. He offered to double Cole's salary and even let him direct his own pictures, a dream deal for any Hollywood writer, but to get it, Cole had to break with the Communists. "All I can say, Mr. Mayer, is thanks," Cole replied. "You're a very generous man. I wish I could go along with you, but I can't."

"You're nuts!" shouted Mayer, standing and pointing to the door. "Goddam crazy Commie! Get out! Goddam it, *Get Out!*"[27] Mayer related the incident to Roy Brewer, who brought it up in a radio debate with Cole. The Communist screenwriter denied the story vehemently at the time but bragged about it in his waning years.

Many people in the film industry rallied to the unfriendlies' defense. Gene Kelly chaired a "Keep America Free" rally. "I think it is not only the freedom of the movie industry and the professional integrity of its workers that is at stake but the whole future of cultural and civil liberties in America," said Kelly, who appeared at the rally with Bartley Crum, Robert Ryan, Marsha Hunt, and Albert Maltz.[28]

"Let us remember that America was born on a battleground for freedom," said actor Larry Parks, one of the unfriendlies, at a PCA rally attended by Gene Kelly, Lionel Stander, Edward G. Robinson, and Paulette Goddard. "This is our heritage! Let's fight for it!" At the same rally Burgess Meredith read a resolution stating that "this committee is set up without limit or definition to its powers" and has "consistently abrogated civil rights and democratic procedure guaranteed by the constitution." With a huge American flag as a backdrop, Gene Kelly led a crowd of 5,000 people in the pledge of allegiance, after which the crowd sang a reverential version of "America," led by actress Marsha Hunt. On October 17, 1947, the day after the Committee witnesses departed for the capital, the *People's Daily World* editorialized that "the film colony, it has turned out, will not be cowed. . . . As the drama unfolds, the people will see the villains in the piece even if Rankin and Thomas do not wear mustaches."[29]

Some in the film colony would get the best seats in the house.

15

"The Glittering Names of Hollywood"

ON OCTOBER 20, 1947, THE HOTTEST TICKET in Washington, D.C., was for the Caucus Room of the old House Office Building. In the streets outside, police grappled with movie fans who were trying to catch a glimpse of the stars, headlined by Gary Cooper and Robert Taylor. Cooper starred in *Morocco* with Marlene Dietrich and appeared in *Beau Geste* and *For Whom the Bell Tolls*. Fans had adored Taylor in *Magnificent Obsession, Billy the Kid,* and *Bataan.* Police had their hands full trying to keep the fans in line.

More than a few of the celebrities and dignitaries in the three hundred spectator seats wore sunglasses, not so much to hide their identity, but to shield their eyes from the lights set up for a battery of eleven newsreel and television cameras. The Committee had even taken the normal bulbs out of the chandelier and stuck in bigger ones. As a result, unfriendly witness Gordon Kahn wrote, the illumination was "as sharp and shadowless as an operating theatre."[1] This entire show—witnesses, committee, aides, and audience—was crammed into a forty-by-eighty-foot room.

"I want to emphasize at the outset of these hearings," said chairman Parnell Thomas, "that the fact that the Committee on

Un-American Activities is investigating alleged Communist influence and infiltration in the motion-picture industry must not be considered or interpreted as an attack on the majority of persons associated with this great industry. I have every confidence that the vast majority of movie workers are patriotic and loyal Americans."

As he ended his opening remarks he said: "Now I want to make it clear to the witnesses, the audience, the members of the press, and other guests here today that this hearing is going to be conducted in an orderly and dignified manner at all times. But if there is anyone here today or at any of the future sessions of this hearing who entertains any hopes or plans for disrupting the proceedings, he may as well dismiss it from his mind."[2]

Testimony began with the friendly witnesses, and it quickly became apparent that movie content would be the emphasis and speechmaking the order of the day. "Ideological termites have burrowed into many American industries, organizations, and societies," said studio mogul Jack Warner. "Wherever they may be, I say let us dig them out and get rid of them. My brothers and I will be happy to subscribe to a pest-removal fund. We are willing to establish such a fund to ship to Russia the people who don't like our American system of government and prefer the communistic system to ours."

But Warner was defensive about *Mission to Moscow,* the "first Soviet production from an American studio," which whitewashed Stalin's crimes. "That picture was made when our country was fighting for its existence, with Russia as one of our allies. It was made to fulfill the same wartime purpose for which we made other pictures," Warner said, adding that if *Mission to Moscow* was subversive, so were the American ships carrying food and guns to the Russian allies. "The general feeling as I found it in Washington," Warner went on to say, "was a tremendous fear that Stalin might go back with Hitler because he had done it before." Warner couldn't remember if Ambassador Davies had contacted Warner first or if Warner had contacted him, but it was "not without foundation" that the government wanted the picture made. But he added that the movie was "not for posterity."

Warner acknowledged that John Howard Lawson wrote propaganda into his scripts. Lawson, Warner said, "tried to swing a lot of things in there, but to my knowledge there wasn't anything."[3]

Investigator Robert Stripling asked Motion Picture Alliance founder Sam Wood if there was any question in his mind that John Howard Lawson was a Communist. "If there is," said Wood, "then I haven't any mind." In the same vein, Morrie Ryskind later testified that "if Lester Cole isn't a Communist, I don't think Mahatma Gandhi is an Indian."[4]

Studio mogul Louis B. Mayer, head of MGM and the highest-paid man in America, attacked Communism and defended the movies as a force for the public good. "In 1938 we made *Ninotchka,* and shortly thereafter, *Comrade X,* with Clark Gable and Hedy Lamarr," said Mayer. "Both of these films kidded Russia."

Mayer took some heat for his film *Song of Russia,* another worshipful wartime presentation, which he said was "made to be friendly" to the USSR. The mogul said the movie had no political implications, despite the beliefs of Committee investigator Robert Stripling and actor Robert Taylor that the film was full of Communist propaganda.[5]

Despite her two-fisted prose against Communist propaganda set forth in her *Screen Guide for Americans,* Ayn Rand had never seen *Song of Russia,* so the Committee screened it for her. Of all those who testified, friendly and otherwise, she was the only one who had actually lived under Soviet Communism, and *Song of Russia* struck her as most unlike the Russia in which she had grown up. "Anything that sells people the idea that life in Russia is good and that people are free and happy would be Communist propaganda," she said, noting that *Song of Russia* portrayed an idealized state where farmers owned their own land and priests operated freely, with no interference from the secret police. In response to a character in the film who says, "The culture we are building here will never die," Rand commented, "What culture? The culture of concentration camps. . . . You are telling people that it is all right to live in a totalitarian state."

The film portrayed the Polish border as a happy place, Rand said, not "an occupied, destroyed, enslaved country which Hitler and Stalin destroyed together." Rand asked the Committee to imagine a happy, music-filled love story set in Nazi Germany. "Would you say that was propaganda or not, when you know what life in Germany was like and what kind of concentration camps they had there?" The wartime alliance against Hitler, she said, did not mean that the American people should be told lies about the Soviet Union. Toward the end of her remarks, Rand said, "It is almost impossible to convey to a free people what it is like to live in a totalitarian dictatorship."[6]

Although he had not lived directly under Communism, Roy Brewer knew firsthand about the Party's studio labor offensive. During the Committee hearings, Brewer joined with James Cagney and Robert Montgomery in an attempt to explain privately to the Committee how Communist publicists had attached actors' names to various causes and events without the actors' knowledge. Brewer's formal testimony, however, was continually delayed. The Committee wanted to showcase the glamour people, but, more seriously, it loathed both unions and those New Dealers who had worked for the Roosevelt Administration. Brewer had been involved with both.

Veteran actor Adolphe Menjou blasted *Mission to Moscow* and *North Star* and told the Committee, "We have in California what I call the lunatic fringe, the political idiots, the morons, the dangerous Communists, and those who have yet to be convinced." But Menjou reserved most of his wrath for Stalin, whom he compared to Al Capone: "He committed the murders and then killed the witnesses." Film clips of the hearings show Menjou saying, "I think the Texans would kill them on sight," giving the impression that "they" were members of the Hollywood Party. In fact he was referring to Stalin's henchmen Vishinsky and Molotov.

Menjou had checked his facts with Sidney Hook, the Marxist scholar who had turned against the Party. Menjou himself struck a scholarly pose and recommended that Americans read for themselves *Das Kapital, The Red Prussian,* Freda Utley's *The Dream We Lost,* William Z. Foster's *Toward a Soviet America,* Arthur Koestler's *The Yogi and the Commissar,* and Victor Kravchenko's *I Choose Freedom.* Menjou had never met John Howard Lawson, he said, but he did not judge writers by the committees on which they served. "There are some excellent writers among those leftist writers," Menjou said. "Some of them have contributed much to some of our finest motion pictures."[7]

"Communists are notable for two things," said conservative writer Rupert Hughes. "One is slavish obedience to their orders and demands of slavish obedience from others." Hughes recalled that, during the Nazi-Soviet Pact, screenwriter Herb Biberman had attacked him as a "bloody-minded degenerate trying to get the blood of American boys spilled on foreign soil."[8]

In his testimony, former *New Yorker* writer James McGuinness dismissed *Song of Russia* as "a form of intellectual lend-lease," but he praised Dalton Trumbo's work on *A Guy Named Joe* and *Thirty Seconds over Tokyo.* McGuinness talked about Party moves during the Nazi-Soviet Pact and noted that the "controlling group" of the Screen Writers Guild, a group dominated by the Party, had supported Herb Sorrell. "Had they succeeded," he said, "they would have had a tight hold on many of the important guilds and unions, the craft unions within the industry."

McGuinness recounted the changes in the Party's attitude toward writers that manifested after the publication of Jacques Duclos's letter in 1945 and noted that as a result of these changes, "Mr. Albert Maltz was forced to eat his own words, disciplined, and had to confess error and return to what he termed the Marxist basis for all writers." Said McGuinness, "The only group in the United States organized for the purpose of thought control is the Communist group, and if they ever got control of the industry nothing would ever appear on the screen but their own conception of what was best for all of us."[9] Maltz's articles and the attacks on him by Mike Gold were made part of the record, but no Committee member opted to pursue the case.

With the testimony of actor Robert Taylor, the proceedings swung back to *Song of Russia*. While Taylor said he never turned down a film Louis B. Mayer wanted him to make, he said he objected to *Song of Russia,* which he believed to contain Communist propaganda. "I certainly do believe that the Communist Party should be outlawed," the combative Taylor told the Committee. "If I had my way about it they would all be sent back to Russia or some other unpleasant place and never allowed back in this country."[10] Loud applause from the gallery followed.

Director and writer Fred Niblo recounted his fights with the Party, which he argued should be banned. "I think it is grotesque that a Russian political party enjoys a legal existence as an American political party in this country. . . . It is a secret organization no less than the Ku Klux Klan. I myself feel that I am sick and tired of being harassed and irritated and even smeared by enemies of my country in my own country."[11]

Robert Montgomery testified that a small but militant minority of Communists had been active in the talent guilds since 1933. As for the Communist Party, he said, "I consider it a subversive group just as I considered the German American Bund a subversive group."[12]

George Murphy told the Committee that, after the Chicago conference about the studio strike, the CSU distributed pamphlets that featured three characters, Ronnie, Eddie, and George— Ronald Reagan, Eddie Arnold, and George Murphy—smeared as "producers' men."

Ronald Reagan told the Committee that Bill Hutcheson of the Carpenters' Union had offered to run "Sorrell and the other Commies" out of town if the IA's Richard Walsh gave in to Hutcheson's demands. Reagan said he did not believe that the Communists had used the screen for propaganda but neither did he advocate outlawing the Party. "I detest, I abhor their philosophy but I detest more than that their tactics, which are those of the fifth column, and are dishonest," he said, "but at the same time I never as a citizen want to see our country become urged, by either fear or resentment of this group, that we ever compromise with any of our democratic principles through that fear or resentment. I still think that democracy can do it."[13] Reagan's testimony led Waldo Salt, one of the unfriendlies, to snort, "It was enough to make you puke."[14]

In brief testimony, Gary Cooper noted that Communists in Europe had used his name without his knowledge. He was asked whether the Party should be outlawed. "I have never read Karl Marx and I don't know the basis of Communism, beyond what I have picked up from hearsay," he said. "From what I hear, I don't like it because it isn't on the level. So I couldn't possibly answer that question."[15]

Director Leo McCarey said movies should be entertainment, not propaganda, and if they were used for political purposes we would be doing the same thing Soviet Russia was doing. The Soviets, he said, had objected to a character in *Going My Way* and *The Bells of St. Mary's*.

> "Bing Crosby?" asked Robert Stripling.
> "No, God," replied McCarey
> "Do you believe Congress should outlaw the Communist Party in the United States?" asked Committee Chairman Parnell Thomas.
> "I definitely do," said McCarey, "and I hope something is done about it because at this time it is a very dangerous thing."[16]

Journalist Howard Rushmore, formerly of the *Daily Worker*, explained how the Party chain of command worked. Rushmore didn't know whether Edward G. Robinson was a Communist but could testify that he was a favorite of the Party. "[V. J.] Jerome once told me to always defend Robinson, even if he was in a bad picture, with a bad performance," said Rushmore. "I didn't question Jerome's orders, so I went ahead and did that."[17]

In his testimony, writer Oliver Carlson also provided detailed information about Party operations, but the press continued to focus on what was said about the studio heavyweights. Studio boss Walt Disney mentioned the four anti-Hitler movies he had made during the war but quickly changed the focus of his testimony to the studio labor dispute: "A Communist group was trying to take over my artists, and they did take them over," Disney said. "Herbert K. Sorrell was trying to take them over." After his standoff with Sorrell, Disney said, he found himself smeared in the *Daily Worker, PM* (a leftist publication based in New York), and even in "some Commie periodicals in South America, and generally throughout the world all of the Commie groups began smear campaigns against me and my pictures."[18]

Despite the grandstanding and occasional buffooneries, many in the Communist Party thought the testimony of the friendlies was scoring some hits. In its damage-control campaign, the Party looked to tap all of its Hollywood resources, particularly those liberals who saw the Committee as a menace to the entire movie industry.

John Huston, Philip Dunne, and their fellow liberal director William Wyler wrote a statement in support of the witnesses and against the Committee and ran it as an ad in the Hollywood trade papers. Others of similar mind rallied to them, and the group that emerged was called Hollywood Fights Back.

The group included a veritable Who's Who of show business: Frank Sinatra, Humphrey Bogart, Lauren Bacall, Groucho Marx, Burt Lancaster, Myrna Loy, Larry Adler, Ira Gershwin, Marsha Hunt, Jane Wyatt, Paul Henreid, Sterling Hayden, Evelyn Keyes, Peter Lorre, Moss Hart, Danny Kaye, Henry Fonda, Walter Wanger, Gregory Peck, Paulette Goddard, Burgess Meredith, John Housemann, and many others. It also included four U.S. senators:

Harley Kilgore of West Virginia, Elbert Thomas of Utah, Glen Taylor of Idaho, and Claude Pepper of Florida.

Dunne, Wyler, and Huston needed a savvy publicist to make their case with the press and the public. They tapped Hollywood public relations man Henry Rogers, a liberal who volunteered his services. Rogers issued a statement decrying the Committee's attempt "to smear the motion picture industry." The hearings were wrong, the statement said, because "any investigation into the political beliefs of the individual is contrary to the basic principles of our democracy. Any attempt to curb freedom of expression and to set arbitrary standards of Americanism is in itself disloyal to both the spirit and the letter of the Constitution."

As Rogers later wrote, "Our public relations strategy was to make certain that our motives were recognized and understood, and that no one would infer that we were Communist dominated or influenced. We were good Americans who protested the manner in which the House Committee on Un-American Activities was conducting its investigation."[19]

Hollywood Fights Back launched a number of gala fund-raising events, and John Huston used some of the money that came in to sponsor two radio broadcasts, directed by Norman Corwin, the leftist radio impresario. A host of notables took part in the broadcasts, including Archibald MacLeish, Judy Garland, Frederic March, Cornel Wilde, Groucho Marx, Gregory Peck, William Holden, Lucille Ball, Burt Lancaster, Robert Ryan, Myrna Loy, Frank Sinatra, Ira Gershwin, Edward G. Robinson, Robert Young, Melvyn Douglas, Joseph Cotten, Van Heflin, Bennett Cerf, Clifton Fadiman, Burl Ives, George S. Kaufman, Richard Rodgers, Oscar Hammerstein, and Charles Boyer. Thomas Mann, Helen Keller, and Albert Einstein sent written statements of support.

"It's always been your right to read or see anything you wanted to. But now it's getting kind of complicated," said Judy Garland during one broadcast.[20] "Once they get the movies throttled," said Frank Sinatra, "how long will it be before the Committee goes to work on freedom of the air? How long will it be before we're told what we can say and cannot say into a radio microphone? If you make a pitch on a nationwide radio network for a square deal for the underdog, will they call you a Commie?"[21]

The broadcasts were received favorably, but despite the publicity campaign, writers and artists showed no solidarity with the unfriendlies, who had yet to testify. Paul Jarrico said that when the Nineteen were originally subpoenaed, they sent a telegram asking for support from such people as Carl Sandburg, John Steinbeck, William Faulkner, and Ernest Hemingway but failed to receive even a single reply.[22] The press remained divided, with more liberal papers such as the *New York Times* sympathetic to the Nineteen, and more conservative journals such as the *Chicago Tribune* and *New York Daily News* opposed. Hollywood Fights Back drew considerable criticism, much of it fueled by groups such as the American Legion. In response, Hollywood Fights Back changed its name to the Committee for the First Amendment. MGM reportedly received so many letters denouncing Katharine Hepburn that Louis B. Mayer told her that he couldn't use her until she was accepted by the public again.[23]

ED DMYTRYK AND ADRIAN SCOTT, two of the Nineteen, asked attorney Bartley Crum of the Progressive Citizens of America to represent them during the hearings. Crum saw the hearings as a chance to test the principle that, while it was not against the law to be a Communist, it was against the Constitution to ask citizens to reveal their political affiliations.

Two of the other attorneys for the Nineteen, Martin Popper and Ben Margolis, were both Communists. As Margolis later admitted, the Party lawyers who were defending the Nineteen welcomed non-Communists Crum and Robert Kenny, a former California attorney general, to the defense team. In addition to their legal expertise, Crum and Kenny were charming and respected figures, well known to the public and used to dealing with the press.

Behind the scenes, the Party lawyers ran the show, meeting secretly and, according to Philip Dunne, getting their orders directly from Party bosses in Moscow.[24] The lawyers, who included Jeff Kibre's former colleague Charles Katz, laid down the policy that the Nineteen should act as a unit, a strategy presaged in the *People's Daily World* articles that had pushed for a "united front." With the exception of writer Howard Koch, the Nineteen went along with the policy. Adrian Scott and Ed Dmytryk, though not then in the Party, decided that solidarity with their other comrades offered the best way out of their current tangle. Party members had convinced them that they would be called Communists whatever they did, so they might as well throw in their lot with the rest.

The Committee for the First Amendment swelled to five hundred members, and while the friendlies were still testifying, the group decided to send some star power of its own to Washington. The twenty-nine members who would fly to D.C. included Humphrey Bogart, Lauren Bacall, John Garfield, Danny Kaye, Paul Henreid, Sterling Hayden, Ira Gershwin, Richard Conte, and Gene Kelly.

The group from the Committee for the First Amendment knew they would fail if they were perceived as a Communist front, and they took careful measures to eliminate that perception. John Huston said that he questioned each member of the group about his or her political affiliations before asking the person to come on-board and was satisfied that none was a Communist.[25] Bogart too was concerned. "Before we left Hollywood," he said, "we carefully screened every performer so that no red or pink could infiltrate and sabotage our purpose."[26]

Howard Hughes, Katharine Hepburn's old flame, offered his airplane, but the group turned it down, most likely because of Hughes's relation to Rupert Hughes, a conservative, and the Party campaign against Hughes's movie *The Outlaw*.

John Huston chartered a Lockheed Constellation named, ironically enough, *Star of the Red Sea* to transport the group to

Washington. Comic and delegation member Danny Kaye stayed in character on the flight by dancing down the aisles and clowning. At stops in Kansas City, Pittsburgh, and Philadelphia, adoring throngs awaited the stars, who addressed the crowds through a megaphone. The sense of mission and esprit de corps ran high, but the Committee for the First Amendment publicist Henry Rogers told Huston and Dunne that they might have problems. "It's great for you and Phil Dunne to be our spokesmen, but I don't see how we're going to keep some of our other people quiet. And once they start talking, there is no way that we can control what the press is going to print."[27]

Rogers told Dunne and Huston that he was worried about Bogart, who had already had dealings with the Committee under Dies and was known for being headstrong and opinionated. Bogart's speech for Roosevelt in 1944 brought sackfuls of hate mail, most of it saying actors should not have opinions, and if they did, they should keep them to themselves. The combative Bogie had responded with a piece called "I Stuck My Neck Out" for the *Saturday Evening Post.*

> "[Bogart] feels that he's the most politically sophisticated guy in our business," said Rogers, "and you know how he goes off half-cocked sometimes. And let's face it, reporters are going to be much more interested in talking to Humphrey Bogart than they are going to be in talking to John Huston or Phil Dunne. I'm not worried about the others. Danny Kaye, Gene Kelly, Evelyn Keyes, Betty Bacall, and the others will all shift the questions put to them over to the two of you."
>
> "Betty's the answer," said Huston. "If we make a big deal out of all this with Bogie, he'll think we are trying to censor him. I'll talk to Betty. She'll get him to keep his mouth shut. . . ."[28]

The actions of the House Committee prompted the group from the Committee for the First Amendment to put on a show of their own at their Washington hotel. By one account, Danny Kaye gave a "sidesplitting performance" as chairman Parnell Thomas, with

Bogart playing Robert Stripling, and June Havoc, Geraldine
Brooks, Sterling Hayden, and Marsha Hunt cast as hostile witnesses.[29] But the antics of the unfriendlies, who were beginning
their testimony, also proved troubling. What the stars saw acted
out in the Caucus Room proceedings was not the eloquent constitutional defense they had been expecting.

John Howard Lawson told the Committee he was proud of
Blockade, "in which I introduced the danger that this democracy
faced from an attempt to destroy democracy in Spain in 1937." But
he refused to answer their questions about Party membership.
"You are using the old technique, which was used in Hitler's
Germany, in order to create a scare here," said Lawson.[30]

Soon Parnell Thomas's gavel was pounding like a jackhammer.
Movie representative Eric Johnston followed Lawson. "Hollywood
is weary of being the national whipping boy for congressional
committees," said Johnston. "We are tired of having irresponsible
charges made again and again and again and not sustained. If we
have committed a crime we want to know it. If not, we should not
be badgered by congressional committees."[31]

It emerged that Edward Cheyfitz, one of Johnston's assistants,
had been in the Communist Party. Johnston said his aide had left
the Party in 1939 over the Nazi-Soviet Pact, but Stripling cited a
Daily Worker article from May 1941 in which Cheyfitz opposed
aid to Britain. The revelation deflated Johnston's testimony.

Dalton Trumbo had brought copies of his screenplays, which he
sought to introduce into the record. "Too many pages," said Chairman Thomas, who refused to let Trumbo read his written statement. The wealthy screenwriter, who during World War II had
eagerly discussed his politics with the FBI and agreed to inform
the FBI on "antiwar" writers, would not say whether he was a
member of the Screen Writers Guild, nor of the Communist Party.
The Remarkable Andrew, Trumbo's Pact novel, would have proved
enlightening fare, but the Committee, had they thought of it,
never got the opportunity. "This is the beginning of an American

concentration camp," yelled Trumbo as he was led away, to the accompaniment of Thomas's gavel.[32]

Next, in the midst of the unfriendlies, came Roy Brewer. Thomas declined to let the IA man read his formal statement, and Committee members found themselves having to ask the witness the meaning of such film industry terms as *grip*. Brewer provided background on Jeff Kibre's meetings with Ella Winter, told how Herb Sorrell had taken over from Kibre, and laid out the ensuing Conference of Studio Unions dispute. Brewer recalled that during the 1945 strike at Warner Brothers, John Howard Lawson, John Wexley, Sidney Buchman, Lewis Milestone, Dalton Trumbo, John Garfield, Robert Rossen, and William Pomerance had joined the pickets.

Back in Los Angeles, Herb Sorrell did not welcome the publicity. "Roy Brewer is an unmitigated liar just as is Walt Disney," snarled Sorrell in a telegram to the Committee, "and I demand that I be subpoenaed and given the opportunity not only to refute their statements, but to tell what I know about who is actually responsible for Communism in the motion picture industry."[33] But Sorrell's subpoena envy went unfulfilled.

In a surprise move, the Committee allowed Albert Maltz to read his statement, in which he noted that his novel *The Cross and the Arrow* had been issued in a special edition for American servicemen. His film *Pride of the Marines* had premiered at Guadalcanal Day banquets. His *Destination Tokyo* had been adopted by the navy as an official training film, and *The House I Live In* had been given a special award by the Academy "for its contribution to racial tolerance." For all this, Maltz said, "this committee urges I be blacklisted in the film industry—and tomorrow, if it has its way, in the publishing and magazine fields also." Said Maltz, "I would rather die than be a shabby American, groveling before men whose names are Thomas and Rankin, but who now carry out activities in America like those carried out in Germany by Goebbels and Himmler."

No one on the Committee asked Maltz about his own criticism of those two Germans from 1939 to 1941, nor about his own groveling and about-face over the "What Shall We Ask of Writers?" article and the ensuing inquisition. But Maltz, like the other unfriendly witnesses, had come to play offense, not defense. He tagged Stripling as "Mr. Quisling."[34]

Alvah Bessie told the Committee, "General Eisenhower himself has refused to reveal his political affiliation, and what is good enough for General Eisenhower is good enough for me." As Bessie was leaving, an angry Stripling growled that "General Eisenhower would not ever think or dream or stoop to ever being a low-down Communist." The gallery applauded, and Thomas did not call for order.

Samuel Ornitz likewise struggled with the question about membership in the Screen Writers Guild and the Party before being gaveled down and dismissed. Herb Biberman wrapped himself in the American flag, proudly declaring, "I was born within a stone's throw of Independence Hall in Philadelphia, on the day when Mr. McKinley was inaugurated as President of the United States." Though assuring the Committee he would be detailed in other answers, he lasted less time than Ornitz. "You have only one idea," Biberman told the Committee, "to cause strife in the industry."[35]

While Parnell Thomas's cigar-smoking grandstanding was alienating the press, the unfriendlies' equally bellicose performances drained sympathy from their supporters. The Nineteen soon faced new problems. While the group of witnesses was in Washington, a local paper reported that Sterling Hayden was a Communist. The report was correct.

The news about Hayden and the witnesses' defiance in the Committee had stretched the tolerance of Humphrey Bogart, who thought the Committee for the First Amendment had been used. "You fuckers sold me out," he yelled at Danny Kaye when they returned to Hollywood.[36] As their publicist Henry Rogers had feared, Bogie began talking to the press, with nobody writing his lines.

"I am not a Communist," he later explained. "I detest Communism as any other decent American does. I have never in my life been identified with any Communistic front organization. I went to Washington because I thought fellow Americans were being deprived of their constitutional rights and for that reason alone." He came to see the trip as "ill-advised, foolish, and impetuous, but at the time it seemed the thing to do."[37]

The testimony of Edward Dmytryk, Adrian Scott, and Ring Lardner Jr. followed the now-familiar pattern of bellicose defiance. Screenwriter Lester Cole blasted the Committee and was followed by Bertolt Brecht, dressed in a suit and smoking cigars, which he apparently thought would impress Thomas. The playwright and poet was accompanied by an interpreter, David Baumgardt of the Library of Congress, who spoke English little better than Brecht, leading to some comic moments as the Committee probed the content of Brecht's works and his relationship with Hanns Eisler. "I cannot understand the interpreter any more than I can the witness," whined Parnell Thomas.

Brecht, who in 1935 had told Sidney Hook that Stalin's victims deserved to be shot even if they were innocent, had gained fame with *Three Penny Opera*, written with Kurt Weill. Brecht collaborated with Hanns Eisler on *Die Massnahme* ("The Measures Taken"), an agitprop musical about four agitators who are faced with a decision about a delinquent comrade. "We must shoot him and throw him into the quicklime pit," the agitators decide. Later they say, "We shot him and threw him into the quicklime pit. And when the quicklime had eaten him, we returned to our work." In the final chorus is the line "And our work was happy, and you have spread the teachings of the classics, the ABC of Communism."[38] Scripts like this led Ruth Fisher to title an article about the author "Bert Brecht, Minstrel of the GPU."

During Brecht's stay in Hollywood, which he called the "world center of the narcotics trade,"[39] the German playwright proposed a film about Reinhard Heydrich, gauleiter of Czechoslovakia. The idea eventually became *Hangmen Also Die,* starring Lionel Stander, the Party's model actor. According to his chess partner John Wexley, Brecht demanded credit for the film, though he never worked on the screenplay. Wexley described Brecht as an egotist who loved to be the center of attention, often sporting a jacket he had brought from China that made him look like a military commissar.[40] Brecht's girlfriend complained about having to wash his neck and ears herself, and actor Charles Laughton's wife, Elsa Lanchester, described Brecht's teeth as "little tombstones sticking out of a black mouth."[41] Ella Winter compared him to a monk in a worker's cap and complained about his reeking cigars, which he chewed to the end.[42]

When the Committee asked if he had ever applied to join the Communist Party, Brecht said, "No, no, no, no, no, never." He acknowledged meeting with Gerhart and Hanns Eisler but was evasive about Grigory Kheifetz, a skilled Comintern agent, Soviet consul, and *rezident* of Soviet intelligence in San Francisco who also made appearances in Hollywood. Brecht claimed not to have heard of the *New Masses,* nor to know who played the lead in *Hangmen Also Die.* The playwright's clever testimony, a masterpiece of improvisational stagecraft and evasion, confirmed that the Committee had not given him or his pro-Communist works the attention they deserved. But after the series of defiant harangues from the other unfriendly witnesses, the Committee was relieved that the playwright had at least answered questions. At the end of Brecht's session Thomas said, "Thank you very much, Mr. Brecht. You are a good example to the witnesses of Mr. Kenny and Mr. Crum."[43]

The most stunning testimony of the day came not from any current or former Communist, nor from anyone in Hollywood, but from Parnell Thomas himself. With many witnesses yet to be heard, the Committee chairman announced on October 30, 1947, that the first phase of the hearings was concluded. The proceedings, he said, would resume in the near future, with testimony from sixty-eight others and new information about propaganda in the films.

Thomas floated a story in the press about shutting down the hearings for fear of massive Communist demonstrations. The truth was, the hearings that Committee thought would make them stars were bombing in the press, even in conservative journals.

"We had won, to an even greater extent than we had hoped for," said Henry Rogers. "This was a total victory for our side." Journalist Eric Sevareid said the pressures of the press and public opinion had forced the hand of Thomas. The Communists were also claiming victory.[44]

"The super-colossal extravaganza of the Un-Americans was going to blow the lid off Hollywood," crowed the *People's Daily World* in a front-page editorial two days after the hearings suddenly ended. According to the Communist journal, which published the statements Lawson and Biberman had been forbidden to present to the Committee, star power had turned the tide.

"The glittering names of Hollywood, names emblazoned on a thousand theater marquees, went on the radio, flew to Washington, issued statements. The whole film colony united in demanding the end of the witch-hunt . . . and suddenly, without notice, Rep. Thomas called off the hearings. . . . Will liberty-loving Americans now press for the total abolition of this un-American committee, of this evil instrument for thought control and suppression?"[45]

In the magazine of the Screen Writers Guild, Lillian Hellman penned an editorial called "Judas Goats," in which she argued that "there has never been a single line or word of communism in any American picture at any time." She called the hearings a "honky tonk show" and "a sickening, sickening, immoral and degraded week." In the spirit of Mike Gold, Hellman took issue with the friendly witnesses not on their politics but on their art. "Act is not the correct word for what Mr. Taylor does in pictures," she wrote, also blasting "the professionally awkward stammering of Mr. Gary Cooper."[46]

Bertolt Brecht's collaborator Hanns Eisler, whose evasive testimony had led the House Committee to Hollywood in the first place, took up a theme that would become part of Party agitprop for years to come. "This witch-hunting will be stopped by the American People," he said.[47]

Eleven unfriendlies had testified, but thereafter those who had defied the Committee became known first as the "Unfriendly Ten," and then, in a more permanent legacy, as the "Hollywood Ten."

"A Horrendous Story
of the Persecution"

BEFORE THE HEARINGS, studio bosses had bragged that "half-assed" congressmen were not going to tell them what to do; then they told the Committee that the industry was tired of being a whipping boy. The statement the studios issued after a November 27 meeting at the Waldorf-Astoria in New York bore a different tone:

> Members of the Association of Motion Picture Producers deplore the action of the 10 Hollywood men who have been cited for contempt by the House of Representatives. We do not desire to pre-judge their legal rights, but their actions have been a disservice to their employers and have impaired their usefulness to the industry. We will forthwith discharge and suspend without compensation those in our employ, and we will not reemploy any of the 10 until such time as he is acquitted or has purged himself of contempt and declares under oath that he is not a Communist.
>
> On the broader issue of alleged subversive and disloyal elements in Hollywood, our members are likewise prepared to take positive action.

We will not knowingly employ a Communist or a member of any party or group which advocates the overthrow of the government of the United States by force or by any illegal or unconstitutional methods.

In pursuing this policy, we are not going to be swayed by intimidation or hysteria from any source. We are frank to recognize that such a policy involves dangers and risks. There is the danger of hurting innocent people. There is the risk of creating an atmosphere of fear. Creative work at its best cannot be carried on in an atmosphere of fear. We will guard against this danger, this risk, this fear.

To this end we will invite the Hollywood talent guilds to work with us to eliminate any subversives, to protect the innocent; and to safeguard free speech and a free screen wherever threatened.

The absence of a national policy, established by Congress, with respect to the employment of Communists in private industry makes our task difficult. Ours is a nation of laws. We request Congress to enact legislation to assist American industry to rid itself of subversive, disloyal elements.

Nothing subversive or un-American has appeared on the screen, nor can any number of Hollywood investigations obscure the patriotic services of the 30,000 loyal Americans employed in Hollywood who have given our government invaluable aid in war and peace.

So the studios would not hire Communists after all, and their sycophantic swoon, a victory for the Committee, created problems for many in Hollywood. The Hollywood Ten, in particular, now faced more serious woes.

That same month, Congress held a special session concerning the need for funds to help block Stalinist expansion in Europe, and at that time HCUA chairman Parnell Thomas asked for a citation of contempt for Albert Maltz, one of the Hollywood Ten. In the last speech before the vote, Richard Nixon said that the only two relevant issues were whether the Committee had the right to ask questions and whether the witnesses had refused to answer such questions. The vote to cite Maltz with contempt passed 346 to 17, and soon the other nine witnesses were similarly charged, with the vote passing by landslide margins. Bertolt Brecht, the eleventh witness, had fled to East Germany, where Gerhart Eisler had also been welcomed. There Brecht would enjoy full cooperation from the Communist regime in staging his plays, along with an Austrian passport, a West German publisher, and a Swiss bank account.

After John Howard Lawson and Dalton Trumbo were convicted, the rest of the witnesses waived jury trials. All were convicted and sentenced to one year, except for Herb Biberman and Ed Dmytryk, who at the hands of a more lenient judge each received six months. The Ten appealed, touching off endless activity and a steady stream of briefs filed on their behalf.

Roy Brewer, meanwhile, knew that there was more to the story than the Hollywood Ten. He and other anti-Communists were concerned that the full story of the Party's offensive in the studios had yet to emerge. If it did not, he feared, the antilabor Republicans might launch blanket attacks on unions, including his own, the IA. Brewer and his allies made a case for new hearings, not before the HCUA, but before the House Committee on Education and Labor, which was chaired by Fred Hartley of New Jersey and included both John F. Kennedy and Richard Nixon. Carroll D. Kearns of Pennsylvania chaired a special subcommittee of the House Committee on Education and Labor on "Jurisdictional Disputes in the Motion Picture Industry." The subcommittee was composed of Gerald Landis of Indiana, Thomas Owens of Illinois, O. C. Fisher of Texas, and John Wood of Georgia, who was a veteran of the 1947 HCUA hearings.

While no movie stars showed up for the subcommittee hearings in February 1948, the proceedings did feature some entertaining testimony, much of it from Herb Sorrell. The Conference of Studio Unions boss told the committee how, barred from the studio by court order, he had taken to the skies with a bullhorn. "I got in my airplane and rode around the studios a thousand feet high and I talked down very successfully with this because at a thousand feet it was legal."[1] But on the Communist issue his testimony proved unconvincing. When asked if the *People's Daily World* was a Communist publication, Sorrell said, "Some claim it is, and I am inclined to think it is Communist. . . . I can't swear to it. I take it and I will continue to take it."[2]

FBI handwriting experts had confirmed that a Communist Party card bearing the name of Herb Stewart was actually signed by Herb Sorrell. Asked about the signature on the Party card, he said, "[It] looks pretty much like I wrote it."[3] But on other points he held the line. He described Rena Vale, who had identified him as being present at a Communist meeting, as a "confused female," adding, "Later I am told she went to the insane asylum."[4]

Sorrell acknowledged that in his various strikes a number of actors, writers, and directors, "who may or may not be Communist," had "helped us substantially." John Howard Lawson had been the most prominent of these, but when Sorrell was asked if he knew Lawson, who had walked Sorrell's picket lines, with whom Sorrell had appeared at many events, and who had been featured in the *People's Daily World,* Sorrell said, "I have met him two or three times. I can't tell you where I met him. All I know is that he has a great big nose."[5]

Confronted with the long dossier of evidence of his activity in Communist front groups before, during, and after the Nazi-Soviet Pact, Sorrell replied: "Well, I tell you, I belong to a lot of things I thought were good and that have been called Communist-front organizations and maybe they were, I don't know. They were good. The things I belonged to were good. Maybe they were Communist front organizations. . . . I just don't know just what harm they could do. That hasn't been explained to me yet."[6]

Roy Brewer also appeared before the subcommittee. In lengthy testimony, Brewer provided details of the studio wars, one of the longest disputes ever to take place in American labor. His testimony was complicated by his reports of shifting alliances due to changes in the Communist Party line. Some committee members remained confused, and Sorrell stood his ground in the face of the evidence, even though his influence was fading steadily. Brewer's influence, however, began to grow as the hearings finished in March 1948.

Former Communists Ben Gitlow and Jay Lovestone welcomed Brewer as an ally against the Party, though Lovestone, like Whittaker Chambers, believed that the Communists would prevail in the end. David Dubinsky, of the Ladies Garment Workers Union, was a determined anti-Stalinist fighter. "You fight 'em, and anybody who fights 'em is my pal," the cigar-chomping Dubinsky told Brewer.[7]

Brewer had added another key ex-Communist to his staff. Howard Costigan had been a secret Party member running the Washington Commonwealth Federation, which the Party controlled. He broke with the Party over the Nazi-Soviet Pact and in 1944 ran for Congress against Hugh DeLacy, a Party member who won the election with help from Hollywood front groups. The defeated Costigan came to Los Angeles, where Brewer, whom he had met the previous year in Seattle, gave him a job organizing groups to oppose the Party.

Brewer also networked with Irving Brown, a labor activist who in the late 1930s had organized strikes at General Motors and Ford. During the war, Brown had gone to Europe, where he had worked with labor leaders in the Resistance. Still in Europe after the war, he found himself battling the Stalinists and worked to avert Communist-sponsored general strikes in both Italy and France, where the Confédération Générale du Travail, a major union, enjoyed the backing of the Communist Party and its celebrity spokesman, singer–actor Yves Montand.

The International Rescue and Relief Committee (IRRC), set up to aid victims of the Nazis, was now aiding victims of Stalinism. Roy Brewer served as vice chairman of the IRRC's southern California committee, whose Hollywood contingent included

Harpo Marx, Joan Fontaine, Henry Fonda, and James Cagney. In April 1948, the group hosted Arthur Koestler, the man the Party loved to hate, and who refused to be intimidated by the death threats he received during his stay in the movie capital.

Koestler mocked Henry Wallace, the Party's candidate of choice for U.S. president and said the turning point in Wallace's career had been his Madison Square Garden speech, in which he deliberately omitted passages critical of the USSR. The author of *Darkness at Noon* went on to attack Stalin and Communism directly, but the evening also provided some unexpected drama.

Koestler had met American poet Langston Hughes in the Soviet Union and told the crowd at the IRRC event he had received word that Hughes had died. As it happened, Hughes was in the audience, standing beside Roy Brewer. "Arthur, I'm not dead," said the poet, sending the audience into laughter and applause.[8] Koestler became a kind of Sherpa guide on Communism for many in the studios, including Budd Schulberg, who told Koestler that he hated the Communists but did not like to attack the Left. Koestler told him he had to get over that. "They're not left," he said; "they're East."[9]

On a more practical level, Brewer also took lessons from his rival Herb Sorrell. During the studio disputes, the anti-Communists didn't have an overarching labor organization like Herb Sorrell's Conference of Studio Unions. Tapping his allies, Brewer now set out to create the Hollywood AFL Film Council, composed of seventeen unions and representing more than 30,000 workers. If new jurisdictional disputes arose, the council would settle them with the cooperation of the American Federation of Labor. While things were quieting down on the back lots, Brewer and his allies turned their attention to the political front, where the Party propaganda machine was supporting Henry Wallace in his 1948 bid for the U.S. presidency.

Brewer, his ally Howard Costigan, and Ronald Reagan launched the League of Hollywood Voters, throwing its support behind Harry Truman and those Democratic candidates who had declined support from the Communist Party. Reagan chaired the organization, with Brewer as vice chairman and Costigan as executive secretary.

Howard Costigan was still smarting from the Hollywood Party's support for his opponent, Hugh DeLacy. "They sent a crew up my way to take care of me," he said. "I'm down here to take care of them." He found Wallace's candidacy useful because it helped isolate the Communists from liberals and other leftists.[10]

California congresswoman Helen Gahagan Douglas, wife of Melvyn Douglas, helped Brewer, Costigan, and Reagan set up the league. Her attention to the plight of migrant workers put her on friendly terms with Roy Brewer, who through the Hollywood AFL Film Council produced a documentary titled *Poverty in the Land of Plenty* about the farm workers on the Di Giorgio family's vast farms near Bakersfield. When *Poverty* was shown on television, the wealthy family sued for libel, the first such case as a result of a television program. The film also led to a rift between Brewer and Jack Tenney, the former left-wing musician who had become a Red-hunting state senator, heading the California version of the House Committee.

Douglas had been part of HICCASP but eventually came to criticize the Party. "Communism has no place in our society," she said. "Communist methods are foreign to ours."[11] As for the situation in Europe, "no sooner had the shooting stopped than the expansionist policies of the Soviet Union created a new threat to the security of Western Europe."[12]

During the 1948 campaign, the League of Hollywood Voters made a nationwide broadcast for Truman and later brought the Democratic presidential candidate to a Hollywood function. The support helped Truman, who at that time was unpopular with many liberals because of his imposition of a loyalty oath for government workers. When Truman won the election, Lucille Ball, Desi Arnaz, George Jessel, Kay Starr, Birnie Foy, Gregory Peck, Humphrey Bogart, Lauren Bacall, Pat O'Brien, and other stars turned out for the League's victory banquet.

While upbeat about the election returns, stars and back-lot workers alike worried about the state of the industry. That year in the famous "Paramount decision," the studios lost control of their theater chains, and box office receipts continued to plummet, prompting *Life* magazine to report that the prospect of another investigation of Hollywood was like "a group of marooned sailors on a flat desert island watching the approach of a tidal wave."[13] With the Communists now exposed through the Wallace candidacy, the film industry could present a united front against them.

Roy Brewer helped form the Motion Picture Industry Council (MPIC), which embraced eleven organizations representing all phases of the industry, from labor to executives. Members included Gene Kelly, Walter Pidgeon, and William Holden. Edward Cheyfitz, the former Communist who worked for movie-industry representative Eric Johnston, also supported the group, which softened Louis B. Mayer's opposition to studio labor's participation in the MPIC. Revisionists have portrayed the council as a toady of the House Committee on Un-American Activities, but the group resisted attempts at state control.

Senator Edwin C. Johnson of Colorado submitted a bill that would apply a "purity test" to moviemakers. The bill would forbid the portrayal in movies of people who might have violated legal statutes governing morals. Johnson also pushed for an elaborate licensing system for motion picture producers and even for actors and actresses. Brewer, an early chair of the Motion Picture Industry Council, denounced such measures as "the first step toward totalitarianism." His stance won him new friends at UCLA's *Daily Bruin*, which had been one of his toughest critics during the studio labor disputes.[14] But as Brewer's stature increased, Party organs and front groups continued their onslaught against him.

"The western Communists hate Roy Brewer more than they would a combination of Trotsky, Truman, and Tito," wrote labor writers Murray Kempton and Victor Riesel. Brewer received support as well. Kempton and Riesel hailed him as "Lincolnesque" and "labor's antidote for Communism." His campaign against the screen Stalinists had, in their opinion, "saved the movie industry from a fate worse than political death."[15]

Had the Conference of Studio Unions prevailed, the labor writers believed, the Hollywood Party would have pushed for one enormous industrial-style union that included everyone from producers to grips. Such a union would have helped Party insiders control industry workers and influence movie content as well.

THE INCLUSION OF ANTI-NAZI RESISTANCE HERO Marshal Tito of Yugoslavia in Party demonology reflected tectonic shifts on the international scene that would prove crucial to the Party's operations in Hollywood. Tito claimed that Stalin's terror surpassed that of Genghis Khan and let it be known he would steer an independent course. That earned Tito the unalloyed wrath of the Soviet boss, who still occupied half of Europe. In 1948, Communists in charge of the police and militia seized power in Czechoslovakia, which had already ceded territory to the USSR. The Communist coup led to mass arrests, persecution, and a vicious purge campaign that eventually included Rudolf Slansky, the Czech Party's general secretary.

By then Stalin had repackaged traditional Russian anti-Semitism as anti-Zionism and had contemptuously dubbed Jews "rootless cosmopolitans." Ethnic minorities such as the Chechens and the Ingush, the Kabardins and the Balkans, the Kurds and the Crimean Tartars had all been sacrificed. Now it was the Jews' turn.[16] The victims included Grigory Kheifetz, the former Comintern agent and spy who had been mentioned in the 1947 HCUA hearings. For no other reason than that he was a Jew, Kheifetz was thrown into a labor camp, from which he did not emerge until the mid-1950s.[17]

At the time, novelist Howard Fast knew that the purges were truly multicultural. "Chaim Suller returned from the Soviet Union to tell me a horrendous story of the persecution, not only of Jews, but of others—executions without trial, whipping, torture—all of this under the benign rule of Josef Stalin."[18] Stalin's terror campaign prompted Morris Childs, a key member of the American Communist Party, to become a double agent and work for the FBI.[19] In Hollywood, the Party's show-business allies were well aware of the situation but took a different course.

On Paul Robeson's 1949 trip to Moscow to celebrate the 150th anniversary of poet Aleksandr Pushkin's birth, the Soviets denied a visa to Bruno Raikin, the singer's official accompanist, who was a Jew. Robeson made the trip anyway, but once in Moscow had difficulty contacting his Jewish friends, including actor–director Solomon Mikoels. Mikoels, with writer Itzak Feffer, had been hosted by Hollywood Communists in 1943 for the express purpose of denying Soviet anti-Semitism.

Unbeknownst to Robeson, in 1948, Stalin had ordered Mikoels's murder; the director's smashed and mutilated body had signaled the dictator's personal touch. Feffer was still alive, and in a meeting at Robeson's hotel, he gestured frantically to tell the singer that the room was bugged. The writer told Robeson that the Soviet secret police had murdered Mikoels and other Jewish cultural figures. Then he drew a hand across his throat to signify his own fate. Robeson did nothing, and when he returned to the United States, he again denied that anti-Semitism existed in the USSR.[20] Three years later, Feffer was shot, one of countless victims of Stalin's terror, Jewish and otherwise.[21]

Writer Isaac Babel was forced to sign testimony that his former mistress had given him the plans to assassinate Stalin and Voroshilov. The poet Nina Hagen-Torn, daughter of a Russified Swede, was imprisoned in 1937 and then again in 1947. Poet Anna Akhmatova, as part of the campaign against her, was called part nun, part harlot. Singer Liria Ruslanova's popularity placed her on a par with an Ella Fitzgerald or Edith Piaf, but fame could not prevent her from a ten-year prison term. Anzoya Feodorova, one of Stalin's favorite actresses and winner of a Stalin award, got twenty-five years for falling in love with an American. Stalin placed the purged entertainers in the same prisons that held hardened criminals.[22]

It was experiences like these, a terror that Westerners could not fathom, that Boris Pasternak described in *Doctor Zhivago*. "One day Larisa Feodorovna went out and did not come back," he wrote. "She must have been arrested in the street at that time. She vanished without a trace and probably died somewhere, forgotten as a nameless number on a list that afterward got mislaid, in one of the innumerable mixed or women's concentration camps in the north."[23]

The gulag system of labor camps also included a number of Americans who had moved to the Soviet Union in the 1920s and 1930s to help build socialism. Many perished, including Lovett Fort-Whiteman, a black American Communist, sent to Sevostlag prison camp near Magadan, in northeast Siberia.

By counts based on newly revealed Soviet archives, some 1,500 writers disappeared, including the poet Osip Mandelstam; the scholar and scientist Pavel Florensky, known as the Russian Leonardo Da Vinci; and novelist Boris Pilnyak, whose works were pulled from every library and bookshop. Those who did not perish found their works banned in their own country. The Party issued a decree condemning composer Dimitri Shostakovich for "formalism," and party boss Zhdanov told him what sort of music the Party wanted him to play.[24]

On September 27, 1949, the Soviets exploded an atomic bomb that had been built with secrets stolen from the United States and Britain by Communist spies such as Klaus Fuchs, whose American contact was Harry Gold, a key figure in the Rosenberg case. The worst mass murderer in human history now possessed nuclear weapons, with full approval of some leading lights of the day. Danish physicist Niels Bohr had urged that the Soviet Union be given the secrets of the bomb. So did Supreme Court justice Felix Frankfurter and the British ambassador in Washington, Lord Halifax, on the grounds that such a move would promote peace.

The American Communist Party picked up this theme, and around it they were able to marshal Hollywood star power. In March 1949 the Party sponsored the "Cultural Conference for World Peace" at the Waldorf-Astoria Hotel in New York. Among the boosters of this event were some forty Hollywood people, including Lillian Hellman, Marlon Brando, José Ferrer, Judy Holliday, and Lee J. Cobb. Bandleader Artie Shaw also took part, later explaining that the Party was "trying to get some pretty big names, names that were prominent before the public, and I guess I was a name they wanted to have there."[25]

WHILE STALIN'S PURGES CLAIMED MORE VICTIMS, the new People's Republic of China gave the Soviets a powerful new ally. Mao Tse-Tung paid tribute to the Soviets by appearing at Stalin's seventieth birthday celebration in 1949. The following June, North Korea's Kim Il Sung invaded South Korea, with full support of Stalin and the Chinese Communists.

American forces were practically as ill prepared for this invasion as they had been for Pearl Harbor. Seoul fell quickly, and American boys from New York and Kansas City were soon falling victim to well-trained and well-equipped Communist troops backed by Mao Tse-Tung's vast legions. The line of the American Communist Party, promoted in I. F. Stone's *Hidden History of the Korean War*, was a familiar inversion of reality. South Korea and the United States, Party writers said, had invaded North Korea, a peaceful democratic country that was now struggling to defend itself.

IN AMERICA, THE HISS–CHAMBERS CASE, with testimony of microfilm hidden in a pumpkin, and the Coplon, Remington, and Wadleigh spy trials brought shocking revelations of Soviet espionage and American laxity.[26] Coplon, for example, was given a job with access to sensitive Justice Department and FBI data about Soviet espionage despite her membership in the Young Communist League. In 1949 Elizabeth Bentley, a Vassar alumna who spied for the Soviets, named more than forty government employees who had played parts in an espionage ring that she ran during the 1940s. Though Bentley was attacked by the Left as a mentally sick fantasist, and maligned for decades by revisionist writers such as Victor Navasky and David Caute, her accusations have been verified by Soviet archives.[27]

That year also saw the appearance of *The God That Failed,* a book in which former high-profile Communists stated their case and bared their souls. Former Comintern scribe Arthur Koestler explained that he came to Communism as to a spring of fresh water, but crawled out of a poisoned river that was strewn with the wreckage of flooded cities and the corpses of the drowned. French novelist André Gide, a former Party devotee, now saw little choice between Communism and Fascism and wrote that the human mind and spirit had never been less free and more tyrannized than it was in the USSR. Black American novelist Richard Wright revealed his disillusionment with the USSR, as did Italian writer Ignazio Silone. American journalist Louis Fischer, who called Stalin the supreme slave master, pointed out that the Soviet Union was like one huge company town, in which the workers had no recourse.

The influential *God That Failed,* Elizabeth Bentley's spy revelations, Stalinist purges and anti-Semitism, the Berlin blockade, the fall of China—these events had no discernible effect on the Party faithful in Hollywood. Dalton Trumbo still claimed that in the Soviet Union, 3,500,000 Jews lived under the protection of laws that banned discrimination of any kind.[28] By some accounts, the events put the Hollywood Ten in the mood for purges of their own.

John Howard Lawson, Herb Biberman, and Alvah Bessie called a meeting at the home of Albert Maltz, where they subjected director Robert Rossen, one of the original Nineteen, to the same kind of inquisition Albert Maltz had endured in 1946. The Party objected to Rossen's film *All the King's Men,* an Oscar winner in 1950, and to its theme of "Power corrupts," although inter-Party rivalries and simple jealousy may also have fueled the attack.

Rossen, in any case, found his views on dictatorship reinforced by inquisition. According to Edward Dmytryk, Rossen walked out of the meeting, telling the others to "stick the whole Party up your ass!"[29]

Ed Dmytryk also objected to the Hollywood Independent Citizens Council of the Arts, Sciences and Professions (HICCASP) using the Ten as martyrs for purposes of fund-raising, with the Party grabbing the lion's share of the take. Needing work and money himself after the studios' about-face, Dmytryk went to England to direct two films. There he was exposed to people who had suffered under Communism and learned the fate of novelists, directors, and playwrights whom Stalin had hailed one day and jailed the next.

During that time, writer Victor Kravchenko sued a French newspaper, *Les Lettres françaises,* that had charged that his book *I Choose Freedom* was full of lies. The Communists tried to get Ed Dmytryk to testify on their side, about the repression and persecution in the United States. He turned them down three times. When Dmytryk returned to the United States, Herb Biberman asked him to rejoin the Party, but Dmytryk refused. Biberman also asked Dmytryk to co-sign a letter asking that the other eight of the Hollywood Ten be paroled. Dmytryk agreed, because he did not consider it a political act. But Biberman gave a copy of the letter to the Communist press, and its publication led many to assume that Dmytryk still stood with the Party.

Meanwhile, the Supreme Court, still packed with Roosevelt appointees, twice refused to consider the cases of the Ten and let their convictions stand. Lester Cole and Ring Lardner Jr. served their time at Danbury, Connecticut, where a familiar figure soon joined them.

Parnell Thomas, the patriotic and cigar-smoking Committee chairman with the thundering gavel, had been found guilty of embezzling government funds through a kickback scheme. The Committee boss had been exposed by columnist Drew Pearson, who had earlier pushed Thomas to carry on with the Hollywood hearings. Thomas pleaded no contest to the charges, did not take the stand, and was sentenced to three years.

After eighteen days in a D.C. federal penitentiary, Dmytryk was transferred to Mill Point, West Virginia, where he joined Clifford Odets and Howard Fast, the Party's favorite novelist, who were also serving contempt raps.

Prison allows time for reflection. The director had been sentenced on June 29, 1950, four days after the Communists invaded South Korea. Albert Maltz, Dmytryk's former Party comrade, no longer questioned the Party line and adopted the official position that South Korea had attacked the North. This only drove Dmytryk further from the Party, and when the Chinese entered the war, he swore an affidavit before his lawyer, Bartley Crum, and the prison superintendent:

> I declined to answer the question as to Communist affiliations because of a duty which I thought I owed to all Americans to preserve what I believed was a constitutional privilege of substance.
>
> However, in view of the troubled state of current world affairs, I find myself in the presence of an even greater duty and that is to declare without equivocation where I stand towards my own country. In the discharge of that duty I want to make it perfectly clear that I am not now nor was I at the time of the hearing a member of the Communist Party, that I am not a Communist sympathizer and that I recognize the United States of America as the only country to which I owe allegiance and loyalty.[30]

News of the affidavit reached Bessie and Biberman, who were doing time in Texarkana together. As Bessie tells it, the two did not exactly get along, with the picky Biberman criticizing the way Bessie stood or sat. (Lawson and Trumbo were once handcuffed together, and that surely provided a few sparks, too.) The two split on Dmytryk. Bessie predicted he would become a "renegade."

This infuriated Biberman, who shrieked, "Eddie will *never* go over to the enemy!"[31]

As it happened, Dmytryk was not alone in his feelings. Korea, the purges, the Czech coup, and the spy trials had turned many, both Party members and liberals, into anti-Stalinists. Many found themselves willing to talk about it. They would soon get their chance.

17

Breaking Ranks

WHEN EDWARD DMYTRYK GOT OUT OF JAIL in November 1950, he went to Ike Chadwick, head of the independent producers, who had given the director his first job. Dmytryk told Chadwick that, despite what Chadwick might have heard, he had broken ranks with the Hollywood Ten and wanted to prove it to the toughest anti-Communist in town, Roy Brewer. Chadwick arranged a meeting.

Many in the Motion Picture Industry Council remained skeptical of Dmytryk, and no consensus emerged on how to proceed. Brewer knew that Party attachments remained strong but that some people stayed in or close to the Party only because they believed that they had nowhere else to turn. Brewer wanted to give the director a chance. He proposed that Dmytryk tell his story both to the Committee and to the public, by publishing it in a magazine article. Brewer and Howard Costigan argued that, as a Communist, Dmytryk had used his name and reputation to serve Party causes, and that he was now obligated to use his name publicly to oppose the Party. Dmytryk balked at the prospect but eventually agreed. Privately, Brewer hoped that the article would force the Party to show its hand. His gamble would soon pay off.

"What Makes a Hollywood Communist?," written by veteran Hollywood writer Richard English after two weeks of interviews with Dmytryk, ran in the *Saturday Evening Post* on May 19, 1951. Nine days later, Albert Maltz, who had defended the director in the controversy over *Cornered* and been best man at his wedding in 1948, blasted Dmytryk in a *Hollywood Reporter* ad, contradicting everything the director had said in his interviews and adding wild charges, such as the claim that Dmytryk had said it was time for progressives to "go underground." By this action, the Party sought to discredit Dmytryk and use him to teach the lesson that you could not break with the Party and survive in the film industry. But the fury of the Party's attack had the opposite effect, convincing some doubters that Dmytryk's story of breaking with the Ten had been on the level.

Some wanted Dmytryk to respond to Maltz in kind, but Brewer argued that an ongoing exchange of charges and countercharges would only play into the Party's hands. After some heated sessions in the Motion Picture Industry Council, Brewer prevailed. Brewer, Ike Chadwick, Ronald Reagan, and three others signed a public statement titled "You Can Be Free Men Again!" to let others know that if they broke Party ranks they would not stand alone.

> When the Communist Party traps an American into its unholy conspiracy, it is almost unbearably hard to break away. The Party sees to that, for the Party must enforce its discipline or die.
>
> The Communist Party is now trying to destroy Edward Dmytryk for breaking with the party and exposing its secrets to the proper government agencies. Dmytryk is not the first ex-Communist to be called "faker" and "liar" and "scoundrel" and "perjurer." These same accusations have been leveled by the Communist Party against such militant ex-Communists as Arthur Koestler, Louis Budenz, Elizabeth Bentley, and Whittaker Chambers.
>
> In each case, the records of these persons show that their disillusionment with Communism came slowly, but with it came determination to help destroy the menace which once had trapped them. The attack against Dmytryk merely

confirms what veteran fighters against Communism already know, namely that the party has been hit where it hurts.

The statement also revealed the plan for the *Saturday Evening Post* article and attacked the "Big Lie," the Party accusation that Dmytryk had said it was time for all progressives to go underground.

> The attack on Eddie Dmytryk was not unexpected and it came as no surprise to those who know how the Communist Party operates. But the Communist Party has failed in its effort to destroy Edward Dmytryk. Were it otherwise, it would be a victory for the Communist Party and a defeat for Americanism.
>
> We will be surprised if there are not other attacks by the Communist Party on other former Communists who have the guts to stand up and be counted and to tell the truth to the proper government agencies. It takes courage and desire and time for an American to work free of the tentacles of the Communist Party. And it takes help. But there is a way out. To any Communist Party member who may be seeking that way, we say: "You too can be free men again!"

Writer Richard Collins, still under the influence of Party smear campaigns, approached Dmytryk's defenders with some trepidation. He had expected to find Brewer a fire-breathing ideologue and discovered instead a quiet and reasonable man who was willing to listen and who was politically a liberal Democrat.[1] After Dmytryk and Collins, many others followed. The willingness of so many people to testify, the changes on the world and national scenes, and the evident failure of the 1947 hearings prompted, in 1951, a new series of congressional inquiries on Hollywood.

John Wood of Georgia, who had served on the 1947 House Committee on Un-American Activities, was named chairman of the new committee. The new lineup included Francis Walter of Pennsylvania, Morgan Moulder of Missouri, Clyde Doyle and

Donald Jackson of California, James Frazier of Tennessee, Harold Velde of Illinois, Bernard Kearney of New York, and Charles Potter of Michigan. This group, mindful of past hearings, was less prone to theatrics than the 1947 Committee but still wanted to play on their home field, the same old House Office Building where Dalton Trumbo had predicted the American concentration camp. The first witness to testify before the 1951 Committee was Victor Jeremy Jerome, the cultural commissar who had founded the Party's studio section nearly twenty years earlier.

"I do not wish to be a party to answering a question that will just heighten a so-called war spirit in this country," said Jerome when asked whom he would support in the event of a conflict between the United States and the Soviet Union. The Party boss admitted to being in Hollywood for nine months in 1936 but declined comment on what he was doing there. He also declined to answer questions about his late colleague, Party organizer Stanley Lawrence, and whether Jerome had organized a commission for ascertaining the loyalty of Party members during the Nazi-Soviet Pact. When asked if he knew Sam Moore, a figure in the Hollywood Writer's Mobilization, V. J. Jerome replied, "I decline to answer the question on the grounds of possible self-incrimination."

While the 1947 unfriendlies hailed the First Amendment and free expression, the 1951 witnesses leaned on the Fifth Amendment, protection against incrimination. Director Carl Foreman, of *High Noon* fame, denied that he was a Party member at the time of testimony but refused to answer about other times. This became known as the "diminished Fifth." Director Robert Rossen said that he was not a Communist Party member and denied sympathy with them, but he would not say whether he had been a member in the past. This became known as the "augmented Fifth."

This Committee was pressing witnesses not just to outline their own activities, but also to name others who had been in the Party, a practice that got the hearings dubbed "a new kind of talky." Anyone who was named as a member of the Communist Party would be invited to testify and explain. The testimony of Larry Parks, one of the Nineteen "unfriendlies," revealed the tensions involved, particularly for actors.

"It's like taking a pot shot at a wounded animal, because the industry is not in as good shape today as it has been," said Parks, who had starred in the 1949 *Jolson Sings Again* and had taken a high-profile role in support groups for the Hollywood Ten.

> I think my career has been ruined because of this, and I would appreciate not having to. . . . Don't present me with the choice of either being in contempt of this Committee and going to jail or forcing me to really crawl through the mud to be an informer, for what purpose? I don't think this is a choice at all. I don't think this is really sportsmanlike. I don't think this is American. I don't think this is American justice. I think to do something like that is more akin to what happened under Hitler, and what is happening in Russia today. . . . So I beg of you not to force me to do this.[2]

But Parks became one of many to name other Party members.

While V. J. Jerome stood as a veritable wall of stone, Howard Da Silva, the Party's straw-boss among the actors, found himself in the mood for speeches. He praised the Federal Theatre Project as "the advent of a magnificent period, and I think some of the greatest work that ever came out, came out at that time; truly a people's theatre." As for the Committee, he said, "I think any attempt to investigate so-called subversive organizations is an attempt to pull wool over the American people's eyes." It was "the old Army game to say 'Look what is happening there, and meanwhile we pick your pockets and drop atom bombs.' That is the real function."[3]

Will Geer, a veteran of such pictures as *Tall Target* and *Barefoot Mailman*, followed a familiar theme. "The word 'Communist,' is an emotional, hysterical word of the day, like the word 'witch' in Salem." The Communists, he said, were "being persecuted now like the Mormons, the Jews, the Quakers, the Masons . . . even radical Republicans in Lincoln's day." Geer took the Fifth, as did writer Waldo Salt, one of Albert Maltz's inquisitors, but not before answering that he did not belong to the Ku Klux Klan. Actor Lloyd Gough, who had been a favorite of the Conference of Studio Unions, took the Fifth on questions such as "Who played the principal role in *Body and Soul?*"[4]

Herta Uerkvitz, an architectural researcher for the movies, told the Committee that her being named as a Communist reminded her of "a tale on witch hunts where a five-year-old child was condemned because a man testified that he saw devils running out of her mouth."[5] She also took the Fifth, a tactic avoided by some higher-profile witnesses.

Sterling Hayden was represented by Martin Gang, an entertainment lawyer who had a reputation for clearing people accused of Communist affiliations, allowing them to continue working. "I had become susceptible to and, in a sense perhaps, a victim of the idea that they had a form of democracy in mind," Hayden told the Committee about the Hollywood Communists. "I found the belief is that they have the key, by some occult power, to know what is best for people, and that is the way it is going to be. . . . When I learned about this and began to think about and digest it a bit, I decided to get out, and I got out."[6] Hayden told them about actress Karen Morley's attempt to get him to rejoin the Party or, failing that, to contribute money.

At the time of the hearings, Hayden was seeing a psychiatrist he identified as "Doc" in his book *Wanderer*. The psychiatrist is without doubt Phil Cohen, something of a mystery character in Party circles, whose patients also included Lloyd Bridges, John Garfield, Richard Collins, and Collins's former wife, Dorothy Comingore, among many others. Cohen hailed from Seattle, where he had joined the Party as an organizer among blacks. Though he dropped out of the Party, he remained their approved therapist, perhaps because the Party rejected professional analysis and Cohen lacked full M.D. accreditation. For reasons that remain unclear, he came to collaborate with Martin Gang and FBI investigator William

Wheeler in clearing those who wanted to cooperate with the Committee. In many cases, they wanted to cooperate because of his ministrations, which included socializing with his patients. Joan LaCour, wife of Adrian Scott, said Cohen "got me slightly swacked on brandy to get me to open up."[7]

According to writer Norma Barzman, Cohen was the shrink everybody went to and who eased them into whatever they wanted to do in front of the Committee.[8] Or as Party official Charles Glenn put it, Cohen made people feel comfortable about informing,[9] leading some to believe Cohen had been working for the FBI all along. He was tagged a "stoolie," a term the Party lifted from prison parlance and that Party members hurled at friendly witnesses as they appeared. But not all witnesses needed therapeutic coaxing to testify.

Director Elia Kazan, still a man of the Left but a staunch anti-Stalinist, had experienced manipulation during the 1940s from both the Party and the Hollywood studios.[10] By 1952, Kazan was prepared to openly take a stand. In executive session, he gave information on his own Communist background but declined to name others. He subsequently changed his mind and decided to submit a complete statement. "I have come to the conclusion that I did wrong to withhold these names before, because secrecy serves the Communists, and is exactly what they want," the director explained. "The American people need the facts and all the facts about all aspects of Communism in order to deal with it wisely and effectively. It is my obligation as a citizen to tell everything that I know."

Kazan explained, "I had enough regimentation, enough of being told what to think and say and do, enough of their habitual violation of the daily practices of democracy to which I was accustomed. The last straw came when I was invited to go through a typical Communist scene of crawling and apologizing and admitting the error of my ways." The invitation had come from a Communist functionary brought in for the occasion.

That night, he continued, "[I] had a taste of police state living and I did not like it." The experience "also left me with the passionate conviction that we must never let the Communists get away with the pretense that they stand for the very things which they kill in their own countries."[11]

Kazan not only told his story but urged others to do the same in an April 12, 1952, notice in the *New York Times*:

In the past weeks intolerable rumors about my political position have been circulating in New York and Hollywood. I want to make my stand clear:

I believe that Communist activities confront the people of this country with an unprecedented and exceptionally tough problem. That is, how to protect ourselves from a dangerous and alien conspiracy and still keep the free, open, healthy way of life that gives us self-respect.

I believe that the American people can solve this problem wisely only if they have the facts about Communism. All the facts.

Now, I believe that any American who is in possession of such facts has the obligation to make them known, either to the public or to the appropriate Government agency.

Whatever hysteria exists—and there is some, particularly in Hollywood—is inflamed by mystery, suspicion and secrecy. Hard and exact facts will cool it.

The facts I have are sixteen years out of date, but they supply a small piece of background to the graver picture of Communism today.

I have placed these facts before the House Committee on Un-American Activities without reserve and I now place them before the public and before my coworkers in motion pictures and the theater.

Seventeen and a half years ago I was a twenty-four-year-old stage manager and bit actor, making $40 a week, when I worked.

At that time nearly all of us felt menaced by two things: the depression and the ever growing power of Hitler. The streets were full of unemployed and shaken men. I was taken in the hard times version of what might be called the Communists' advertising or recruiting technique. They claimed to have a cure for depressions and a cure for Nazism and Fascism.

I joined the Communist Party late in the summer of 1934. I got out a year and a half later.

I have no spy stories to tell, because I saw no spies. Nor did I understand, at that time, any opposition between American and Russian national interest. It was not even clear to me in 1936 that the American Communist Party was abjectly taking its orders from the Kremlin.

What I learned was the minimum that anyone must learn who puts his head into the noose of party "discipline." The Communists automatically violated the daily practices of democracy to which I was accustomed. They attempted to control thought and to suppress personal opinion. They tried to dictate personal conduct. They habitually distorted and disregarded and violated the truth. All this was crudely opposite to their claims of "democracy" and "the scientific approach."

To be a member of the Communist Party is to have a taste of the police state. It is a diluted taste but it is bitter and unforgettable. It is diluted because you can walk out.

I got out in the spring of 1936.

The question will be asked why I did not tell this story sooner. I was held back, primarily by concern for the reputations and employment of people who may, like myself, have left the Party many years ago.

I was also held back by a piece of specious reasoning which has silenced many liberals. It goes like this: "You may hate the Communists, but you must not attack them or expose them, because if you do you are attaching the right to hold unpopular opinions and you are joining the people who attack civil liberties."

I have thought soberly about this. It is, simply, a lie.

Secrecy serves the Communists. At the other pole, it serves those who are interested in silencing liberal voices. The employment of a lot of good liberals is threatened because they have allowed themselves to become associated with or silenced by the Communists.

Liberals must speak out.

I think it is useful that certain of us had this kind of experience with the Communists, for if we had not, we should not know them so well. Today, when all the world fears war and they scream peace, we know how much their professions are worth. We know tomorrow they will have a new slogan.

Firsthand experience of dictatorship and thought control left me with an abiding hatred of these. It left me with an abiding hatred of Communist philosophy and methods and the conviction that these must be resisted always.

It also left me with the passionate conviction that we must never let the Communists get away with the pretense that they stand for the very things which they kill in their own countries.

I am talking about free speech, a free press, the rights of property, the rights of labor, racial equality and, above all, individual rights. I value these things. I take them seriously. I value peace, too, when it is not brought in at the price of fundamental decencies.

I believe these things must be fought for wherever they are not fully honored, and protected whenever they are threatened.

The motion pictures I have made and the plays I have chosen to direct represent my convictions.

I expect to continue to make the same kinds of pictures and to direct the same kinds of plays.

The testimony and ad drew the full wrath of the Party, with Kazan finding himself attacked in the *Daily Worker* and accused of selling out for money by Lillian Hellman, who called his testimony "hard to believe for its pious shit."[12] A stream of anonymous letters smeared Kazan as a "rat" and "squealer." Other former Party members would also become targets.

Director Edward Dmytryk outlined the differences between 1947 and 1951, with attention to the Korean War. One thing that had spurred him to testify, he said, was the open declaration of some, such as Paul Robeson, that they would not fight for the United States against the Soviet Union. "I don't say all members of the Communist party are guilty of treason," he said, "but I think a party that encourages them to act in this capacity is treasonable. For this reason I am willing to talk today."[13]

Richard Collins explained that he had told Paul Jarrico, his former writing partner, he would not give any names during his testimony if Jarrico would give Collins his personal assurance that in the event of a war between the United States and the Soviet Union, Jarrico would do nothing to help the Soviet Union. "Since he could not give me this assurance," Collins said, "I would not give him mine."

Collins cited Albert Maltz's February 1946 *New Masses* article, which objected to the Party's art-as-weapon doctrine, as "a completely reasonable plea," something that "came out of Maltz's guts, since it was something he had to write." The effect of the subsequent Party inquisition, Collins testified, was to strike fear into Communist writers. The incident, the changes brought on by the Jacques Duclos letter, and the change in the Party line spurred Collins to leave the Party.[14]

Meta Reis Rosenberg had been a liaison between the Hollywood Writer's Mobilization and an organization called the Victory Committee. She described Party member Abe Polonsky as "a very brilliant writer" but testified that the Party brooked no opposition. "The minute you disagree they begin to call you names, and this is a form of intimidation. . . . There is no really independent thinking among the rank and file."[15]

When asked if Richard Collins had perjured himself when he named his former partner as a Party member, screenwriter Paul

Jarrico took the Fifth at the advice of the ever-present Ben Margolis. But when asked about his current projects Jarrico readily delivered a blurb. "The last screenplay on which I was employed was *The Las Vegas Story*, with Jane Russell and Victor Mature. I urge you all to see it."[16]

Writer Martin Berkeley told the Committee how Lionel Stander, the "International"-whistling Communist actor, had introduced him to "comrade Harry Bridges" and how Donald Ogden Stewart, Dashiell Hammett, and Lillian Hellman had been assigned to a group known as Party members at large. Berkeley also addressed a claim by Herb Biberman that the movies had suffered from the absence of talented people such as himself, and that the movies were now obsessed with sex, a theme from the *People's Daily World* movie special.

"I don't know whether they are uninterested in sex in the Communist Party, but I vaguely remember some of the pictures that Mr. Biberman made. He said we were only concerned with melodrama, and I couldn't understand why the absence of ten men or the purging of twenty-five or thirty, which I hope is done soon, from the industry is going to make the quality of our product any worse, because I believe that the product that we are turning out today is as good or better than it ever was."

Berkeley told the Committee that the picture most affected by the Party was *Blockade*, a "silly . . . badly made, badly written picture."

In long testimony, Berkeley charted Party efforts to influence the IA, described the fights in the Motion Picture Democratic Committee over Stalin's invasion of Finland, and estimated that groups such as the Hollywood Anti-Nazi League and the Joint Anti-Fascist Refugee Committee had siphoned "millions" of dollars into Party coffers. He detailed the flip-flops of the Nazi-Soviet Pact and told of travails with George Willner, the Communist agent who had sabotaged his work. He also recalled how the Party had moved NLRB official William Pomerance into the Screen Writers Guild.

What really gave Berkeley a lofty rank on the Party's demon list was the way he spun off names like a Rolodex, providing the Committee with the names of more than 150 Party members.[17]

Budd Schulberg told how Party organizer Stanley Lawrence had led him into a Marxist study group, and how the Communist Party had tried to influence his writing. When asked how the Committee should deal with those seeking to disentangle themselves from the Party, he said: "I think that since many of these people obviously in a sense are in nowise really subversive. They got into something they really didn't understand and once they are out, they should help in every way. Industries should not be encouraged to crack down on them. I think the people in Hollywood still are frightened about hiring some of these people."[18]

Frank Tuttle, director of *This Gun for Hire, Swell Guy, Roman Scandals,* and many other films, testified about life in the Hollywood Party. "There is a kind of mental incest in the Communist Party groups. You see and talk only to people for the most part who are either Communist or close to the Communist way of thinking. Many people bring up problems that are straw men because they knock them down with a stock answer. It was not until then I was able to reestablish myself as an independent thinker."[19]

Michael Blankfort, who wrote *Broken Arrow,* told the Committee how the Party pressured him to review favorably the plays that they liked, but he didn't. The disagreements would cost him. The *New Masses* and *Daily Worker* denounced his third novel, *The Widow Makers,* as anti-Communist.

Journalist Harold Ashe, who had worked with the Motion Picture Artists Committee, lit into Stanley Lawrence. When Lawrence came to Hollywood, the Party organizer claimed to be an expert in underground work. "Later independent investigation of mine revealed that he had been a Los Angeles taxicab driver," Ashe said. "I might add that he knows less about underground work than my six-year-old girl."

Ashe also blasted the Party's work schedule, in testimony that surely articulated the rage of many. "I felt as early as the end of

1936 that the Communist Party was a betrayer of the working class, and I think so today. . . . I was being badly exploited by the Party, working about sixteen to eighteen hours a day." Ashe provided detailed testimony on Jeff Kibre and the Party's involvement in the trade-union issue. Before he finished he took some swings at those picketing the hearings. "I think it is the surest kind of hypocrisy that these Communists picketing out there today talk about this committee denying them the right to think. They haven't got any right to think. They gave it to Stalin."[20]

Michael Wilson, the Berkeley grad in philosophy who regarded Hollywood as the "big money tit," had contributed to *It's a Wonderful Life* and other films. But in testimony Wilson revealed the level of seriousness with which Hollywood writers approached their craft. "I did a number of Hopalong Cassidy pictures, which are those that are now corrupting our children on the television screens of the nation," said the member of the Party's B team and a self-proclaimed man of peace. "This Committee is beating the drums of war," he said. "I don't believe that we prepare for peace by preparing for war, and in my humble opinion, if the profits were taken out of war, I believe there would be a lot less war hysteria in this country today."[21]

The Committee was growing weary with that line, along with past claims of opposition to fascism. "Now, I fought against fascism for five years," said Representative Donald Jackson from California. "Mr. Potter [Committee member from Michigan] lost two legs. We didn't do it from a soap box. We did it out where deeds were being performed against fascism."[22]

Stanley Rubin, a writer who had worked on *South to Katanga, Flying Cadets, Mister Dynamite, Bombay Clipper,* and other films, recalled Michael Wilson leading classes in which he "painted the followers of Trotsky as liars, assassins, and villains incarnate," warning the rank and file to purge any Trotskyites from among their friends and acquaintances. [23]

Karl Tunberg, president of the Screen Writers Guild, recounted the knock-down, drag-out battles with Communists that took place in bitter all-night sessions. "We have really been through the mill on fighting these people," he testified.[24]

Musician David Raksin, who had scored *The Secret Life of Walter Mitty, Forever Amber,* and *The Magnificent Yankee,* explained how he had been turned against the Party when Stalin disciplined composers Shostakovich and Prokofiev. "They were men of great talent," he said, "and . . . if they chose to explore paths which led off the beaten track and if they chose to indulge in experiments as artists which were not immediately comprehensible to people who were not schooled in listening to music, they should be permitted to do this, and . . . this was the very breath and blood of art, and the position of the Communist Party at the time seems to have been that these men were servants of something and, at all costs, had to be made to toe the line."[25]

Actor Jeff Corey, named in the Committee hearings by colleague Marc Lawrence, said he knew that actor "who played an informer, with great verisimilitude, in a picture called *The Asphalt Jungle.*" Corey, who did not want to be televised and objected to the photographers, described himself as "an actor of some sensitivity." Claiming he had been "grey-listed if not completely blacklisted," he stood on the First and Fifth Amendments, along with Article 18 of the United Nations General Declaration of Human Rights.[26]

Tough-guy actor Edward G. Robinson appeared as a voluntary witness. The actor had spoken at so many benefits for front groups, reading speeches often written by Party members, that the *Examiner* refused to let him speak at one of their "I Am an American Day" celebrations. The rejection crushed Robinson, who had never ceased regarding himself as a fine patriot. "I was duped and used. I was lied to," Robinson said. "But I repeat, I acted from good motives."[27]

Waiting for Lefty author Clifford Odets, once the golden boy of agitprop theater, was working as an art critic. Odets told the Committee he knew Michael Blankfort, a critic for *New Masses.* "I knew him vaguely. But I didn't like him. That is because he was a budding playwright too, I think. He wrote scurrilously of my plays." Odets, who once had several plays running at once, also wandered into Party theories of art. "A Marxist believes that if you would straighten out your ideology in terms of Marxist orientation, then when you do that, you will no longer have structural flaws. . . . John Howard Lawson very thoroughly believes that. I do not. I do not think that if you spoil your inner life by Marxian ideology that you will have no structural difficulties in your play."[28]

In his testimony, Martin Berkeley had named "my old friend Dashiell Hammett, who is now in jail in New York for his activities," and "that very excellent playwright Lillian Hellman," who had since been subpoenaed.[29] In a letter to the Committee, Hellman said, "I do not like subversion or disloyalty and if I had ever seen any I would have considered it my duty to have reported it to the proper authorities. But to hurt innocent people whom I knew many years ago in order to save myself is to me inhuman and indecent and dishonorable. I cannot and will not cut my conscience to fit this year's fashions, even though I long ago came to the conclusion that I was not a political person and could have no comfortable place in any political group."

The woman who accused Elia Kazan of peddling "pious shit" added: "I was raised in an old-fashioned American tradition and there were certain homely things that were taught to me: To try to tell the truth, not to bear false witness, not to harm my neighbor, to be loyal to my country, and so on. In general, I respected these ideals of Christian honor and did as well with them as I knew how."[30] Her letter offered to waive invocation of the Fifth if she was asked only about herself, but she refused to answer a direct question about her Communist Party membership, or whether she knew V. J. Jerome or John Howard Lawson.

Abe Burrows, the *Guys and Dolls* coauthor who had taken heat for satirizing the Party, appeared with attorney Martin Gang. The Communists, said Burrows, "sounded like superpatriots, completely superpatriots. It wasn't until later that they began to show themselves. That iron fist in the intellectual glove now began to show itself, and people began to recognize what they were."[31]

Karen Morley had acted in *Black Fury, Scarface, Washington Masquerade, Arsene Lupin,* and *M.* Represented by Vito Marcantonio, she took the Fifth, rounding out more than 4,000 pages of Hollywood testimony during which the subpoena envy of 1947 proved little in evidence. As actor Marc Lawrence observed, "Anybody who had the guts to say 'I'm a Communist and you want to cut my throat because that's what I believe?' That's gutsy. But nobody said that."[32]

While the ongoing talky proved informative and even entertaining, the heavy drama took place beyond the cameras.

18

"Those Witches Did Not Exist; Communists Do"

DURING WORLD WAR II, American technical workers had been encouraged to go overseas and help the allies. If Americans worked outside the United States for eighteen months and only returned once a month, whatever income they earned was exempt from tax. Actors and directors soon discovered this loophole, called the "eighteen month clause," and took full advantage of it; Gene Kelly was one of the first, followed by Gary Cooper, Ward Bond, Gene Tierney, Gregory Peck, Claudette Colbert, Errol Flynn, Kirk Douglas, and directors Howard Hawks, John Huston, and William Wyler among others.[1] For most people, money was the primary motive, but many people suspected that some of those who left America after the war were fleeing the Committee, which Hollywood Party members were indeed doing.

Rather than testify before the 1951 Committee, many in the Hollywood Party packed up and fled abroad. Paul Jarrico opted for Czechoslovakia, but Mexico, England, and France were the usual destinations of choice. Dalton Trumbo went to Mexico; screenwriters Ben and Norma Barzman found that French intellectuals, even non-Communists, hailed them as heroes. In a country where being a Communist was more acceptable, they found good company with Yves Montand and Simone Signoret, who backed the Party line, performed at Party events, and denounced the United States at every opportunity as an imperialistic bully.[2]

While some American Party members remained abroad for years, others returned to Hollywood. Dalton Trumbo had earned two months off his prison sentence and before decamping to Mexico retreated to the Lazy T, his ranch in the Tehachapi Mountains of California. His friends found that, apart from his jailhouse pallor, the writer picked up his previous lifestyle as though he had never left. Joan LaCour, Adrian Scott's wife, found Trumbo guzzling booze, popping uppers and downers, and working simultaneously on eight scripts under four or five pseudonyms.[3]

Trumbo later admitted what everyone in Hollywood knew, but no one had ever mentioned: he had been working steadily since the blacklist began.[4] While in prison, even, Trumbo had been busy writing scripts and smuggling them out. In 1951 he coscripted Joe Losey's *The Prowler*, and then, working from Mexico, where he sent his children to an exclusive private school, he wrote under such pseudonyms as Marcel Klauber, Sally Stubblefield, and Les Crutchfield, while working on films such as *Roman Holiday, The Carnival Story, The Green-Eyed Blonde,* and *The Young Philadelphians*. Writing as Robert Rich, he wrote the story for *The Brave One*, which won an Oscar in 1956.

Trumbo also admitted that "others of my kind had also been working," and "the major studios were openly in the black market."[5] The record backs him up. Michael Wilson won an Oscar for his work on the screenplay of the 1951 *A Place in the Sun*, which starred Montgomery Clift and Elizabeth Taylor. Twentieth Century Fox's 1951 lineup included *Wait Till the Sun Shines, Nellie*, with Albert Dekker, who also appeared in *As Young As You Feel*. Abe Polonsky, part of the Party's A team, wrote *I Can Get It for You Wholesale;* Michael Gordon directed it, as he also directed *Secret of Convict Lake.*

Columbia's 1951 offerings included *Sirocco,* with Lee J. Cobb and Zero Mostel, and *Santa Fe,* directed by Irving Pichel, who was one of the original Nineteen and who, as part of the Hollywood Writer's Mobilization, had called for a boycott of Hollywood films while promoting Soviet offerings such as *Russia on Parade.* Howard Da Silva and Luther Adler, a veteran of *Cornered,* starred in *M,* which was directed by Joe Losey. In 1950, Sterling Hayden starred in a movie directed by John Huston, *Asphalt Jungle,* which helped launch the career of Marilyn Monroe.

Gene Kelly's high-profile lobbying for the Hollywood Ten and support for Herb Sorrell did not hurt him. Rather, MGM's 1951 *Singing in the Rain* gave him the role that made him famous. And MGM's *Kind Lady* was cowritten by Edward Chodorov, a member of the Communist Party and veteran of the Hollywood Anti-Nazi League. United Artists continued to employ such Party stalwarts as Hugo Butler, Guy Endore, Morris Carnovsky, and Paul Trivers on works such as *High Noon, He Ran All the Way,* and *The Second Woman.*

WHILE THE HOLLYWOOD TEN and others who defied the Committee opted for the black market, others took the route of Ed Dmytryk and sought out Roy Brewer. The IA man had become a force in the Democratic Party.

Senator Joseph McCarthy's wild accusations led President Truman to dub the Wisconsin senator "the greatest asset that the Kremlin has,"[6] a view with which Brewer, Reagan, Howard Costigan, Sidney Hook, and other anti-Communist liberals readily agreed. The Wisconsin Republican never had anything to do with Hollywood, but the infamous senator did have his imitators around the studios.

By the time of the second batch of hearings, in 1951, Hollywood had come to host a cottage industry of amateur Red-hunters. But when the Party sought to tar Roy Brewer with the Red-baiting brush, Brewer's allies rushed to his defense. In a series of articles on the Hollywood situation, James Bassett wrote that Brewer was "a million miles from being a Red-baiter."[7] The *Omaha World Herald*, familiar with Brewer's past in the labor movement, said he was "not one of those who front for Tories, or find pinkos and Reds behind every bush."[8]

Brewer's tough but careful approach gave him a reputation as someone approachable, and he intervened in the case of Larry Parks. Brewer believed that Parks had taken the rap for his wife, Betty Garrett, who was active in Progressive Citizens of America but was never named as a Party member, and whose career thrived while her husband's foundered. While actors suffered most from the blacklist, their career difficulties could not always be attributed to politics in a town so enslaved to fashion, where the "in" and "out" crowds change almost daily. When Brewer went to Ben Kahane at Columbia, the executive told him that Parks simply wasn't worth the money his agent was demanding.

The Parks case caused a division in the Motion Picture Alliance. John Wayne thought Larry Parks had been given a raw deal and read a statement in support of the actor. On the other hand, gossip columnist Hedda Hopper, an actress who hadn't performed since 1942, remained a "once a Communist always a Communist" type. She opposed support for Parks and continued to attack Edward Dmytryk long after he had broken with the Party. When Brewer prevailed on the Parks issue, Hopper dropped out of the MPA.

According to Martin Gang, Brewer was "the one voice of sanity in that group, and he was also, personally . . . a decent and honest man."[9] But Brewer would cross swords with a powerful group on his own side, the American Legion.

In those tumultuous days of the early 1950s, the Communist Party and its support groups held no monopoly on picketing and protesting. The American Legion, which had chapters coast to coast, had become prime movers. The Legion had begun picketing movies, such as *Monsieur Verdoux* with Charlie Chaplin, that they thought bore excessive involvement by Communists, anti-Americans, or both. The Legion also targeted *Moulin Rouge*, directed by John Huston and starring José Ferrer.

Brewer had previously met with Huston, who, like Humphrey Bogart, had come to feel he had been used by the Communist Party. "It was a long time afterward that I discovered that the real reasons behind the behavior of the 'Ten' in Washington, and when I did I was shocked beyond words," the director wrote to a colleague. "It seems that some of them had already testified in California, and that their testimony had been false. They had said they were not Communists and now, to have admitted it to the press would have been to lay themselves open to charges of perjury. . . . And so, when I believed them to have engaged to defend the freedom of the individual, they were really looking after their own skins. Had I so much as suspected such a thing, you may be sure I would have washed my hands of them instantly. But, as I said before, the revelation was a long time coming."[10]

In José Ferrer's testimony to the Committee in 1951, where he was represented by Abe Fortas, Ferrer had agreed with Brewer's testimony about Party use of front groups. While Ferrer had climbed on the good-cause bandwagon too readily, his name had been used without his knowledge or approval. Convinced of Huston's and Ferrer's sincerity, and in a gesture of support, Brewer crossed an American Legion picket line at the Los Angeles theater that was showing *Moulin Rouge*. The action influenced other former Party members or supporters to approach him.

Irving Pichel, one of the original Nineteen, wrote Brewer to thank him for putting in a good word, as did screenwriter William Kozlenko, a friend of Clifford Odets. After securing a contract with MGM, Kozlenko bought a home in Beverly Hills where he hosted chamber music concerts. The Party tried to use these events to recruit new members, and Kozlenko evicted them en masse.

ROY BREWER MET OR EXCHANGED CORRESPONDENCE with Kirk Douglas, Lloyd Bridges, Vincent Price, Philip Dunne, William Wyler, Kim Hunter, Marsha Hunt, Gene Kelly, Lee J. Cobb, Yip Harburg, and many others. Walter Wanger, the *Blockade* producer and Committee for the First Amendment veteran who had feuded with the Motion Picture Alliance, was ready to bury the hatchet. "Having known so many of the leading figures of your group intimately and for many years, I never questioned their integrity or the honesty of their purpose," he wrote, explaining that his quarrel had been with the MPA statement of purpose. "The Communists made a use of it which I never anticipated," Wanger said. "I was guilty of wishful thinking as was many another who hoped that Russia, our then ally, could be made into a friendly neighbor. If my words hurt your group, or any member of it, I can now only express regret and join with you in shoveling the earth over that dead issue."[11]

Lloyd Bridges (no relation to Harry) explained that Columbia had brought him to California from New York, but that he had been disappointed to find only small parts. At the Actor's Lab he met Roman Bohnen, who told him that if he joined the Communist Party he would be identifying with humanity and become a better actor. In a letter to Brewer, Bridges compared it to joining a church on impulse and then neglecting to officially drop out.

Brewer never knew who would be on the line when the phone rang. One call came from Jules Goldstone, the agent of Lena Horne, who had been named by artist John Vogel as the most beautiful woman in America in 1950. Horne had been denied a spot in a benefit for Adlai Stevenson, the Democrats' hope for the presidency, and wondered if Brewer could do anything about it.

Brewer had been asked to chair the Hollywood committee that backed Stevenson, agreeing to the condition that nobody who had been a regular participant in events staged by Communist front groups could be involved in the Stevenson benefit. Horne had appeared in so many front-group activities that she been dubbed the "female Paul Robeson." In a long letter to Brewer, Horne revealed that her family had known the singer, and that her grandmother, a social worker, had helped him obtain a scholarship.

Horne's own career success had brought certain feelings of obligation toward other blacks. Robeson suggested she become more involved in social causes, such as the Council for African Affairs. Carlton Moss, the *Negro Soldier* producer, took Horne to her first HICCASP meeting and exploited her insecurities to the point that she would appear for any cause she thought might benefit blacks.

Moss secured Horne's permission to write her biography, but Horne rejected the first draft on the grounds that it gave too much attention to the inequalities of her upbringing. But she granted Moss another chance before she left for Europe. When she returned, the book had been finished but she rejected it again and told Moss that she would block publication. Horne told Roy Brewer that Moss introduced her to southern California Communist Party boss Pettis Perry, who suggested she join the Communist Party. Horne explained to Brewer that she felt exploited by this offer.[12]

CURIOUSLY, ROY BREWER'S OWN BACKGROUND and affability led some to believe they could exploit him. Simon Lazarus, a theater manager, aimed to mine the economic potential of the blacklisted writers. If the major studios wouldn't use them, then he would. "They're like gold in the streets," Lazarus said. "We'll make good pictures and we'll make money."[13]

Lazarus had run theaters for thirty years and had been one of the first to negotiate with the IA projectionists, something he thought would give him leverage with IA leader Roy Brewer, now the veteran of an effective anti-poverty documentary, *Poverty in the Land of Plenty*. Lazarus duly appeared in Brewer's office with George Schaeffer, business agent of IA Local 150, explaining that he wanted to set up a company to make labor films and sought the cooperation of union crews. Brewer was interested and asked who would be involved. It would be Michael Wilson, one of the unfriendly witnesses and a Communist Party member, who had compared U.S. movies on the Korean War to Nazi films.[14] Momentarily stunned, Brewer told the pair that only "over my dead body" would anybody connected with the Communist Party make films about American labor with the cooperation of his union. Lazarus and his team decided to do it their way.

The picture they wanted to make was *Salt of the Earth*, written by Michael Wilson, directed by Herb Biberman, produced by Paul Jarrico, and financed by the Mine, Mill, and Smelter Workers of America, one of eleven unions the CIO had expelled in 1949 because of Communist domination. In the film, Will Geer plays a disreputable-looking sheriff, and Irving Hentschel, the evangelical Communist who confronted Brewer in the early days, worked as a technician on the project. Haskell Wexler, a self-described "Old Commie" who had made films for the Electrical Workers Union, helped process the film.[15]

The story was based on a 1950 strike against Empire Zinc in Hanover, New Mexico, in which the workers won substantial wage increases. In *Salt of the Earth*, the noble Mexican-American miners battle the venal, racist Anglo owners, who scorn the miners as "tamale eaters." In the original story, the miners had faults of their own, but Herb Biberman cut those scenes. When the evil mine owners prevail against the courageous pickets, the women take up the cause.

"The women's skirts billow in the wind, like unfurled flags," reads Wilson's screenplay, "like the tattered banners of a guerrilla band that has come to offer its services to the regular army." The women sing "The Union Is Our Leader" and "Solidarity Forever." The narrator, Esperanza Quintero, played by Mexican actress Rosaura Revueltas, says at one point: "He said the bosses would try to split the Anglo and Mexican-American workers and offer rewards to one man if he would sell out his brother. . . . There was only one answer to that, Charley said—Solidarity. The solidarity of working men."

IA projectionists boycotted the movie, which premiered in Toronto and New York, as well as Europe. The French *L'Humanité*, a Party paper, gushed that the film "will convince you that in

America the flame of mankind still burns."[16] In America even favorable critics at the *New York Times*, *Los Angeles Daily News*, and *San Francisco Chronicle* qualified their praise by admitting the picture was politically slanted. Critic Pauline Kael said the film was "as clear a piece of Communist propaganda as we have had in many years . . . a proletarian morality play."[17] Even Stefan Kanfer, a left-wing revisionist, described the dialogue as "clanking agitprop prose."[18] But in his review, John Howard Lawson called it "a signpost on the road to a more living and abundant film culture."[19] When he finally saw it, Roy Brewer actually liked the film, which, despite the projectionists' boycott, received wide distribution in Latin America and duly attained political cult-film status.

ABOUT THIS TIME BREWER GOT A CALL from Zsa Zsa Gabor, who was in France to make a film called *Public Enemy Number One*, which the *Daily Worker* helpfully explained was "not the life story of Roy Brewer."[20] The director was American Jules Dassin, a man Gabor's agent, Paul Kohner, had claimed was a Communist. Brewer told Gabor that she should do whatever she thought was right, but that Dassin had fled from the House Committee, and it was likely that the picture might have a hard time being released in America. Irving Brown, Brewer's union ally, got involved, and there was an approach made to Dassin to see if he would sign some sort of statement. He refused and was subsequently fired. The Communist press in France lugged out its big guns.

The April 20, 1953, edition of *L'Humanité* led with quotes from Charlie Chaplin, who had fled the United States in 1952, claiming that he wouldn't return "even if Jesus Christ was president."[21] Chaplin blasted "a press that is sold out and the lies of the powerful reactionary groups." These had created an atmosphere "in which free minds know only persecution." Brewer was described as "one of the most notorious FBI stool pigeons amongst American movie workers" and Irving Brown as "the Yankee contriver of trade union splits in France." The whole affair showed "the colonialist methods which they have already illustrated in other fields." And, of course, it was all reminiscent of Goebbels and Hitler. The French Communist Party produced pamphlets along the same lines and handed them out at the Cannes Film Festival.

Gabor finished the picture, a spoof of American gangster movies, and Brewer never heard from her again. Jules Dassin married Melina Mercouri, the actress of left-wing inclinations who eventually became minister of culture in her native Greece. Meanwhile, back stateside, Party intrigues were working their way into American culture.

CARL FOREMAN INTENDED *High Noon* to be a parable of someone who had stood up to the Committee. The film, starring Gary Cooper and Lloyd Bridges, was a favorite of President Eisenhower, and Communist publications denounced it as a glorification of individualism. The Party also denounced a series of anti-Communist films such as *I Was a Communist for the FBI, My Son John, Red Snow,* and *Big Jim McClain.* One such anti-Communist film, *Man on a Tightrope,* was based on the actual case of a troop of circus players who escaped from Communist Czechoslovakia. The script was written by Robert Sherwood, who won an Oscar for *The Best Years of Our Lives* in 1946. Elia Kazan disliked the project but directed it anyway, casting Adolphe Menjou as a member of the Soviet secret police.

Kazan's colleague Arthur Miller found in *The Devil in Massachusetts,* by Mario Starkey, the material that would become *The Crucible.* The play showcased the by-now-familiar "witch-hunt" theme, a parallel rejected by, among others, Elia Kazan's wife, Molly. "Those witches did not exist. Communists do," she wrote. "Here, and everywhere in the world. It's a false parallel. Witch hunt! The phrase would indicate that there are no Communists in the government, none in the big trade unions, none in the press, none in the arts, none sending money from Hollywood to Twelfth Street. No one who was in the Party and left uses that phrase. They know better."[22]

While Miller pursued these themes, Elia Kazan teamed with Budd Schulberg, a boxing enthusiast who had been hanging around the waterfront in Hoboken, New Jersey. Schulberg had bought the rights to Malcolm Johnson's Pulitzer Prize–winning series, "Crime on the Waterfront," and had written a screenplay then titled *Bottom of the River*. They shopped it with little success. "I'm not going to make this picture," said Darryl Zanuck. "Who gives a shit about longshoremen?"[23]

After striking out with the studios, Kazan and Schulberg ran into independent producer Sam Spiegel, who was staying at the Beverly Hills Hotel in a room across the hall from theirs. They pitched the project to him and to their delight he went for it. The lead went to Marlon Brando, and the picture that emerged was *On the Waterfront*, shot on location in Hoboken for less than one million dollars, a bargain even by the standards of the time.

Terry Malloy, played by Brando, blows the whistle on the mob that runs his union. Johnny Friendly, played by Lee J. Cobb, is the local crime boss, bumping off those who don't play "D and D"— deaf and dumb. A crime commission is investigating the corruption, and a priest, Father Barry, played by Karl Malden, urges the men to testify.

"Now boys, get smart," says Barry. "Now getting the facts to the public, testifying for what you know is right against what you know is wrong. And what's ratting to them is telling the truth for you. Now can't you see that?" Those who keep silent, Barry says, share the guilt.

After his brother, Charlie the Gent, played by Rod Steiger, falls victim to the mob, Terry decides to talk, leading to the film's showdown scene.

"You ratted on us, Terry," says Johnny Friendly.

"From where you stand, maybe," Terry shoots back. "But I'm standing over here now. I was rattin' on myself all those years and I didn't even know it. . . . You're a cheap, lousy, dirty stinkin' mug. And I'm glad what I done to you. You hear that? I'm glad what I done."

The Communist press understood the symbolism of *On the Waterfront* and erupted in venom that was typified by John Howard Lawson's review in the *Hollywood Review*. "It is not surprising," wrote Lawson, "that the most subtle doses of McCarthyite poison are concocted by men who wear the livery of the informer." In Lawson's opinion, Kazan and Schulberg were "men of talent," but "they have ceased to be men" and their film "points the way to the death of film art."[24]

Lester Cole later wrote that, for Kazan, "informing on his friends was hardly enough. With Budd Schulberg, fellow stoolie, to write it for him, he directed *On the Waterfront,* a film designed to justify stoolpigeons and slander trade unionism."[25]

But Kazan had seen it all coming. "*On the Waterfront* was my own story," Kazan explained many years later. "Every day I worked on that film, I was telling the world where I stood and my critics to go and fuck themselves."[26]

The picture nobody wanted to make proved more than a contender, winning seven Oscars, including Best Picture, and Best Supporting Actor and Actress for Brando and Eva Maria Saint. Kazan and Schulberg took laurels for Best Director and Best Screenplay.

Kazan enjoyed his vengeance, but Marlon Brando had some misgivings. Brando credited Kazan with teaching him to act and considered him the ultimate actor's director. But Brando had been wary of the role. "I was reluctant to take the part because I knew what Gadg [Kazan] had done and knew some of the people who had been deeply hurt." But at the time he did not grasp the film's deeper meaning. "What I didn't realize then was that *On the Waterfront* was really a metaphorical argument by Gadg and Budd Schulberg: they made the film to justify finking on their friends."[27]

The year after *On the Waterfront,* Arthur Miller sent Kazan a copy of his play *A View from the Bridge,* about a waterfront worker who informs out of jealousy. Kazan wrote back that he would be honored to direct it. Miller shot back that he didn't want Kazan to direct—he had only sent it "because I wanted you to know what I think of stool pigeons."[28]

STALIN, MEANWHILE, provided an international backdrop for the continued hearings on Communism. In Czechoslovakia, high-level Communists, eleven of them Jews, were put on trial as Zionists, Trotskyites, and enemies of the people. Josef Frank, assistant secretary general of the Czech Communist Party, was accused of being a Gestapo agent while still an inmate at Buchenwald. The eleven hanged included Otto Katz, editor of a Czech Communist daily. In America, some people were deeply affected by these events, while others clung to the Party line.

In her testimony during the hearings, which continued into 1953, Dorothy Comingore, Richard Collins's first wife, said she was proud of her role in *Citizen Kane,* claimed her forefathers had fled the Inquisition in Spain, and said that "another world war would be organized insanity."

> "Were you ever a member of the Communist Party?" asked Committee counsel Frank Tavenner.
> "Don't you get bored asking the same question?"
> "I get bored with the replies," Tavenner said. When the counsel asked Comingore if she was now a Party member, the actress replied, "You are cute."[29]

There were no further questions. Later that year Comingore was arrested on a prostitution charge.[30]

Party member and screenwriter Silvia Richards had been disturbed by Trofim Lysenko, the quack geneticist who opposed Mendel's Law and who under Stalin became president of the Lenin All-Union Academy of Agricultural Sciences and the director of the USSR's Institute of Genetics. Not only had Lysenko's theories been taught, but their implementation played a role in ruining a Soviet agriculture that was already damaged by other political dogmas. "Another thing which has changed the feeling in town a great deal are the recent Prague trials and the use of anti-Semitism which is involved," Richards said.[31]

Several witnesses, including Leopold Atlas, mentioned the Albert Maltz incident when the hearings shifted to New York in May 1953.

Bandleader Artie Shaw told the Committee, "I hate to admit I was a dupe—I don't like the word—but I think that just about accurately states my position in these matters."[32]

Television director Mortimer Offner was asked if he knew Leo Townsend, who had cooperated with the Committee. "You are referring, I take it, to the stool-pigeon screenwriter that testified before this committee in Hollywood?" Offner said.[33]

An intriguing but seldom mentioned witness testified in New York. Journalist Cedric Belfrage, a British citizen, had written for *Picture Goer* in England, where he also served as film critic for the *London Daily* and *Sunday Express*. While working as stringer for the *New York Sun* and British movie fan magazines, Belfrage met Lester Cole. "He and I hit it off instantly," Cole wrote.[34]

Belfrage also knew Elizabeth Bentley. Bentley's controller and lover, Soviet agent Jacob Golos, or "Yasha," wanted to turn Belfrage, who was then working for the British intelligence service, over to Bentley's control. In her book, Bentley said that Belfrage had been turning over valuable British intelligence data, most of which Bentley saw and reviewed before relaying it to the Soviets. Belfrage refused to answer Committee questions about Bentley.

Lionel Stander, appearing with attorney Leonard Boudin, asked that the television cameras and lights be turned off. "I am a professional performer," the Party's model actor explained, "and I only appear on TV for entertainment or for philanthropic organizations, and I consider this a very serious matter that doesn't fit into either category."

Stander began his career in silent movies but had arrived at the hearings bursting with dialogue, claiming to have exposed racketeers George Browne and Willie Bioff a week before right-wing columnist Westbrook Pegler. "I am not a dupe, or a dope, or a moe, or a schmoe," Stander said. "I am not ashamed of everything I said in public or private." He called John Leech, an early defector from the Party, a "psychopathic liar" and then turned on Marc Lawrence, who had testified that Stander told him he would score with the ladies if he joined the Party.

"Because by using psychopaths—and I have the letter here giving the mental history of Marc Lawrence, who came from a mental sanitarium, he suffered a mental breakdown." Stander charged that the Committee had relied on "a whole stable of informers, stool pigeons, and psychopaths and ex-political heretics who come in here beating their breast and saying 'I am awfully sorry; get me back into pictures.'"[35]

Other entertaining testimony came from songwriter Jay Gorney, who was represented by future left-wing congresswoman Bella Abzug. Gorney started to sing the First Amendment and when interrupted said, "Well, Mr. Tavenner, you have allowed other singers. . . . They have sung long songs—trained pigeons, I call them."[36]

Robert Gladnick, organizer for the Ladies Garment Union, had been in the Young Communist League and identified Joe Springer, also known as Joe Saul, who had organized a Communist school at Crestline to teach sabotage methods.[37] The Nazi-Soviet Pact had pushed Gladnick away from the Party. "In 1939 Molotov went to Berlin and said Nazism was a question of taste, and any man who could swallow that statement that Nazism or fascism was a question of taste, I think he'll do anything Moscow wants him to do," Gladnick said, adding, "the Communist is not an independent thinker. He is not a radical. He will be a monarchist if the Communist line is monarchism. He will be a fascist when the line is fascism."[38]

In executive session testimony, William Alland, Orson Welles's former partner, explained how Virginia Mullen, who had led him into the Party, suggested that he color his show with propaganda. "Nothing that could be considered anti-Russian would be tolerated. To glorify, or not even to glorify, to attempt to show in a good light an American tycoon, for instance—by 'tycoon' I mean a big businessman, big corporation—to show him as being a gentleman or a kind man, a liberal man, would have been considered taboo."[39]

Alland told the Committee that, in the Party, "you begin to feel it, to misrepresent, under circumstances, is a virtue rather than an evil."[40] Another expression of that mind-set came from Dalton Trumbo, who wrote in 1956 that "the important thing about a lie is not that it be interesting, fanciful, graceful, or even pleasant, but that it be believed."[41]

When asked by the Committee about the Communist Party, writer Arnaud D'Usseau responded, "Mr. Tavenner, did you ever seen a film called The Informer—a very fine film made by John Ford?" A question came up about anti-Semitism in the USSR. "There was a director named Eisenstein," D'Usseau said. "I believe he is a Jew. This man was given millions upon millions of rubles, or dollars, to make any number of pictures. I don't think this suggests that there is anti-Semitism in the Soviet Union."[42] For D'Usseau, the presence of one Jewish director settled the issue.

Zachary Schwartz, who worked as an artist for Warner Brothers, Disney, and Columbia, recalled the anti-Semitism he had faced growing up in Los Angeles. "It is a terribly destructive thing for a child to have thrown in his face, day after day, that he is a 'kike' and a 'sheenie.'" Schwartz had been attracted to the Party because it seemed to be the only organization around that opposed anti-Semitism. But by 1948 and the founding of Israel, Schwartz noted an anti-Semitic drift among Communists. He charged that the current Communist Party was as anti-Semitic as Hitler,[43] a theme that also appeared in the testimony of Robert Rossen, one of the original Nineteen, who had had second thoughts since taking the Fifth in his 1951 testimony.

"I don't think, after two years of thinking, that any one individual can even indulge himself in the luxury of individual morality or pit it against what I feel today very strongly is the security and safety of this nation," Rossen said. Rossen recalled the lurches of the Nazi-Soviet Pact, and the visits of Solomon Mikoels and Itzak Feffer, and how they had fallen out of favor.

The victims of the recent Czechoslovakian show trials were "all hung, in my opinion, for being Jews, and nothing else—I don't think they were traitors to the Soviet Union," Rossen said. "The Soviet Union knew that by raising the word 'Jew' and raising the word 'traitor' it was specifically inciting the people of these various countries, which had been hotbeds of anti-Semitism for hundreds of years. . . . I think the act was done deliberately."[44]

Judy Holliday, though not a Party member, had taken a high-profile role in support of the Ten and had appeared at a number of events sponsored by front groups. When asked why she had changed her mind, she explained: "I read about spies and people really working against the government and then I began to realize the seriousness of the accusations which I once thought were directed at me. . . . We are in a state of extreme tension now, things aren't the same as they once were. I mean, Douglas MacArthur signed a big ad in the *New York Times* congratulating the Red Army. That was then, see?"

Holliday had contributed to People's Songs, a Party-backed group, but only to get them off her back. "I gave them a dollar after much nagging and pestering. I dislike folk songs intensely. I think the People's Songs are terrible. I have no interest in it at all. . . . I just hated their stuff."[45]

Burl Ives, a self-described "missionary" for American folk music, had been on the board of People's Songs and, in a voluntary appearance before a Senate committee, sang the only one he said he knew.

> *I'm a-gonna cross the ocean wide,*
> *With a Springfield rifle by my side*
> *When Hitler's beat you can be my bride*
> *And I told her not to grieve after me.*

Ives explained his participation in the second Hollywood Fights Back broadcast. "I had heard the first broadcast and there were so many names, a great many names which were obviously very good Americans, and not left wing, that I concluded that it would be a proper thing for me to do," he said. For his part of the broadcast, the singer read a Drew Pearson column. Later, on a European tour, he found himself in Rome on May Day, and the experience changed his thinking.

In Rome, "there was a great deal of resentment of the United States, that you could feel as well as see, and this annoyed me very much. And it was through my experience there with this feeling against my country that I began to realize that there is not this space where anybody who has been a liberal can escape to and say 'I will have no part of this thing.'"[46]

At the end of the testimony, it appeared that more than three hundred Communists had been active in the Hollywood talent guilds, a number far greater than what the most zealous Red-hunters had thought possible. This did not count key figures in the state and Los Angeles branches of the Party, nor the hundreds of others on the back lots. Not a single witness had openly defended Communism, the USSR, or Josef Stalin.

IN JOSEF STALIN'S FINAL DAYS, he accused Jewish doctors of plotting a medical assassination against him. The KGB deployed for mass action against Soviet Jews, and only Stalin's death in March 1953 prevented a new wave of purges and executions. The Party faithful paid tribute to the man who had guided the first land of socialism for more than thirty years.

"Oceans of tears have been shed by people all over the world," said California Communist Party boss William Schniederman.[47] "The oppressed of all five continents must have felt their heart-beats stop when they heard that Stalin was dead. He was the embodiment of their hopes," gushed Bertolt Brecht, Stalin

Prize–winner and court playwright of East Germany's Communist regime.[48] Brecht had it exactly backward.

The death of Stalin inspired East German workers to revolt, in the first of the postwar anti-Stalinist uprisings. True to form, Brecht backed the Soviets as their tanks and machine guns crushed the revolt of his own countrymen. The German workers received no support from the American Communist Party, which was at the time taken up with the defense of Communist spies Julius and Ethel Rosenberg, who were executed on June 19, 1953.

"While the whole world and I were fighting for the Rosenbergs," said Simone Signoret years later, "there were heaps and heaps of Rosenbergs in the USSR. And those who orchestrated the anti-American witch hunt here knew perfectly well what was going on in Soviet Russia."[49]

The Party's Over

PICKETS FROM THE CONFERENCE OF STUDIO UNIONS continued until 1952, but by then Hollywood's labor wars were long over. During the 1930s, under Jeff Kibre, the Party had failed to take over the IA, and during the following decade, under Herb Sorrell, again it failed to displace the major film industry union. The union conflict left the studios strewn with casualties. A jurisdictional dispute that had originally involved fewer than one hundred workers had cost some 9 million man-hours and at least $20 million in lost wages. There had also been at least $110,500,000 in lawsuits.[1]

Jeff Kibre, who had first revealed that Hollywood cartoonists had been organized by the Communist Party, became an officer in the CIO's Fishermen and Allied Workers, where he got involved in a price-fixing scandal. He was listed as a delegate to four CIO conventions and eventually appeared in Washington, D.C., working as a lobbyist for Harry Bridges. Kibre also showed up in Alaska at the time when the District Early Warning (DEW) line was being constructed. Kibre took the Fifth Amendment before a government committee in 1956[2] and was little heard from after that. By that time the AFL and CIO had rejoined, further isolating the Communist Party. The Mine, Mill, and Smelters Union that had backed *Salt of the Earth* merged into the AFL-CIO-affiliated Steelworkers Union in the late 1960s.

On January 21, 1952, the Painters' International Union lifted the charter of Local 644, a move that left Herb Sorrell without his business agent's job. He sued for breach of contract, lost, and ended up where he started, painting houses in Los Angeles as a private contractor. It is not known whether he hired exclusively union painters. Sorrell's wife was a churchgoing woman, and during the 1960s, Sorrell himself turned to religion. But the CSU boss who had flown over the battle scenes in his airplane never told what he knew about the studio wars. Roy Brewer believed that, if Sorrell had gone public, he would have placed himself in danger. Sorrell died in 1971 in Burbank, where his troops had fought their biggest battle. Harry Bridges, Sorrell's ally, had even more to reveal, but he died in 1990 at the age of 89 without ever having told his story.

Willie Bioff, the corrupt union man who shook down the moguls and discredited anti-Communists, turned evidence in a case against Frank Nitti, a lieutenant of Al Capone. When paroled, Bioff changed his name to Bill Nelson and moved to Phoenix. One day in November 1955, he started his truck and it blew up, throwing his dead body twenty-five feet from the wreckage. Though unsolved, the press and police considered the murder a mob hit.

Albert Dekker, the actor–politician who first attacked Roy Brewer, later turned to him for help in finding work. But Frances Farmer's former costar had some problems that proved beyond assistance. On May 5, 1968, at age sixty-two, Dekker locked himself in the bathroom, dressed in women's underwear, wrote obscenities on his body in red lipstick, manacled his wrists, and hanged himself from the shower curtain.[3]

Hugh DeLacy, another CSU booster, became the only member of Congress to ever take the Fifth Amendment before the House Committee. After one term in Congress, DeLacy moved to Ohio and worked for Henry Wallace. He later wound up in southern California, building houses.

While actors, directors, and writers continued to approach Brewer, the union man found his policies challenged by IA boss Richard Walsh. Turned down for an AFL position in 1953, Brewer resigned his union post and took a job with Allied Artists, a small independent studio. At Allied, Brewer worked as a branch manager for $350 a week, good money for the day but a fraction of what any of the Hollywood Ten had made in their prime. While many of humbler origins had risen to greater heights, the Left seized on the move as a payoff. "This sterling trade-union leader," wrote Alvah Bessie, "went on to his reward and became a studio executive himself."[4]

It had not been Brewer's decision to come to Hollywood, and it wasn't his decision to leave. In 1955, ten years after he first arrived in Hollywood, Brewer's new boss at Allied, Steve Broidy, transferred him to New York City.

The following year, in a study on blacklisting written with the socialist Michael Harrington, and which itself became the subject of Committee hearings, John Cogley wrote that Roy Brewer had dominated the motion picture industry more than any individual had ever succeeded in doing. After Brewer moved to New York in the early months of 1955, no one in Hollywood really took his place.[5] During his stay in New York, he helped produce *The Fearmakers*, with Dana Andrews, about a man who returns from Korea to find his company infiltrated by Communists.

Actor Ward Bond, who often played heavies, became head of the Motion Picture Alliance (MPA), which attempted to have witnesses who took the Fifth Amendment expelled from the Screen Writers Guild. The Motion Picture Industry Council, which Brewer had founded, sided with the screenwriters against the move, leaving the MPA without much clout. That proved small compensation for the Hollywood Party, which was still predicting the dawn of American concentration camps and a reign of terror, while simultaneously pursuing their case in American courts.

After the 1947 hearings, the Hollywood Ten initiated two lawsuits challenging the industry's policy of not hiring Communists.

Neither came to trial. In 1949, the Screen Writers Guild brought a similar suit against the producers, which was eventually dismissed in 1953. In cases involving Lester Cole and Paul Jarrico, the employers successfully claimed that the plaintiffs had breached the morals clause of their contract and had become objects of public disapproval.

In *Wilson v. Loew's Inc.*, filed by Michael Wilson, Anne Revere, Gale Sondergaard, Guy Endore, and nineteen others in March 1953, the plaintiffs claimed they had been blacklisted and sought $52 million in damages. They lost in the district court, the court of appeals, and the Supreme Court, which still bore a solid core of New Deal liberals.[6]

Other projects provided lessons in show-business economics. To slip in the odd line of propaganda or block anti-Communist films was one thing. For the Party to make and market movies from scratch, movies that the American public would want to see in a competitive marketplace, was another matter altogether. According to Paul Jarrico, the Party was looking for a film to showcase Paul Robeson. But the projectionists' boycott had made *Salt of the Earth* a money-loser, killing off other ambitious projects. As Jarrico put it, "we lost our shirts" on the film.[7]

The defections of key members and the scattering of the faithful left the Party ill prepared to accept the new blows that were soon to arrive. Revelations of Stalin's bloody reign were nothing new, but they proved harder to ignore when they came from new Soviet Communist leader Nikita Khrushchev, in a 1956 report to the twentieth Communist Party Congress.

"It was not all capitalist and Trotskyite propaganda after all," said Los Angeles Party official Dorothy Healey. "Wretched, bloody crimes had been committed."[8] When Peggy Dennis, wife of Party leader Eugene Dennis, read the Khrushchev speech, she wrote, "The last page crumpled in my fist, I lay in the half darkness and I wept . . . for a thirty-year life's commitment that lay shattered. I lay sobbing low, hiccoughing whimpers."[9]

Even after the speech was printed in both *Time* and the *Daily Worker,* some Party members rejected it as capitalist propaganda. But Khrushchev's denunciation of Stalin's crimes pushed still others out of the Party.

Howard Fast, dubbed "Big Brother's U.S. Pen Pal," by *Time,* had won the Stalin Peace Prize in 1953, the only American winner other than Paul Robeson.[10] In 1954, Fast became a staff writer for the *Daily Worker,* but his true crisis came two years later. Khrushchev's revelations of Stalinist terror so wracked Fast that he wrote *The Naked God,* a soul-wrenching work as powerful in places as such anti-Stalinist classics as *The New Class,* by Milovan Djilas, and *The God That Failed.*

No Communist, Fast wrote, doubted the validity of Khrushchev's report, which "itemizes a record of barbarism and paranoiac bloodlust that will be a lasting and shameful memory to civilized man." If one were to understand Communism, Fast said, one must begin not with social science but "naked terror, awful brutality, and frightening ignorance."[11]

The author and screenwriter blasted "Stalin and the collection of hangmen and murderers around him." The Communist Party, "based on pseudo-religious cant, cemented with neurotic fear and parading ritualistic magic as a substitute for reason," had become "a prison for man's best and boldest dreams."[12]

After Fast had renounced the Party, a number of Eastern Bloc refugees sought the author out. "They spread before my already tortured eyes such a picture of terror, injustice, and sheer nightmare as to make the Khrushchev speech appear to be only a moderate outline of the never-to-be-itemized whole." The only people who resisted the revelation of Stalin's crimes, wrote Fast, were wealthy Communist sympathizers, "the mental revolutionaries, the parlor pinks, the living-room warriors, the mink coated allies of the working class." These he called "sick people, who had seen no other death than a painted corpse in a funeral parlor, no other violence than an auto crash—these people lusted for an Armageddon their mad dreams had promised them."[13]

But the writer found room for personal repentance. In *The Naked God* he recalled his participation in the inquisition of Albert Maltz, who was "treated as if he had committed a crime." While Fast said that the Communist Party should cease to exist, he praised America as "a land where the individual, in his work and in his rights, is recognized and defended."[14]

The Naked God proved to contain more verisimilitude than Fast's novels. The wealthy Lillian Hellman, like Bertolt Brecht and Paul Robeson, shrugged off Khrushchev's revelations, and Fast's departure from the Party left Dalton Trumbo "deeply annoyed."[15] Both Ella Winter and Anna Louise Strong, disillusioned with the Soviet Union, transferred their loyalty to Mao Tse-Tung and his Communist regime as the new keeper of the flame.

Khrushchev, meanwhile, was no reformer. He himself had taken part in the purge and terror campaigns and, once in power himself, maintained the internal repressions and the former dictator's colonial policies and, in a new spirit of militancy, threatened to bury the West. When Hungarians took to the streets against Soviet rule in 1956, Khrushchev sent troops and tanks to crush their revolt as the West stood by and watched.

The Soviet invasion of Hungary and the execution of Imre Nagy and other leaders greatly disturbed Yves Montand, who had toured the USSR at the time of the Hungarian revolt. The singer and actor started speaking out against the USSR and the French Communist Party, which backed Khrushchev's action. Montand confided his doubts to Ben and Norma Barzman, the American Communist screenwriters who were still in France. The pair said they didn't listen. "We had a hard time dealing with it," said Norma Barzman. "I don't remember why we remained so blind."[16]

Khrushchev's revelations likewise failed to affect Charlie Chaplin, who was living on royalties in Switzerland and remaining pro-Soviet to a fault. The USSR showed its gratitude by opening a Chaplin museum in Moscow,[17] and during Chaplin's paternity suit with Joan Berry, the Soviets launched a Chaplin festival and blamed his troubles on the Trotskyites and the Hearst press.[18]

By 1956, as Paul Jarrico explained, "there were not even enough people left to sit down as a group and figure out what we had done wrong."[19] That he had to ask what they had done wrong reveals something about the mind-set of the Hollywood Party. Jarrico said, "I was the head of the Party in the sense that I presided over its liquidation. . . . Even the slowest of us realized that the accusations against Stalin and Stalinism had been true—though we denied they were true—and that we had been defending indefensible things. That, I would say, was the end of the Party."[20]

Jarrico spoke the truth. The Hollywood Party had denied or defended all: the Moscow trials, the Ukraine famine, the Nazi-Soviet Pact, the invasion of Poland, the invasion of Finland, the surrender of German Jewish Communists to the Gestapo in 1940, the execution of Jewish antifascists as "spies for Hitler," the Katyn massacre of Polish officers, the mass execution of Russian prisoners of war, the Czech coup, Zhdanov purges and the Berlin blockade, the crushing of the Hungarian revolution. They did all this while earning a good living, substantial fortunes in some cases, in the very country they attacked as repressive and fascist. As Richard Grenier put it, in the dialectic of the Hollywood Left capitalism is evil—except for the three-picture deal with Paramount, the Malibu mansion, the swimming pool and tennis court, the Mercedes Benz. Or, as Marx himself might have framed it: From each according to his credulity, to each according to his greed.

Those whose creed had been *Stalin mit uns* could not, like other parties, openly announce their agenda. They had enjoyed spectacular success using liberals to serve their causes, but no longer could the industrious Communist tail wag the lazy liberal dog. By 1958, Paul Jarrico gave up and quit. Surveying the wreckage, Dalton Trumbo said, "I doubt that there are five members of the Communist Party left in all of Hollywood."[21] It had been a war, and they had lost. Howard Fast wrote that by the end of 1957 the Communist Party of the United States had for all practical purposes ceased to exist.

"The right wing rolled over us like a tank over wildflowers," said Karen Morley, who in 1954 ran for lieutenant governor of New York with the American Labor Party, a Party front that opposed the Marshall Plan and NATO and backed the North in the Korean War.[22] Morley failed to win the post, and her theory about the victory of the Right was not quite true.

The right-wingers had played a role but had committed blunders that played straight into the hands of the Party. Rather, it was the ex-Communists and anti-Communist liberals who shouldered the heavy ideological fighting, the polemical commando raids, the union sectarianism, battling the Party's smear campaigns all the way. And it was ordinary rank-and-file union men who actually fought it out in bloody battles in the streets outside Warner Brothers, Paramount, Columbia, and MGM.

Party organizer and agent John Weber credited Roy Brewer as the one who had "smashed" the Hollywood Party.[23] A man described as a "hayseed movie house projectionist"[24] and "lunch-bucket Democrat"[25] had prevailed over a thirty-year cultural and labor initiative, backed by the Soviet Union through a vast and powerful organization, glittering with star power, whose leaders not only thought themselves possessed of matchless intelligence and superior sophistication, but believed their infallible Marxist doctrine assured them of victory.

Nothing like it had ever occurred in American labor, culture, or politics, but in accounts of the time it would wind up, as they say, on the cutting-room floor. And though the Party's Hollywood apparatus lay in ruins, it would still win some victories in the long run, aided by the zeitgeist of the following decade.

Part 4

The Sequel

He who controls the present controls the past.
He who controls the past controls the future.
—George Orwell, *1984*

"The Chronicle of Some Mythical Kingdom"

KIRK DOUGLAS OPTIONED, with his own money, Howard Fast's novel *Spartacus*. The eager Fast cut a deal to write the screenplay, which Douglas found "a disaster, unusable. . . . It was just characters spouting ideas."[1] Douglas turned to Dalton Trumbo, a writer of legendary speed, capable even in the pre-computer age of cranking out forty pages a day, and asked him to revise the script.

Douglas disguised Trumbo's work under the name of Eddie Lewis, who was one of the actor's own partners. Howard Fast hated the changes to the *Spartacus* script and called a meeting of all the department heads, in which he lectured with chalkboard and pointer, telling set designers and wardrobe people what they had done wrong. Douglas had found Fast hard to work with, but he also later ran into trouble with Trumbo.

After *Spartacus* had been released in 1960, the actor wanted Trumbo to script Edward Abbey's novel *The Brave Cowboy*, but the screenwriter was then working on *Exodus* with Otto Preminger. "Remember when we were working on *Spartacus*, we fucked Preminger?" Trumbo told Douglas. "Well, now it's your turn to get fucked."[2]

Otto Preminger openly announced that he had hired the prolific screenwriter to work on *Exodus,* making Dalton Trumbo the first person to emerge from the shadows of the blacklist, which would not survive the new decade.

The nation was involved in a land war in Asia, "knee deep in the big muddy," as Pete Seeger put it, against Communist forces that were backed by the Soviet Union. Unlike in World War II and Korea, the lines of this conflict did not seem so clearly drawn. Many Americans were not eager to be drafted into this war, in which the United States and its South Vietnamese allies often came across as the bad guys. The war became The Cause for the New Left, which fought it out on the home front of street and campus. The counterculture screamed, "Make love, not war," and many paid heed. "Be the first one in your block to have your boy come home in a box," sang Joe MacDonald of Country Joe and the Fish. Bob Dylan composed "Masters of War" and other mumbled manifestoes that caught the imagination of the Baby Boom generation, whose members were rejecting the materialistic consumer society their Depression-era parents had created.

With the revived peace movement mobilized against U.S. involvement in Vietnam, anti-anti-Communism came into vogue, and the fortunes of those with leftist credentials began to turn around. But in Hollywood, some who had once sided with the Communists seemed to disown them in later years.

Katharine Hepburn had supported Herb Sorrell, Henry Wallace, and the Hollywood Ten, going so far as to write a letter in support of Ring Lardner Jr. when he was in prison. When Lardner next saw Hepburn, in 1964, while trying to talk Spencer Tracy into taking a role in *The Cincinnati Kid,* he thanked her for writing the letter, but Hepburn said she didn't remember it and refused to talk about it.[3] But like others, he no longer needed her support.

Ring Lardner Jr. won an Oscar for *M*A*S*H* in 1970, while Waldo Salt earned Academy Awards for *Midnight Cowboy* and *Coming Home,* in addition to writing the films *Tauras Bulba* and

Wild and Wonderful. Michael Wilson wrote the screenplay for *Bridge on the River Kwai,* which was credited to Pierre Boulle, author of the novel on which the film was based. Wilson launched the *Planet of the Apes* movies and wrote the 1969 *Che!,* about Argentinean Communist Che Guevara. Dalton Trumbo wrote *Papillon,* in which he briefly appears as a prison commandant.

Despite his continued success, Trumbo may have felt what Howard Fast in *The Naked God* called the "degradation of the soul." In 1970, Trumbo won the Screen Writers Guild Laurel Award; he made his new feelings known in his acceptance speech. "The blacklist was a time of evil. . . . No one on either side who survived it came through untouched by evil. . . . There was bad faith and good, honesty and dishonesty, courage and cowardice, selflessness and opportunism, wisdom and stupidity, good and bad on both sides. . . . In the final tally we were all victims because almost without exception each of us felt compelled to say things he did not want to say, do things he did not want to do, to deliver and receive wounds he truly did not want to exchange. That is why none of us—right, left, or center—emerged from that long nightmare without sin." He went on to say that there had been no heroes or villains during the blacklist, "only victims."

The mink-coated, perpetually smoking Lillian Hellman continued to work in films, scripting *The Chase,* which followed what Pauline Kael called a classic America-is-evil scenario. While even her opponents conceded her stage talents, Hellman's screen work failed to ignite either audiences or critics. *The Chase,* said Rex Reed, was "the worst thing to happen to movies since Lassie played a war veteran with amnesia."[4] Hellman's bank account continued to swell, and she kept busy seeing expensive analysts and suing her enemies. Her politics remained aggressively pro-Soviet.

In 1969, the year after Soviet tanks crushed the Prague Spring uprising, Hellman attacked novelist Anatoli Kuznetsov for fleeing the Soviet Union and seeking asylum in England. The astonished Kuznetsov explained to Hellman that "the Soviet Union is a fascist country. What is more, its fascism is much more dangerous than Hitler's . . . tens of millions of bloody victims, a culture destroyed, fascist anti-Semitism, the genocide of small nations, nothing but murder, suicides, persecution trials, lunatic asylums, an unbroken series of tragedies from Gumilev to Solzhenitsyn."[5] There is no record of a reply from Hellman.

After scouring Hellman's political apologia, *Scoundrel Time*, biographer William Wright noted that the "offhand nonchalance with which she dismisses forty years of rigorous Stalinism is so stunning. . . . The deceased and discredited Stalin is all she renounces, not Russia, and not Communism."[6]

Hellman experienced cinematic beatification in the 1977 *Julia*, in which Jane Fonda was cast as the playwright. Hellman learns to write, with the aid and comfort of Dashiell Hammett, played by Jason Robards. She becomes famous, flaunts her wealth, buys mink coats. When her childhood friend Julia falls victim to the Nazis, Lilly bravely risks herself to aid the anti-fascist cause. Aside from two fleeting mentions, viewers could easily conclude that Communism did not exist. Hellman's *crie de coeur* when she learned that the Soviet motherland had been invaded remains cinematically unexplored.

John Howard Lawson taught at Stanford and other universities and authored *Film in the Battle of Ideas*. Interviewed by Victor Navasky in 1974, three years before his death, the Hollywood Party's enforcer said that he still thought Marxism was "the noblest set of ideals ever penned by man" and that he still "considered it to be an honor to be a member of the Party." He criticized the silence on Polish anti-Semitism and claimed he would have spoken out if he had known about the gulag.[7]

In 1965 Lester Cole wrote *Born Free* and found that the project had made him an expert on movies about pets. Ironically, another Party man, Hugo Butler, had written *Lassie Come Home*, which his wife considered an example of socially conscious cinema.[8] Cole went on to write film criticism for Communist Party publications, which he represented at film festivals in Moscow. He spent time in East Germany, which he punctiliously called the German Democratic Republic. In his 1981 memoir, *Hollywood Red,* he praised North Korean cinema and charged that "the reasons the persons give for leaving [the Party] cannot be accepted as genuine." Looking back, he said he took solace from Friedrich Engels's statement: "Until there is world socialism, man remains in a state of his prehistory."[9] Cole, ever "unfriendly," also turned on Trumbo for his "only victims" speech.

"This outrageously lofty, ecclesiastical benediction from 'on high' upon the scum of the industry and the most vicious, Jew-baiting would-be-Negro-lynching Ku Kluxers in Congress starred what was to develop, over the years, into open hostility among members of the ten," snarled Cole, who saw Trumbo as a victim "of his own rhetoric." Cole made that point directly to Trumbo, which prompted Trumbo to respond with a letter saying: "I'd rather you didn't drop around the house any more. . . . I'm not going to have you scaring my kids to death in one of your goddam fits."[10]

Budd Schulberg went into Watts after the riots and joined with local blacks to start a class for young writers. The group produced a book, *From the Ashes: Voices of Watts.* Cole says he heard Schulberg on a radio show and called in as Lester, a man interested in birds.

"Canaries, yes. A bird you really know. . . . You know all about canaries because you are a canary! Aren't you the canary who sang before the Un-American Committee? Aren't you that canary? Or are you another bird, a pigeon—the stool kind?"

In Cole's account, the dumbfounded Schulberg stammers, "L-l-ester? Lester Cole. . . . I've been wanting to see you all these years. I want to explain. . . ."

"Just sing, canary, sing, you bastard."[11]

Whether this actually happened is uncertain, but one can guess.

Alvah Bessie, a sometime film critic for the *People's Daily World*, worked for Harry Bridges, then in a San Francisco nightclub. The "great explainer," Samuel Ornitz, Party point man for denials of Soviet anti-Semitism, wrote novels before he died in 1957.

Albert Maltz became an admirer of East Germany, a country he said was "moving into the sunlight of fraternalism, of peaceful, constructive labor, of independence from imperialism."[12] Maltz wrote *Two Mules for Sister Sarah* and other films but never returned to screenwriting prominence, though he did show a relapse of sorts. During the thaw that enabled Solzhenitsyn to publish, he praised Boris Pasternak's *Doctor Zhivago,* only to later attack it as not worth reading when conditions again froze over. The book was not published in the Soviet Union until 1988. To the end of his days, Maltz disowned his "What Shall We Ask of Writers?" article from *New Masses* and defended his retraction.

Maltz was as enraged by Trumbo's "only victims" line as Mike Gold had been about Maltz's *New Masses* article. "My position was that if it was a question of being a 'hero' or a shit, you can't really say the decision not to be a shit is heroic," said Maltz, who believed himself a hero.[13] He wrote so many hostile letters to Trumbo that Trumbo's wife, Cleo, refused to accept them. Victor Navasky showed the screenwriter some of Maltz's anti-Trumbo material, who looked it over and replied, "Fuck Albert Maltz."[14]

The internecine squabbles of the Hollywood Party paled beside their sulfuric hatred of those who had turned against Communism. These people were shunned, read out of the human race, and ruined wherever possible.

"There was an unwritten code among blacklisted writers prohibiting fraternization with people who had testified as 'friendly witnesses' and 'named names,'" said Julian Zemet, writer of *Sierra Sue* and *Saigon*.[15]

The Party took vengeance on Hollywood therapist Phil Cohen, ruining his business. He eventually moved to Santa Barbara and taught in a community college. Black novelist Chester Himes also felt Party wrath over his novel *Lonely Crusade,* which mocked Communist union organizers. In the best Stalinist style, the abuse was retroactive. "Martin Berkeley I always thought was a pig when he was a Communist and a pig when he stopped being a Communist," writer Isobel Lennart told Victory Navasky.[16]

When Ed Dmytryk appeared at the 1988 Barcelona Film Festival, Jules Dassin, John Berry, and others walked out of a panel on which the director appeared, calling him "scum," and "Judas." Said Walter Bernstein, a former Party member and screenwriter for *The Front,* "I'm proud to say that I called him 'garbage' from the stage."[17]

Dmytryk went on to direct *The Caine Mutiny,* with Humphrey Bogart, *Raintree County, The Young Lions, The Carpetbaggers,* and other films. He also wrote two books stating his case, which never changed. "I deserted my comrades *because* they were 'comrades,'" he said in the 1996 *Odd Man Out: A Memoir of the Hollywood Ten,* "because as [Whittaker] Chambers pointed out, American Communists had to be loyal to the Comintern and the Soviet Union."[18]

As the years wore on, Howard Fast distanced himself from *The Naked God,* which never found as wide a readership as his other books. In his memoir, *Being Red,* he said "a very substantial number of the best minds and talent in these United States were party members. . . . Theodore Dreiser, W. E. B. Du Bois, Albert Maltz and John Howard Lawson and Dalton Trumbo . . . dozens of others. . . . I have no right to name them." Said Fast, "We were romantics; like a priesthood," and he included a curious confession: "Long ago, I lost faith in anyone's objectivity, including my own."[19] His dictum that the Communist Party had ceased to exist in 1957 also proved false.

Though membership numbered in the low thousands, the Communist Party USA remained loyal to the USSR, working through such front groups as the United States Peace Council, National

Alliance Against Racist and Political Repression, and the Labor Research Association. These groups secured the cooperation of some union leaders, city officials, and even members of Congress.

During the 1980s, the USSR continued to subsidize the Communist Party USA to the tune of some $2 million a year. They dropped support only when leader Gus Hall, who once criticized ballet as pornographic, attacked Mikhail Gorbachev's glasnost and perestroika reforms as "old social democratic thinking class collaboration." Under glasnost, said Hall, "the editors have gone wild with untruths, especially about history and capitalism."[20]

In the long run, Charlie Chaplin's lobbying for the USSR did not trump his art, even with anti-Communists. When they wanted to add Chaplin to the Walk of Fame, Adolphe Menjou said that he was "too great to keep his name off, despite the fact that he has a hole in his head politically."[21] The Tramp made a triumphant return to America to pick up an Oscar in 1975. Three years later, he was knighted.

Sterling Hayden, probably the only actor who ever cold-called V. J. Jerome, never landed the roles that suited his talents. He left his most lasting impression as General Ripper in Stanley Kubrick's *Dr. Strangelove*, in which he bemoans fluoridation of water as part of a "postwar Commie conspiracy." Hayden went on to play small parts in films such as *The Godfather*. Karen Morley, his Party comrade, remained mired in the deepest fever swamps of the Left.

"There were strong Fascist elements on the march," she said in 1983. "Six concentration camps were set up; the money was allocated for them and actually spent, about a quarter of a million dollars. And it was quite clear who would have been sent to them. It was in this atmosphere that people informed." The same year John Wexley, original writer of the film *Cornered* and the author of a 1955 book on the Rosenbergs, said, "In Texas they made punishment the death penalty—you can look this up if you like—for members of the Party."[22]

Maurice Rapf, the *Song of the South* writer who met Ring Lardner Jr. on a 1934 tour of the USSR, still blames Trotskyites for wrecking the Party and believes World War II was intended to be an imperialist conflict against the USSR. "As for all the revelations about the atrocities that took place in the Soviet Union—the so-called exposé of Stalin—by the time it began, I was no longer a member of the Party anyway—and I don't believe half of it, either," Rapf said, adding that he didn't like what Yeltsin was doing and still believed in class struggle.[23]

During the blacklist, actor Lionel Stander worked as a broker on Wall Street. He later returned to films, appearing in *They Shoot Horses, Don't They?; New York, New York; The Cassandra Crossing; 1941; Joey Takes a Cab;* and *The Last Good Time.* From 1979 to 1984, he played the chauffeur on television's "Hart to Hart." During that stint, he said, "I'm in a television program that is always among the top twenty, that is shown in sixty-seven countries in the world, helping lobotomize the entire world."[24]

Salt of the Earth veteran Will Geer worked on Broadway during the blacklist and was hired openly by Otto Preminger during the 1960s. He appeared in *Black Like Me* and *Jeremiah Johnson* and enjoyed a long and lucrative run on television's "The Waltons."

Some actors who had been in the Party were astonished to find their former Guild opponents in a forgiving mood. John Wayne threw an arm around Jeff Corey and said, "Jeff, it's been too fucking long."[25] Corey also credits Pat Boone with helping him get work. But the studio-imposed blacklist need not have been the end for anyone. As Budd Schulberg and others pointed out, no blacklist existed in journalism, in publishing, or on Broadway, all fields that were open to veterans of the studio wars. Ironically, some came to see the blacklist as a benefit in their lives. "Maybe the blacklist was a good thing," said Zero Mostel. "If I'd kept on making lousy movies I might be the most hackneyed, tired old actor you ever saw today. This way I returned to painting, and I got a chance to do James Joyce and Sholem Aleichem."[26]

Betsy Blair admitted, "It helped me certainly as a person and therefore probably as an actress. Any growth and development, any hardship or diversity, helps."[27]

Marsha Hunt conceded, "On the other hand, my life has gone into new directions that I have found deeply rewarding. The fact is that the blacklist opened up a lot of time for me in which I was able to make all sorts of marvelous discoveries. I was really closeted on a soundstage until then."[28]

Norma Barzman said, "The truth is, thirty years of exile gave our lives a richness they would never have had. . . . We weathered it all pretty well."[29] The Party members fared even better when the histories of their times were written, ghosted, as it were, by the Hollywood Ten.

In his 1970 acceptance speech for the Screen Writers Guild Laurel Award, Dalton Trumbo had not mentioned the Communist Party or his role in it. In 1976, Michael Wilson joined Trumbo as a recipient of the Screen Writers Guild Laurel Award. In his speech, Wilson likewise avoided mention of the Communist Party, in which both he and Trumbo had been high-profile players, but did remember a "great witch hunt," implying that there had been no Communists.

"I fear that unless you remember this dark epoch and understand it, you may be doomed to replay it," Wilson said. Those themes and omissions would form the dominant story line of Hollywood's political past, a kind of western in stark black and white. For those who had been in the Party, history was not something to be studied, but created.

Like the Soviets, who airbrushed Trotsky and other foes of Stalin out of official photographs, the Hollywood Party replaced fact with legend. The Communist Party and its involvement in Hollywood was simply left out. The story only begins when the Committee, a group of black-hatted inquisitors, rides into town, tarring anything that moves with a red brush, persecuting noble idealists, censoring artists, and launching the "dark epoch" of the blacklist, part of the "McCarthy era." That template, plus the appealing plot of Trumbo, Wilson, and others who duped the studios by working through fronts, simply overrode the long and complicated story of the Communist Party's cultural offensive, the front groups, and the studio labor conflicts.

As for "the industry," it was not up to admitting that it had played the role of what Lenin called "useful idiots," duped and bilked by militant Communists. Though it was the industry, not the government, that blacklisted writers and performers, the blacklist legend allowed the studios to pose as victims themselves, a cover-up too intoxicating to pass up.

The blacklist, in huge Ben Hur letters, came to be *the* story, as reflected in the titles of books on the subject: *Hollywood on Trial,* by Gordon Kahn, one of the Nineteen; Alvah Bessie's *Inquisition in Eden; The American Inquisition 1945–1969* by Cedric Belfrage; Larry Ceplair and Steve Englund's *The Inquisition in Hollywood;* David Caute's *The Great Fear;* Stefan Kanfer's *A Journal of the Plague Years: A Devastating Chronicle of the Era of the Blacklist;* and Griffin Fariello's *Red Scare.* In the blacklist story line, the dialogue bristles with phrases such as "witch hunt," "anti-Communist witch hunt," "McCarthyism," "McCarthyite," "McCarthy era," "anti-Communist hysteria," "Red scare," "virulent anti-Communist," and others. Most dredged up the dreary demonology of the times and even perpetuated their smears. Liberal Democrat and New Dealer Roy Brewer found himself constantly attacked as a McCarthyite, a defender of gangsters, and, in the book *Contract on America,* even linked to a conspiracy to kill President John F. Kennedy.[30]

THOSE WHO CHRONICLED THE TIMES DID NOT, like Mitch with Blanche Dubois in *A Streetcar Named Desire,* drag their subjects into the light by revealing their past liaisons. Rather, they offered the kindness of strangers, letting the Party members tell the story, which also got screen time.

The first cinematic attempt to deal with the subject joins the action in the early 1950s, long after the major events had passed. *The Front* (1976) starring Woody Allen and Zero Mostel, was written by Walter Bernstein, the former Communist Party member who, looking back, slyly comments that Party front groups could make one out of two.

The Front opens with black-and-white footage of a smiling Senator Joe McCarthy, who in fact never had anything to do with Hollywood. As Frank Sinatra sings "Young at Heart," viewers see bombs falling, scenes from the Korean War, and then the smiling faces of Joe DiMaggio, Marilyn Monroe, and Dwight Eisenhower, followed by Julius and Ethel Rosenberg. The selection of images seems to assume that no commentary is necessary.

The action picks up with television writer Alfred Miller telling bookie Howard Prince, played by Woody Allen, that he is being blacklisted because "I'm a Communist sympathizer."

"You've always been one," Prince responds.

"It's not so popular anymore," says Miller, without providing any further background for the viewer.

Prince, the bookie, puts his name on scripts by Miller and two other writers. The material is so good that producers and cast alike gush about how brilliant it is. The writers include Herb Delaney, played by Lloyd Gough.

"I'm a Communist," Delaney tells Prince, but the story provides no information about what being a Communist entailed at any time. *The Front* takes place during the early 1950s, at the height of Stalin's anti-Semitic repressions in Europe, but Prince never raises an uncomfortable subject. Indeed, he seems to know little or nothing about politics.

While blacklisted writers could write under fake names, actors could hardly fake their identities. In *The Front*, actor Hecky Brown, played by Zero Mostel, must be cleared by Francis Hennessey, a rigid, inquisitorial type who runs "Freedom Information," in an office plastered with military memorabilia, including an eagle that bears a resemblance to Nazi imagery. Brown explains that he marched in a May Day parade for the express purpose of meeting "this Communist girl with a big ass." But Brown's apologia is not enough for Hennessey, and the actor loses work because producers are caving in to the minions of the inquisitorial Committee. Where he once worked for $3,000 a night, Brown must now perform for a paltry $250. Hennessey pressures the actor to spy on his friend, the bookie Howard Prince. That, combined with the pressure of having to work for chump change, leads Brown to leap out of a window.[31]

After Brown's demise, Prince himself is subpoenaed to appear before the Committee. A yokelish Committee member announces that the Committee's job is "to keep America as pure as we can make it." Though he had cut a deal to cooperate, Howard Prince changes his mind.

He tells the Committee they have no right to ask him these questions and then delivers the payoff line: "And you can all go fuck yourselves," something not a single witness out of hundreds actually said in reams of testimony. The moral of *The Front* is that the Hollywood Ten did the right thing in defying the Committee. As the credits show, many in the cast were themselves blacklisted, but the film, besides its many evasions, refutes the notion that being blacklisted meant that one was necessarily the best in the business.

GUILTY BY SUSPICION (1991), WAS WRITTEN AND DIRECTED by Irwin Winkler, producer of such films as *They Shoot Horses, Don't They?*, *Raging Bull*, *Rocky II*, *Comes a Horseman*, and *The Right Stuff*. The film opens not with a barrage of images but a crawler about the 1947 hearings in which "ten men"—no names or background provided—were held in contempt and imprisoned. Thereafter, the crawler says, nobody called to testify could work unless they cooperated with the Committee and named names, a statement that is at odds with the record.

In *Guilty by Suspicion*, an executive session of the Committee takes place in a dark, smoky back room, presided over by a fat, sweaty, cigar-smoking chairman who is not named. He is a ranting boor with a southern accent, and he claims that no "real American" could hesitate to cooperate.

"When I joined the Party I thought they were trying to help people," says writer Larry Nolan, whose lines in the film are based on pieces of actor Larry Parks's actual Committee testimony. After testifying, Nolan rushes home and starts burning his books, including *The Catcher in the Rye*. Dorothy, Nolan's actress wife, described by the Committee as a "known drunk," commits suicide. Martin Scorcese plays Joe, a director who says he is now and was then a Communist, but as in *The Front*, there the issue ends. Joe leaves for Europe because "it's not my country any more." Robert De Niro plays David Merrill, a successful film director just back from France, where he was apparently so busy and uninformed he knew absolutely nothing about the Committee or the ten men who were imprisoned. Writer and Party veteran Abe Polonsky reportedly took his name off the film when Winkler changed Merrill from a Communist to a liberal.[32]

Viewers learn through another character that Merrill was a decorated navy officer who fought behind enemy lines, a past of which he provides no evidence. Producer Darryl Zanuck wants Merrill to direct a movie for him but there is a problem. "Some guy running for Congress has a hard-on for Hollywood," says Zanuck. Therefore Merrill must be "straightened out" before he can carry on. He finds it all very puzzling.

In the film, the attorney for the Committee is named Ray Karlin. Indeed, the actor is a dead ringer for Roy Cohn, who was the assistant to the late Joseph McCarthy. Merrill has been named as a Communist sympathizer. The Committee reads him names, and Merrill acknowledges that he knows Sterling Hayden and Lionel Stander, but not Howard Da Silva. Two other names on the list are fictitious. Merrill must be a "team player" and "purge himself." But he's having none of it.

"I won't be a fucking stool pigeon," he says. Then trouble starts.

Merrill tries to meet with Zanuck, but a secretary explains that the producer is busy screening *Viva Zapata* with Elia Kazan. The studio pulls his most recent picture and wants him to return his $50,000 fee. He is barred from the studios and flees to New York, where he is rejected by former friends and kept from working. He finds work in a film equipment supply shop, but even there he is hounded by FBI men decked out like the Capone mob.

Merrill's son watches a television news segment about the Rosenbergs. An announcer says the suffering of their two boys is "a small price to pay for the irreparable damage done by their Communist spy parents." After the segment, Merrill's son asks his father, "Are they going to kill you?" They are not, but Merrill must testify.

Merrill's writer friend Bunny will also appear before the Committee and asks Merrill if he can use his name. "It's not enough to eat shit," Bunny says. "They want you to name names."

Merrill concedes to the Committee that he attended a couple of Communist Party meetings in the fall of 1939 but was thrown out of the meetings because he argued too much. If he was arguing against the Nazi-Soviet Pact, in operation at that time, he does not mention it. Merrill further tells them that in 1946 he and his wife attended a "ban-the-bomb" meeting sponsored by the Hollywood Peace Forum. But he won't talk about other people who might have been involved.

"Fuck 'em," he tells his lawyer. The hearing soon turns into chaos. An unidentified but crazed member of the Committee raves about Larry Nolan. "Maybe those books ought to be burned," he says. "Libraries are full of that Communist filth."

The fat Committee chairman says that Ruth, Merrill's schoolteacher wife, is a dangerous woman who must be barred from influencing young minds. "Don't you have any sense of decency?" says Merrill, echoing attorney Joseph Welch's famous retort to McCarthy.

Merrill is dismissed from the room in the style of the Hollywood Ten and emerges triumphant. The film fades to a crawler, which says that "thousands" of lives were shattered, that people were denied the right to earn a living and were forced to live that way for twenty years.

THE FRONT AND GUILTY BY SUSPICION are the major dramatic efforts to emerge from the studios on the subject of the Committee hearings and the blacklist. Both films echo with the sound of axes being ground and a barrel being scraped. Both are intentionally didactic, but viewers learn nothing about Communism, inside or outside of the studios.

The 1982 *Frances,* with Jessica Lange, claims to be based on the life story of actress Frances Farmer and was written by a trio that included Nicholas Kazan, son of Elia Kazan, who was Farmer's former acting partner and director. Here was a chance to dramatize for the first time the bitter revenge and smear campaigns that entertainment Communists launched against those who failed to follow their agenda. The film does note that Farmer won a trip to the USSR in a contest sponsored by a "Commie newspaper," and her mother warns Farmer that the Reds are using her. But viewers do not see the rebellious, headstrong actress reject the USSR as a land half-dead and crawling. Neither is the ensuing Party campaign against Farmer shown to be a contributing factor in her breakdown. The Communist Party nowhere appears as a force in either the Group Theatre or in Hollywood.

VETERANS OF THE STUDIO WARS WATCHED in amazement as the revisionist myth unfolded. Philip Dunne, the first Hollywood figure to testify before the Dies Committee, had been in town for the duration, during which time he had not only seen it all, but been called everything from a crypto-fascist to a radical Marxist. Dunne had even been misidentified as one of the Hollywood Ten, who by the 1980s had become the Hollywood Ten Thousand.

In 1980 Dunne asked, "Has the whole story been told? I had to admit that in my opinion it had not." In fact, he said, "various revisionists had in their accounts of those times so distorted events in which I had played some part that I could almost believe that I was reading the chronicle of some mythical kingdom."[33]

He cited Ceplair and Englund, authors of *The Inquisition in Hollywood,* who were the only revisionists to approach him, but who, like others, ignored his colleagues John Huston and William Wyler. Huston's and Wyler's stories might have spoiled the simplistic blacklist plot.

"Today the Hollywood Ten have been virtually deified," Dunne wrote. "The infamous hearings are presented in books and documentary films as a heroic battle fought by the 'unfriendly' witnesses, the Ten and their numerous successors, against the forces of evil represented by the House Committee on Un-American Activities. This is as much a historical distortion as the theory then popular that they were de facto traitors."[34]

The hatred for those who cooperated with the Committee infected both Hollywood journalism and those who award prizes. Elia Kazan drew constant harassment, though his achievements could not be denied. Kazan's film *A Face in the Crowd,* written by Budd Schulberg, prompted the *People's Daily World* to say, "When two stool pigeon witnesses before the Un-American activities committee conspire to produce one of the finest progressive films we have seen, something more than oversimplification of motives is needed to explain it."[35]

Kazan's *The Visitors,* about a soldier who brings evidence of rape against former buddies, was the first film to deal with the home-front effects of the war in Vietnam. It was well received at the 1972 Cannes Film Festival, but one of the jurors was Joe Losey, the Communist director Kazan had known in his early radical days. Yves Montand, who knew Losey, said Losey still thought "like a 1950s Stalinist."[36] True to form, Losey campaigned against *The Visitors* behind the scenes, and it lost. Later, he admitted he liked the picture.

By the 1990s it was obvious that there were few, if any, parallels to Kazan's body of work. His achievements, however, had not earned him awards from the American Film Institute or the Los Angeles Film Critics Circle. The latter group's vice president, Joe McBride, had distributed copies of Kazan's Committee testimony at a meeting of the group and claimed that to give Kazan an award would be ignoring the moral issue of his informing. While rejecting the director of *Gentleman's Agreement, On the Waterfront, A Streetcar Named Desire, East of Eden,* and *Splendor in the Grass,* the group did see fit to give its highest award to Roger Corman, whose films included such classics as *Swamp Women, Stripped to Kill, Teenage Caveman,* and *Attack of the Crab Monsters.*

While looking at an increasingly short list of candidates for its lifetime achievement award, the prestigious American Film Institute (AFI) also bypassed Kazan. Charlton Heston recalled a time when several directors, Kazan among them, had made the short list. Producer Gail Ann Hurd, attending her first meeting, said, "I know Kazan's a great director, but we can't give this award to a man who named names!"[37] Heston challenged her, saying the award had nothing to do with politics, but Kazan was not selected, and Heston suspects he never will be. "It was a return to Stalinism," said Heston, "a Stalinism of political correctness."[38]

The rejection did not bother Kazan, who said he has won enough awards, but it did disturb critics such as John McDonough, who was ejected from an AFI meeting after writing an article that pointed out the injustices against Kazan by those McDonough called the "new blacklisters." "They bring [embarrassment] upon themselves by excluding from their honor rolls one of the most influential American directors who ever lived," McDonough said on National Public Radio as the fiftieth anniversary of the 1947 hearings approached. "It's time they marshaled some of the courage they claim to admire so much in those who fought the blacklist fifty years ago and spend a little time fighting the blacklist today. Kazan doesn't need their honor, of course. But they need him."[39]

As these events played out, an old Party gambit was staging a comeback. After the 1947 hearings, Herb Biberman claimed that the movies had suffered from the absence of the Ten, a theme that was endlessly repeated in the Party press. Fifty years later, in the 1997 *Tender Comrades,* a book that was released for the fiftieth anniversary of the hearings, Hollywood biographer Patrick McGilligan decked that argument in garish shades of purple.

"It was a cultural holocaust, a tragedy from which the industry has never fully recovered," he said.[40] Moreover, "the blacklist robbed them and us. America's iron curtain rang down on an era. Hollywood movies took a giant step backward; the humane traditions that the leftists had brought with them to Hollywood were jettisoned. The outrage over prejudice disappeared. Violence, which had always been part of film, would become ritualistic. The simple practice of reconstructing a logical narrative took a blow from which Hollywood is still recovering."[41]

That might come as news to Robert Bolt, David Mamet, Paddy Chayevsky, Horton Foote, William Goldman, and other writers of logical narratives. But McGilligan had added a new twist to Biberman's old thesis. "Even today," McGilligan wrote, "there are still risky political subjects that Hollywood won't take on."[42]

That is true, but not in the way Party hagiographers intend. One of the Party's major goals had been to block anti-Communist content in the movies, and even though their Party organization lay in shambles by the mid-1950s, the myths and legends they spawned remained powerful. The major political movement of this century became taboo, even though story material abounded.

Thousands of Germans had risked their lives to flee East Berlin, but the only film to emerge about it was *Night Crossing,* from Disney Studios. Hollywood has never made a single film about any of the dramatic escapes from the Marxist regime of Fidel Castro, who executed rivals such as popular General Arnaldo Ochoa, imprisoned poets such as Armando Valladares, and persecuted homosexuals. The spy novels of William F. Buckley have never been filmed, nor the science-fiction works of C. S. Lewis. On the other hand, left-wing demonology such as *Daniel, Testament, The House on Carroll Street, Salvador, Walker,* and others emerged regularly from major studios, even though the movies lost money.

While scores of films have dealt with the National Socialist regime in Germany, which passed out of existence in 1945, not a single Hollywood film has ever shown Communists committing atrocities. No Hollywood film has dealt with the Ukraine famine, the Moscow trials, or the Zhdanov purges that claimed Feffer, Mikoels, and thousands of others. No Hollywood film has shown the Hungarians rising up against their Soviet oppressors. Outside of *Eleni,* with John Malkovich, there is nothing about Communism in Europe. The only Hollywood film evidence of the Czechs rising in revolt against the Soviets is a short sequence in *The Unbearable Lightness of Being.* The crackdown of a Soviet-backed military junta in Poland on the Solidarity movement yielded one film, *To Kill a Priest,* starring Ed Harris, which failed to detail the politics involved. The legacy of Hollywood Stalinism explains the dearth of movies about Communism.

A movie that showed the atrocities of Communism, in which anti-Communists are heroes, might lead some to conclude post facto that the Committee had been right. It would violate the legend of the blacklist. Clearly, in the area of film content, the Party won, but there was more.

Jane Fonda championed the North Vietnamese regime, Hollywood luminaries feted Nicaraguan Marxist Daniel Ortega, and actor Ed Asner openly raised money for Salvadoran Communist guerrillas, all without the slightest peril to their careers. But during the entire Cold War—through the Soviet invasion of Czechoslovakia in 1968, the persecution of Solzhenitsyn and other writers, and the martial-law crackdown in Poland—not a single Soviet or East European dissident became the object of high-profile celebrity activism in Hollywood. And long after the Cold War had ended, some things remained the same.

The Missing Cast

ON OCTOBER 27, 1997, fifty years to the day since the Hollywood Ten had opened their testimony, the crowd from the posh precincts of Beverly Hills, Westwood, Bel Air, Pacific Palisades, and Santa Monica began streaming into the Motion Picture Academy theater to remember the Hollywood blacklist and pay homage to its victims. They saw footage of the hearings and witnessed Ring Lardner Jr. and Marsha Hunt step out of the past to tell them about the virus that had swept across the nation, which at the time, they said, no longer seemed to be the land of the free and home of the brave.

In *Hollywood Remembers the Blacklist*, the audience saw Oscar master of ceremonies Billy Crystal play actor Larry Parks, John Lithgow play actor Sterling Hayden, and Academy Award–winner Kevin Spacey play writer Paul Jarrico. Then, in a casting *tour de force*, at the end of the evening Paul Jarrico himself took center stage. Jarrico delivered the curtain lines about the good guys and bad guys, with the good guys coming out on top, as the credits started to run on the screen. All told, it was an impressive performance but in the end a cover-up, fueled by a long-standing false-memory syndrome. The veterans who took part in the extravaganza knew that key cast members were missing.

Elia Kazan was still on the scene, living in New York, and not at all resentful about lifetime achievement awards going to Roger Corman instead of himself. The director of *Gentleman's Agreement* and *A Streetcar Named Desire*, who had added novels such as *The Arrangement* to his credits, had won more than enough awards for one lifetime. A decade earlier he had published a massive biography that included many of the details, and he could have related many of its tales that night, with the same ease and wit as Paul Jarrico. Kazan's commentary could have been backed up with clips from *On the Waterfront*, accounts of how it had been his story all along, and recollections of how he had felt the night the film carried the Oscars. But those staging the show had not seen fit to invite him. Nor did they invite Richard Collins, still active and still in the Screen Writers Guild. Collins knew the back story as well as anyone.

Closer at hand was Edward Dmytryk, who was still living in Los Angeles. The director of *The Caine Mutiny* remained lucid enough to write *Odd Man Out: A Memoir of the Hollywood Ten* in 1996. He could have told about joining the Party in the fervent days of World War II, when Americans made common cause with our gallant Soviet allies against Hitler and emerged triumphant. Dmytryk could have told the story of being warned about reading *Darkness at Noon*, lest he violate the Communist *fatwa* against Arthur Koestler. The audience could have heard the story of *Crossfire* and his sessions at the Gotham Cafe with John Howard Lawson. He could have told backstage stories from the days of the Committee, his exile in England, and why he chose to testify. He could have told how he and his children had been shunned by Party members, and how he had been attacked by *The Front* screenwriter Walter Bernstein and others in Barcelona a decade earlier. But Edward Dmytryk did not receive an invitation. Neither did the man who had befriended Dmytryk in his darkest hours.

Kirk Douglas, the ragman's son who became one of Hollywood's enduring symbols, could have recalled how he stuck up for

Dmytryk against the advice of friends. Douglas could have told a few stories because he knew the inner workings of the support groups. So did another star who had been part of the events and had been mentioned in *Hollywood Remembers*.

Lauren Bacall, still elegant and active at seventy-three, had cared for husband Humphrey Bogart until his death from cancer in 1957. Better than anyone, certainly better than Marsha Hunt, Bacall could have explained why Bogie took the position he did and what had gone on backstage more than fifty years ago. Though her presence in the *Hollywood Remembers* program would have been a huge drawing card, the industry producers had not been willing to let her speak.

Frank Sinatra also knew a thing or two about what had happened. The Voice could have recalled his friendship with Albert Maltz and their experience filming *The House I Live In*, the Academy Award–winning film they made together. He could also have described how he had tried to openly hire Maltz in 1960 to write a script for *The Execution of Private Slovik* and how the American Legion had protested. Sinatra had made radio broadcasts for the Committee for the First Amendment and could have told the audience how he saw the campaign unfold.

Bartley Crum, attorney for the Ten, had died in 1959, but his daughter, actress and journalist Patricia Bosworth, had just completed *Anything Your Little Heart Desires*, a revealing memoir about the Committee days. She could have told the audience, as she did in her book, how the Communist Party lawyers had manipulated the publicity campaign around the witnesses and dictated the strategy of defying the Committee. She could have explained how the Party turned against her father, as it had against many others. Bosworth was not extended a casting call.

Actor Robert Vaughn had written a thoughtful book called *Only Victims*—the title taken from Dalton Trumbo's famous speech—and could have supplied a perspective on the subject. He was not invited, and neither was the man who knew the story from above and from below the line, who had for a decade dominated Hollywood, and whose union's logo is on every film that leaves the studios.

Roy Brewer, the hick projectionist and lunch-bucket Democrat from Hall County, Nebraska, had returned to Los Angeles in the mid-1960s and gone back to work for the IA, still carrying his union card after seventy years. At the time of the memorial, Brewer was living in North Hollywood and was the last survivor of the Motion Picture Alliance for the Preservation of American Ideals, outliving Ayn Rand, John Wayne, Ward Bond, John Ford, Clark Gable, and Gary Cooper. Though well into his emeritus years at eighty-eight, Brewer remained lively, with excellent recall. Brewer could have explained about Herb Sorrell, the Conference of Studio Unions, and his meetings with the moguls and told stories about virtually all the hearings and scores of actors and actresses. He could have told how John Wayne stuck up for actor Larry Parks when Hedda Hopper and others wanted to condemn him. But nobody who knew the back story expected Brewer to be invited.

The exclusion of Dmytryk, Bacall, Brewer, and other industry players was not a matter of availability but a question of will and politics. The back story of the Communist Party, how it duped stars and moguls alike and bilked the industry for millions of dollars, could not be allowed to disturb the simple, feel-good tale of the evil Committee and its victims. That refusal left the audience shortchanged, intellectually and emotionally.

The Cold War was over, the Berlin Wall was smashed to pieces and sold as souvenirs, and the USSR was defunct. The wreckage could now be appraised in the light of history. According to Stephane Courtois's *Black Book of Communism,* between 85 and 100 million deaths worldwide during this century could be directly attributed to the ideas launched by Marx and Lenin. Since he did not distinguish between friends and enemies, and had a longer time to operate than his one-time ally Adolf Hitler, Josef Stalin was directly responsible for a large portion of the deathlist. Though for more than half a century the blood of workers, peasants, actors, writers, and directors alike had cried out from the ground unheeded, the story of the millions who had perished in the gulag network of camps was now emerging, sometimes aided by cooperation from the Soviets themselves. Soviet intelligence traffic and the records of the Comintern had become public knowledge.

As those who revealed the records concluded, the essence of American Communism was loyalty to Stalin.[1] The American Party knew what he had done, and they not only played deaf and dumb; they collaborated in covering up his crimes. While others on the American Left, such as Susan Sontag, proclaimed during the 1980s that Communism was fascism, fascism with a human face, and that one could learn more about the true nature of Communism from *Reader's Digest* than the *Nation,* the Hollywood Party still remained silent. As Father Berry had put it in *On the Waterfront,* those who know and remain silent share the guilt.

Given those realities, the fiftieth anniversary remembrance would have been the ideal forum for a simple acknowledgment that Communism had been the grand failure of our time and that its supporters in Hollywood had, at the very least, been misguided.

More than fifty years earlier the industry had blacklisted directors and artists from Nazi Germany, but they were now venerating those who had remained loyal to Stalin and excluding those who turned against him. As the program for *Hollywood Remembers the Blacklist* said, some of those in the Party were indeed talented, but one wonders how much better they would have done without the blinders of Marxism–Leninism. While wielding the incantation of McCarthyism, the Party maintained bitter feuds and fought the old battles, like Japanese soldiers still fighting on, on some deserted Pacific island.

What the film industry impresarios failed to realize was that a reappraisal of Communism would not have hurt their esteem in the eyes of the public but raised it. For that there was a precedent.

One need only look at the actions of Yves Montand, who had welcomed American Communists to France. Montand, a costar in films with Marilyn Monroe and Barbra Streisand, came to realize that he had "been exploited, used to advertise an idea, just like a shampoo or a drink." He came to call Party members "Red Nazis" and in *Paris Match* wrote that if one of those who defended Stalinist atrocities were to seek him out, "I would puke all over him. That's how strongly I feel."[2] He also put his beliefs into action.

In the 1970 film *The Confession,* directed by Costa Gavras, Montand played Artur London, Czechoslovakia's deputy foreign minister, who had been charged in the 1952 show trials, fueled by Stalinist anti-Semitism and resulting in eleven executions. The film includes a scene of faceless policemen scattering the victims' ashes in the snow. "*The Confession* was a farewell to the generous sentimentality of the Left," said Montand, "a Left that had been blind to its own crimes and had cultivated a messianic pose, proposing to bring happiness to human beings, even if it means slaughtering them."[3]

During the 1980s, still at the height of his career, Montand went on French television and summarized his record with the Party by saying: "*Nous étions des cons*" (roughly translated, "We were morons, cretins"). Far from harming his prestige, the confession enhanced it. Once seriously considered for president of France, Yves Montand died in 1991 a national hero.

None of the producers of *Hollywood Remembers the Blacklist* thought to have an actor play Montand giving his heart-wrenching confession. And even half a century after the fact, nobody in supposedly liberal, open-minded Hollywood was up to a similar mea culpa performance. The official story was still a version of *j'accuse.* Instead of a courageous reappraisal with a full cast, the industry impresarios had offered a colorized remake of the myth, in which those who had defended the worst mass murderer in history were still, as Philip Dunne put it, virtually deified. Perhaps that was to be expected.

Hollywood remains a place of fantasy, of dancing shadows, where all dreams are created equal. But it is also a place of shifting fashion and has shown itself capable of change. Films of historical verisimilitude, such as *Schindler's List,* do occasionally emerge. Maybe some day, perhaps in a new century, someone will take the back story of the Hollywood Party and make a movie of it.

Appendix 1

"What Shall We Ask of Writers?"

by Albert Maltz

Originally Published in New Masses *on February 12, 1946*

ISIDORE SCHNEIDER'S FRANK AND EARNEST ARTICLE on writers' problems (*NM*, October 23, 1945) is very welcome. In attempting to add to his discussion, I ask that my observations be taken for what they are: The comments of a working writer, not the presentation of a formal esthetician. It is likely that some of my statements are too sweeping, others badly formulated. I urge that the attention of readers, however, be directed to the problem itself, rather than to formulations which may be imperfect. All who are earnestly desirous of a rich, expanding literature in America have the obligation of charting the course. This common effort must not languish while we search for unassailable definitions.

It has been my conclusion for some time that much of left-wing artistic activity—both creative and critical—has been restricted, narrowed, turned away from life, sometimes made sterile—because the atmosphere and thinking of the literary left wing has been based upon a shallow approach. Let me add that the left wing has also offered a number of vital intellectual assets to the writer—such as its insistence that important writing cannot be socially idle—that it must be humane in content, etc. Schneider enumerated these assets and I take them here for granted. But right now it is essential to discuss where things have gone wrong—why and how.

I believe that the effects of the shallow approach I have mentioned—like a poison in the blood stream—largely cause the problems Schneider mentioned. Indeed, these problems are merely the pustules upon the body, the sign of ill health.

Let me underscore that I am referring only to artistic activity, not to journalism. Schneider differentiates generally between writing for the moment and writing enduring works. There are other ways of phrasing this distinction, but his is a useful one—provided it is not taken with mechanical literalness. For instance, certain works have been written for the moment which nevertheless prove to contain enduring values. Such examples do not alter the true meaning of Schneider's categories.

Schneider went on to state, correctly, that: to report immediate events or to propagandize for immediate objectives is an honorable as well as useful function (John Reed, Ehrenburg). The harm, he added, "is in confusing the two. Some writers have sought to solve a conflict of conscience by trying to do the two in one," (i.e. journalism and art). "They have written books in such a way as also to serve immediate political expediencies. The results showed either in weakened and schematic writing or wasted writing."

In these remarks, Schneider recognizes the problem, describes it accurately—but does not go on to uncover the deep source of it. Left-wing writers have been confused, yes. But why?

The answer, I believe, is this: Most writers on the left have been confused. "The conflict of conscience," resulting in wasted writing or bad art, has been induced in the writer by the intellectual atmosphere of the left wing. The errors of individual writers of critics largely flow from a central source, I believe. That source is the vulgarization of the theory of art that lies behind left-wing thinking, namely, "art is a weapon."

Let me emphasize that, properly and broadly interpreted, I accept this doctrine to be true. The ideas, ethical concepts, credos upon which a writer draws consciously or unconsciously are those of his period. In turn, the accepted beliefs of any period reflect those values which are satisfactory to the class holding dominant social power. To the degree that works of art reflect or attack these values it is broadly—not always specifically—true to say that works of art of have been, and can be, weapons in men's thinking, and therefore in the struggle of social classes, either on the side of humanity's progress, or on the side of reaction. But as interpreted in practice for the last 15 years of the left wing in America, it has become a hard rock of narrow thinking. The total concept, "art is a weapon," has been viewed as though it consisted of only one word: "weapon." The nature of art—how art may best be a weapon, and how it may not be—has been slurred over. I have come to believe that the accepted understanding of art as a weapon is not a useful guide, but a straitjacket. I have felt this in my own works and viewed it in the works of others. In order to write at all, it has long since become necessary for me to repudiate it and abandon it.

Whatever its original stimulating utility in the late twenties or the early thirties, this doctrine, "art is a weapon," over the years in day-to-day wear and tear was converted from a profound analytic, historical insight into a vulgar slogan: "Art should be a weapon." This, in turn, was even more narrowly interpreted into the following: "Art should be a weapon as a leaflet is a weapon." Finally, in practice, it has been understood to mean that unless art is a weapon like a leaflet, serving immediate political ends, necessities, and programs, it is worthless or escapist or vicious.

The result of this abuse and misuse of a concept upon the critic's apparatus of approach has been, and must be, disastrous. From it flow all of the constrictions and—we must be honest—stupidities too often found in the earnest but narrow thinking and practice of the literary left wing in these past years. And this has been inevitable.

First of all, under the domination of this vulgarized approach, creative works are judged primarily by their formal ideology. What else can happen if art is a weapon as a leaflet is a weapon? If a work, however thin or inept as a piece of literary fabric, expresses ideas that seem to fit the correct political tactics of the time, it is a foregone conclusion that it will be reviewed warmly, if not enthusiastically. But if the work, no matter how rich in human insight, character portrayal, and imagination, seems to imply "wrong" political conclusions, then it will be indicted, severally mauled, or beheaded, as the case may be.

Let me give a recent example of this unhappy pattern: When Lillian Hellman's magnificent play, *Watch on the Rhine,* was produced in 1940, the *New Masses'* critic attacked it. When it appeared, unaltered, as a film in 1942, the *New Masses'* critic hailed it. The changed attitude came not from the fact that two different critics were involved, but from the fact that events had transpired in the two years calling for a different political program. This work of art was not viewed on either occasion as to its real quality, its deep revelation of life, character, and the social scene, but primarily as to whether or not it was the proper "leaflet" for the moment.

There is an opposite error, corollary to this: *New Masses'* critics have again and again praised works as art that no one—themselves included—would bother to read now, 10 years later. In fact, it once even gave a prize to such a book. This is not due to the fact that those who have written criticism for the magazine have the abandonment of taste because a shallow approach does not permit it. Literary taste can only operate in a crippled manner when canons of immediate political utility are the primary values of judgment to be applied indiscriminately to all books.

Again, from this type of thinking comes that approach which demands of each written work that it contain "the whole truth." An author writes a novel, let us say, about an unemployed Negro during the depression. The central character, after many harsh vicissitudes, ends by stealing and is sent to the penitentiary. If a book with this content were to be richly rendered, it might be highly illuminating in its portrayal of such an aspect of Negro life in America. But, again and again I have seen such works, justifiably confined to only one sector of experience, severely criticized because they do not contain "the whole truth." Upon examination this "whole truth" reveals itself to be purely political. The narrow critics are demanding that the novelist also show that some unemployed Negroes join the unemployed councils, etc. This demand, which I have seen repeated in varied ways in the pages of the *New Masses*, rests upon the psychological assumption that readers come to each book with an empty head. They know nothing, understand nothing. Therefore, all they will ever know of Negro life in America must be contained in this book. Therefore, if the author has omitted to say that some unemployed Negroes join organizations, it is a deficient book because it doesn't contain "the whole truth," and it doesn't properly fill the total vacuum of the reader's mind.

The creative writer, respecting this type of criticism, is faced with insuperable difficulties. He is confronted with the apparent obligation of writing both a novel and an editorial that will embrace all current political propositions remotely touching his material. Whether or not his character would join the unemployed council is of no matter; whether or not the material and artistic concept of the book forbid the examination of other characters—that, too, is of no matter. By hook or crook the material must be so rendered that the whole political "truth" of the scene is made visible, and the empty-handed reader is thereby won to new horizons—Q.E.D.

This is not a method by which art can be made rich, or the artist freed to do his most useful work. Let those who deny this ask working writers.

From this narrow approach to art another error also follows rather automatically. If, in actual practice—no matter how we revere art—we assume that a writer making a speech is performing the same act as writing a novel, then we are helpless to judge works written by those who make the "wrong" sort of speeches. Engels was never bothered by this problem. For instance, he said of Balzac—I paraphrase—that Balzac taught him more about the social structure of France than all of the economists, sociologists, etc., of the period. But who was Balzac? He was a Royalist, consistently and virulently antidemocratic, anti-Socialist, anti-Communist in his thinking as a citizen.

In his appreciation of Balzac, Engels understood two facts about art: First, as I have already stated, the writer, qua citizen, making an election speech, and the writer, qua artist, writing a novel, is performing two very different acts. Second, Engels understood that a writer may be confused, or even stupid and reactionary in thinking—and yet it is possible for him to do good, even great, work as an artist—work that even serves ends he despises. This point is critical for an understanding of art and artists. An artist can be a great artist without being an integrated or logical or a progressive thinker on all matters. This is so because he presents not a systematized philosophy but the imaginative reconstruction of a sector of human experience. Indeed, most people do not think with thoroughgoing logic. We are all acquainted with Jews who understand the necessity of fighting fascism, but who do not see the relationship between fascism and their own discrimination toward Negroes. We know Negroes who fight discrimination against themselves, but are anti-Semitic. I am acquainted with the curator of a museum who has made distinguished contributions in his scientific field, but who sees no contradiction between his veneration for science and his racist attitude toward Negroes. Out of these same human failings many artists are able to lead an intellectual life that often has a dual character. Ideas which they may consciously hold or reject do not always seriously affect their field work where, operating like a scientist upon specific material, they sometimes handle an aspect of human experience with passionate honesty in spite of the fact that the very implications of what they are writing may contradict ideas they consciously hold.

For instance, in sections of *Grapes of Wrath*, John Steinbeck writes a veritable poem to revolution. Yet we would be making an error to draw conclusions from this about Steinbeck's personal philosophy or to be surprised when he writes *Cannery Row* with its mystic paean to Bohemianism. Similarly, we can point to John Galsworthy, a successful, wealthy, middle-class Englishman. As a thinker, Galsworthy may not have understood the meaning of the phrase "class justice." But as an artist, honestly and earnestly recreating what he saw in English society, he wrote two plays, the *Silver Box* and *Justice,* which gave a searing portrait of class justice in human terms and which no socially conscious, theoretically sagacious, left-wing writer of today has come within 200 miles of equaling.

Unless this is understood, the critics on the left will not be able to deal with the literary work of their time. Writers must be judged by their work and not by the committees they join. It is the job of the editorial section of a magazine to praise or attack citizens committees for what they stand for. It is the job of the literary critics to praise the literary works only.

The best case in point, although there are many, is James T. Farrell. Farrell is, in my opinion—and I have thought so ever since reading *Studs Lonigan* over 10 years ago—one of the outstanding writers in America. I have not liked all of his work equally, and I don't like the committees he belongs to. But he wrote a superb trilogy and more than a few short stories of great quality, and he is not through writing yet. *Studs Lonigan* endures and is read by increasing numbers. It will endure, in my opinion, and deserves to. But if, in my opinion, Farrell is to be judged solely by his personality or his political position, then the *New Masses* is left in the position of either ignoring his work or attacking it. Let's face it. Isn't this exactly what has happened? Farrell's name was a bright pennant in the *New Masses* until he became hostile to the *New Masses*. Very well; for his deeds or misdeeds as a citizen, let him be editorially appraised. But his literary work cannot be ignored, and must not be ignored. And, if Engels gave high praise to the literary work of Balzac, despite his truly vicious political position, is not this a guide to the *New Masses'* critics in estimating the literary work of a whole host of varied writers—Farrell, Richard Wright, someone else tomorrow? What is basic to all understanding is this: There is not always a commanding relationship between the way an artist votes and any particular work he writes. Sometimes there is, depending upon his choice of material and the degree to which he consciously advances political concepts in his work. (Koestler, for instance, always writes with a political purpose so organic to his work that it affects his rendering of character, theme, etc. He must be judged accordingly.) But there is no inevitable, consistent position.

Furthermore, most writers of stature have given us great works in spite of philosophic weaknesses in their works. Dostoyevsky, Tolstoy, and Thomas Wolfe are among many examples. All too often narrow critics recognize this fact in dealing with dead writers, but are too inflexible to accept it in living writers. As a result it has been an accepted assumption in much of left-wing literary thought that a writer who repudiates a progressive political position—leaves the intellectual orbit of the *New Masses*, let us say—must go down hill as a creative writer. But this is simply not true to sober fact, however true it may be in individual cases. Actually it is impossible to predict the literary future of Richard Wright at this moment. At this moment he takes political positions which seem to many to be fraught with danger for his own people. He may continue to do so. But *Black Boy*, whatever its shortcomings, is not the work of an artist who has gone down hill. It is to the credit of the *New Masses* that it recognized this in dealing with the book. Equally, it is impossible to predict now the future literary achievements or failure of James Farrell, of Kenneth Fearing, of Lillian Smith, as it is of Van Tiliburn Clark, of Howard Fast, of Arnold Manoff, of Michael Blankfort. Books must be weighted like new coins—in terms of what they are. No other standard is valid. Writing is a complex process, and the sources of creative inspiration, out of which an artist works, are exceedingly complex. There are many, many reasons why writers grow and sometimes retrogress. The political convictions of a writer, or his lack of political convictions, may have something to do with his growth or creative decline, and certainly will if he writes highly politicized novels (Koestler). But they don't always have to do with it (Marquand—Steinbeck), and any assumption that as a writer's politics go, so inevitably does his art go—forward or backward—is the assumption of naïveté.

I have discussed a number of the general evils which seem to me to flow from the vulgarization and one-sided application of the doctrine, "Art is a weapon." I'd like now to examine its specific effect upon creative writing.

A creative writer, accepting the esthetic standards I have described, almost inevitably begins to narrow his approach to the rich opportunities of his art. He works intellectually in an atmosphere in which the critics, the audience, the friends he respects, while revering art, actually judge works on the basis of their immediate political utility. It is, moreover, an urgent social atmosphere, one of constant political crises. Almost inevitably, the earnest writer, concerned about his fellow man, aware of the social crisis, be-gins to think of his work as only another form of leaflet writing. Perhaps he comes to no such conscious conclusions. But he does so in effect, and he begins to use his talent for an immediate political end. If the end is good, it would be absurd to say that this may not be socially useful. It would also be highly inaccurate to maintain that from an approach like this, no art can result. On the other hand, I believe that the failure of much left-wing talent to mature is a comment on how restricting this canon is for the creator in practice.

The reason for this does not come primarily from the fact that works written for the moment are of interest only for the moment. Sometimes, as I pointed out earlier, they prove to have enduring interest also. It goes deeper—into the way a writer views his task, into the way he views people and events. The opportunity of the artist is conditioned by the nature of art itself. We read textbooks for facts, theories, information. But we read novels, or go to the theatre, for a different purpose. The artist, by the nature of his craft, is able to show us people in motion. This is why we revere good writers. They let us observe the individual richly—a complex creature of manifold dreams, desires, disappointments—in his relation to other individuals and to his society.

The artist is most successful who most profoundly and accurately reveals his characters, with all their motivations clearly delineated.

But the writer who works to serve an immediate political purpose—whose desire it is to win friends for some political action or point of view—has set himself the task not primarily of revealing men and society as they are—the social novelist—but rather of winning a point—the political novelist. I am not saying that an artist should be without a point of view—does not inevitably guide his selection of materials, characters, etc.—the Brothers Karamazov. But there is a difference between possessing a philosophic point of view, which permeates one's work—the social novelist—and having a tactical ax to grind which usually requires the artificial manipulation of character and usually results in shallow writing—the political novelist or political propagandist working in the novel.

One can gain a useful lesson by examining *And Quiet Flows the Don*. The central figure, Gregor, is a man who ends up as the political enemy of the Soviet revolution. I have always remembered a brilliant scene in this book: Gregor, who had fought with the Reds in the Civil War and then gone over to the Whites, returns to his village. He wants no more of fighting or politics. He asks only to live quietly as a farmer. But he is not allowed to remain at peace. Retribution, in the form of a Communist, catches up with him. The Communist comes to his house, listens to Gregor's earnest plea to be left alone and replies, with passion, "No, we will not leave you alone; we will hound you."

One cannot read this scene without sympathizing with Gregor and yearning for the Communist to be more tolerant. Yet—one understands both men. Their characters, history and motivations have been clearly presented. The position each takes is inevitable. The sympathetic insight into Gregor, the humanity of his presentation, does not, however, corrupt the historical point of view in the book. Rather, it deepens it.

The social illumination of this novel and its political meaning, would not be possible with a different handling of Gregor. This is so because profound characterization presents all characters from their own point of view, allowing them their own full, hu-man justification for their behavior and attitudes, yet allowing the reader to judge their objective behavior. This is the special wisdom art can offer us. But if Sholokhov had had a narrow political ax to grind, he would not have allowed Gregor his humanity, he would have wanted only to make the reader hate him, and so the breath of life would have gone from the book. It would have been weaker socially, psychologically, artistically and politically.

The pitfall of the socially conscious writer who uses his art in a shallow manner is that his goal all too often subtly demands the annihilation of certain characters, the gilding of others. It is very, very difficult for him not to handle characters in black and white since his objective is to prove a proposition, not to reveal men in motion, as they are.

Consequently, it is more than likely that he will "angle" character and events to achieve his point. He may not wish to do this. But he is led to it by his goal—led into idealistic conceptions of character, led into wearing rose-colored glasses which will permit him to see in life that which he wishes to find in order to prove his thesis, led into the portrayal of life, not as it is, but as he would like it to be. And this is not only inferior art, but shallow politics as well. His becomes the author of what Engels called "pinchpenny" socialist novels. This is often why "the conflict of conscience," of which Schneider spoke, has resulted so often in a schematic writing or wasted writing and, in not a few instances, in a book or play which must be discarded when a change of newspaper headlines occurs.

This latter calamity is the very symbol of the pitfall dug for the artist by his own narrow approach to his art. I know of at least a dozen plays and novels discarded in the process of writing because the political scene altered. Obviously, the authors in question were not primarily bent upon portraying abiding truths, either of character or the social scene, but were mainly concerned with advancing a political tactic through the manipulation of character. Otherwise, a new headline in the newspapers would not have made them discard their work. I even know a historian who read Duclos and announced that he would have to revise completely the book he was engaged upon. But what type of history was this in the first place?

I am convinced that the work-in-progress of an artist who is deeply, truly honestly recreating a sector of human experience need not be affected by a change in the political weather. A journalist's work, on the other hand, usually is affected. This is not an invidious judgment on the journalist. It is merely the difference between journalism and art. When the artist misuses his art, when he practices journalism instead of art, however decent his purposes, the result is neither the best journalism, nor the best art, nor the best politics.

The great humanistic tradition of culture has always been on the side of progress. The writer who works within this tradition—offering his personal contribution to it—is writing a political work in the broadest meaning of the term. It is not also incumbent upon him that he relate his broad philosophic or emotional humanism to a current and transient political tactic.

He may do so if he wishes. That is up to him. But if he does, he must remember that, where art is a weapon, it is only so when it is art. Those artists who work within a vulgarized approach to art do so at a great peril to their own work and to the very purposes they seek to serve.

Appendix 2

"Change the World"

by Mike Gold

Originally Published in the Daily Worker *on February 12, 1946*

ALBERT MALTZ, WHO WROTE SOME POWERFUL political and proletarian novels in the past, seems about ready to repudiate that past, and to be preparing for a retreat into the stale old ivory tower of the art-for-art-sakers.

If you can extract any other message out of his piece in the current *New Masses,* you are a better mind reader than this columnist.

His thesis is a familiar one, viz: that much "wasted writing and bad art has," for the past 15 years, "been induced in American writers by the intellectual atmosphere of the left wing" and that this bad influence has its central course in our vulgarized slogan: "Art is a weapon."

"It has been understood to mean that unless art is a weapon like a leaflet, serving immediate political ends, necessities and programs, it is worthless or escapist or vicious," he says.

Another charge is we tend to judge works of art solely from the standpoint of the politics of the author.

"Writers must be judged by their work and not by the committees they join."

As an example of our "narrow and vulgar" tendency, Albert says: "The best case in point—although there are many—is James T. Farrell, one of the outstanding writers of America. I have not liked all of his work equally and I don't like the committees he belongs to. But he wrote a superb trilogy and more than a few short stories of great quality, and he is not through writing yet."

299

There's a lot more of such theorizing, but I believe I have given a fair sample of the whole.

It has the familiar smell. I remember hearing all this sort of artistic moralizing before. The criticism of James T. Farrell, Max Eastman, Granville Hicks, and other renegades always attacked the same literary "sins of the Communists," and even quoted Lenin, Engels and Marx to profusion.

One can refuse to answer Maltz on ethical grounds, however. The fact remains that for 15 years, while Maltz was in the communist literary movement, he managed to escape with his talents and get his novels written.

This Communist literary movement in the United States was a school that nurtured an Albert Maltz and gave him a philosophic basis. It gave him his only inspiration up to date. It also inspired and created a Richard Wright, who was born and reared in a humble John Reed club.

The best American writers of the past 15 years received their inspiration, their stock of ideas, from their contact, however brief or ungrateful, with the left-wing working class and this Marxist philosophy.

Maltz's coy reference to the "political committees" on which James Farrell serves is a bad sign. Farrell is no mere little committee server but a vicious, voluble Trotskyite with many years of activity. Maltz knows that Farrell has long been a colleague of Max Eastman, Eugene Lyons and similar rats who have been campaigning with endless lies and slanders for war on the Soviet Union.

It is a sign of Maltz's new personality that he hasn't the honesty to name Farrell's Trotskyism for what it is; but to pass it off as a mere peccadillo. By such reasoning, Nazi rats like Ezra Pound and Knut Hansum, both superior writers to Farrell, must also be treated respectfully and even forgiven for their horrible politics because they are "artists."

There is a lot more one could say, and maybe I'll say it in a later column. Meanwhile, let me express my sorrow that Albert Maltz seems to have let the luxury and phony atmosphere of Hollywood at last to poison him.

It has to be constantly resisted or a writer loses his soul. Albert's soul was strong when it touched Mother Earth—the American working class. Now he is embracing abstractions that will lead him nowhere.

We are entering the greatest crisis of American history. The capitalists are plotting (and the big strikes are a first sample) to establish an American fascism as a prelude to American conquest of the world.

Literary evasions of this reality can afford no inspiration to the young soldiers and trade-unionists, the Negroes, and all the rest of toiling humanity who must fight. The ivory tower may produce a little piece of art now and then, but it can never serve the writer who means to fight and destroy the Hitlers of this world.

Appendix 3

"Moving Forward"

by Albert Maltz
Originally Published in The Worker *on April 7, 1946*

WE LIVE IN A PERIOD OF SOCIAL CONVULSION greater than the world has ever seen. Poverty, depression, colonial enslavement, racism, war, political conspiracy, mass murder—these are the problems with which humanity must deal. In this world of acute struggle, writers, like everyone else, live and work. Since the nature of their work is such that it is capable of influencing the thoughts, emotions, and actions of others, it is right and good that the world should hold them responsible for what they write, and that they should hold themselves responsible.

I have believed this for quite some time now. I have also believed that in our time Marxism can be the bread of life to a serious writer. With these convictions, I published an article in the *New Masses* some weeks ago which was greeted by severe criticism. The sum total of this criticism was that my article was not a contribution to the development of the working cultural movement, but that its fundamental ideas, on the contrary, would lead to the paralysis and liquidation of left-wing culture.

Now these are serious charges, and were not rendered lightly, not taken lightly by me. Indeed the seriousness of the discussion flows from the fact that my article was not published in the *Social Democratic New Leader* (which, to my humiliation, has since commented on it with wolfish approval), but that it was published in the *New Masses*.

In the face of these criticisms, I have been spending the intervening weeks in serious thought. I have had to ask myself a number of questions: Were the criticisms of my article sound? If so, by what process of thought had I, despite earnest intentions, come to write the article in the terms I did?

Intimately connected with these personal questions were broader matters demanding inquiry by others as well as by myself. If the criticisms of my article were sound, why was it that a number of friends who read the manuscript prior to publication and whose convictions are akin to mine had not come to such severe conclusions? And why was it that the *New Masses* accepted the article without comment to me, indeed with only a note of approval from the literary editor? And why was it that even after the criticisms of my article appeared, I daily received letters which protested the "ton" of the criticisms of me, but consid-ered that at worst I only had fallen into a few "unfortunate" formulations?

I have come to quite a number of conclusions about these questions. And if I discuss the process of my arriving at them with some intimacy, I hope the reader will bear with me, since I know no other way of dealing honestly with the problems involved. I particularly invite those who have written me letters of approval to consider whether some of the remarks I have to make about myself may not also appropriate to them.

I CONSIDER NOW THAT MY ARTICLE—by what I have come to agree was a one-sided, nondialectical treatment of complex issues—could not, as I had hoped, contribute to the development of left-wing criticism and creative writing. I believe also that my critics were entirely correct in insisting that certain fundamental ideas in my article would, if pursued to their conclusion, result in the dissolution of the left-wing cultural movement.

The discussion surrounding my article has made me aware of a trend in my own thinking, and in the thinking of at least some others in the left-wing cultural movement, namely a tendency to abstract errors made by left critics from the total social scene, a tendency then to magnify those errors and to concentrate attention upon them without reference to a balanced view of the many related forces which bear upon left culture, and hence a tendency to advance from half-truths to total error.

Let me illustrate this point: In the thirties, as there seems to be general agreement, left-wing criticism was not always conducted on the deepest, or most desirable, or most useful level. Its effectiveness was lowered by tendencies toward doctrinaire judgments and toward a mechanical application of social criticism. And these tendencies must be understood and analyzed if working-class culture is to advance to full flower. But, on the other hand, the inadequacies of criticism, such as they were, are only a small and partial aspect of the left-wing cultural movement as a whole. The full truth—as I have been aware for many years, and as I was thoroughly aware even when writing my article, is this: From the left-wing cultural movement in America, and from the left wing internationally, has come the only major, healthy impetus to an honest literature and art that these last two decades have provided. Compound the errors of left cultural thought as high as you will—still its errors are small as compared to its useful contribution, are tiny as compared to the giant liberating and constructive force of Marxist ideas upon culture. As a matter of sheer fact this is such a self-evident proposition that it does not require someone of my conviction to state it; it has been acknowledged even by reactionary critics who, naturally, have then gone on· falsely to declare that the liberating force of the left culture has run its course and expired.

The total truth about the left wing is therefore the only proper foundation and matrix for a discussion of specific errors in the practice of social criticism and creative writing. It was in the omission of this total truth—in taking it for granted—in failing to record the host of writers who have been, and are now, nourished by the ideas and aspirations of the left wing—that I presented a distorted view of the facts, history and contribution of the left-wing culture to American life. This was not my desire, but I accept it as the objective result. And, at the same time, by my one-sided zeal in attempting to correct errors, and so forth, I wrote an article that opened the way for the *New Leader* to seize upon my comments in order to "support" its unprincipled slanders against the left.

Of all that my article unwittingly achieved, this is the most difficult pill for me to swallow. Misstatements are now being offered up as fresh proof of the old lie: that the left puts artists in uniform. But it is a pill I have had to swallow and that I now want to dissolve.

Who and what keeps artists in uniform? In our society uniforms are indeed fitted for artists at every turn. But how? By a system of education which instructs a whole society in the belief that the status quo is unalterable, that social inequality is normal, that race prejudice is natural; by a social order which puts writing talent at the disposal of Hearst and artistic talent at the disposal of advertising agencies; by a total pressure made up of pressures and intellectual pressures and moral pressures, all designed to harness writers, artists, teachers, journalists, scientists, into willing or confused or frightened support of the established order in society, into maintaining, if need be, capitalist poverty, crime, prostitution, the cycle of wars and depressions—into maintaining all of this by their talent. This is the way in which artists, unless they break loose in conscious and organized protest, are put into one of the many, elegantly cut uniforms offered them by our kings of monopoly, our lords of the press, radio and so forth.

No; it is not the left wing that is guilty of this. On the contrary, the left wing, by its insistence that artists must be free to speak the absolute truth about society, by the intellectual equipment it offers in Marxist scientific thought, is precisely the force that can help the artist strip himself of the many uniforms into which he has been stepping since birth.

This is my conviction, and it has been my conviction for years. For precisely this reason it highlights the contradiction between my intentions in writing my article—and its result. By allowing a subjective concentration upon problems met in my own writing in the past to become a major preoccupation, I produced an article distinguished for its omissions, and succeeded in merging my comments with the unprincipled attacks upon the left that I have always repudiated and combated.

And this, as I said earlier, is the process by which one-sided thinking can lead to total error—it is the process by which objects, seen in a distortion mirror, can be recognized, but bear no relation to their precise features. It was this, among other things, that my critics pointed out sharply. For that criticism I am indebted. Ideas and opinions are worth holding when they are right, not when they are wrong. The effort to be useful involves always the possibility of being wrong; the right of being wrong, however, bears with it the moral obligation to analyze errors and correct them. Anything else is irresponsible.

THE SECOND MAJOR CRITICISM of the thinking in my article revolved about a separation between art and ideology, which was traced in varied terms, through a number of illustrations I had used and concepts I had advanced. I suppose I might claim here that it was merely inept formulation on my part which resulted in an "impression" that I was separating art from politics, the artist from the citizen, etc. But in the course of reading and rereading the criticisms of my article and the article itself, I have come to agree that I did make the separations mentioned, and that I made them not only in the writing, but in my thinking on the specific problems I was discussing.

Once again, this is the result of a one-sided nondialectical approach. Out of a desire to find clear, creative paths for my own work and the work of others, I felt it necessary to combat the current of thought that, in the past has tended to establish a mechanical relationship between ideology and art—a tendency that works particular harm to creative writing because it encourages a narrow, sloganized literature of a living reflection of society. However, in the course of this "contribution," as had been pointed out, I severed the organic connection between art and ideology.

This is not a small matter but a serious one, for if the progress of literature and art is separate from thought, if the ideas of a writer bear no intimate relationship to the work he produces, then even Fascists can produce good art. This is not only contrary to historic fact, but is theoretically absurd. Good art has always, and will always, come from writers who love the people, who ally themselves with the fate of the people, with the struggle of the people for social advancement. It is precisely because Fascists must hate people that 12 years of Nazi Germany produced not one piece of art in any field. It is for this reason that a writer like Celine, the Frenchman who began with a talented work of protest, but who found no constructive philosophy for his protest, ended in corrupt cynicism, in hatred of people, in the artistic sterility of the Fascist. It is for the same reason that the talent of American writers like Farrell and Dos Passos has not matured but has, on the contrary, gone into swift down-grade into sheer dullness as well as the purveying of untruth.

Here I want to interrupt for a word of comment on Farrell. I agree now that my characterization of him was decidedly lax, and that it was the inadvertent, but inevitable, result of the line of thinking in my article that separated art from ideology and politics. I want to make clear, however, that while a "mild attitude toward Trotskyites" was apparently the net effect upon readers of my comments, it was not at all what I had in mind, and it decidedly does not reflect my opinions Actually if I had been attempting a thorough examination of Farrell, there would have been much more to say—and I want to say some of it now.

Farrell's history and work are the best example I know of the manner in which a poisoned ideology and increasingly sick soul can sap the talent and wreck the living fiber of a man's work. This has been clear for quite some time now; his literary work has become weak, dull, repetitious. But precisely because this is so, and because his one outstanding work, *Studs Lonigan*, which ranks high among contemporary American novels—deservedly, I believe—was written before he became a Trotskyite, it is essential to trace dialectically in his work—as in the work of others like him—the process of artistic decay. It was not something I was "cheering" about, but it is something to reckon with as sheer fact that Farrell, Wright, Dos Passos, Koestler, etc. are "not through writing yet," that they are going to produce other books. If no one in America read these authors, one could settle by ignoring them. But this is not the case; they are widely read. As I see it, the effective manner of dealing with their work is not to be content merely with contemptuous references; this will not satisfy those who, ignorant of their political roles, know only their novels.

What is needed is profound analysis of this method and logic by which their anti-Soviet, antipeople, antilabor attitudes enter their work, pervert their talents, turn them into tools and agents of reaction. Only in this manner can other writers be made to see clearly the artistic consequences of political corruption; only in this manner can the struggle for a mass audience be conducted in a truly persuasive and mature manner.

AT THIS POINT I SHOULD LIKE TO ASK A QUESTION particularly of those who read my earlier article with approval, or with only sketchy criticism. What is the sum of what I have been saying until now?

It seems clear to me, as I hope it is already clear to them, that I have been discussing and illustrating revisionism, and that my article, as pointed out by others, was a specific example of revisionist thinking in the cultural field.

For what is revisionism? It is distorted Marxism, turning half-truths into total untruths, splitting ideology from its class base, denying the existence of class struggles in society, converting Marxism from a science of society and struggle into apologetics for monopoly exploitation. In terms of my article I think the clearest summation was given by Samuel Sillen in the *Daily Worker*.

"A hasty reading of the article may give the impression that it merely offers suggestions for correcting admitted defects of the literary left. But a deeper study of the article reveals that these suggestions, some of which might be valuable in another context, are here bound up with a line of thinking that would lead us to shatter the very foundation of the literary left, Marxism. This is the main issue. On this issue we must have utmost clarity.

"While Maltz seems to believe that he is merely criticizing a vulgarized approach to literature, he is in reality undermining a class approach. While appearing to challenge an over-simplified identity between art and politics, he severs their organic relationship in our epoch. In repudiating the 'accepted understanding' of art as a weapon, Maltz whittles down the concept itself to a point approaching nonexistence. In centering his fire on the 'literary atmosphere of the left,' he ignores the basic problem of an honest writer in capitalist society, the 'literary atmosphere of the right.'

"The article cannot be viewed as simply a challenge to a mechanical application of fundamental truths. The truths themselves are crushed under the structure of Maltz's reasoning. What is the main problem of the literary left today? It is to reestablish its Marxist base. In the past few years that base has been sapped by revisionism."

I believe that Sillen's summation is correct. The process he describes here is a revisionist process; it is the result of a failure to deeply break with old habits of thought. This failure was, I believe, at the core of the main tendencies in my article and it was the key to its uncritical acceptance by more than a few in the cultural field, both before and after publication. The intense, ardent, and sharp discussion around my article, therefore, seems to me to have been a healthy and necessary one—and to have laid the foundation whereby a new clarity can be achieved, a new consciousness forged, and a struggle undertaken to return, deeply, to sound Marxist principles. For it is essential that everyone, who appreciates that a healthy culture must be based on the needs of the people and the needs of the working class, appreciate also that Browderism could not lead to such a culture. A literature that would be uncritical of monopoly capital and its effect upon human lives, indeed, a literature based on the concept that monopoly capital can serve the American people progressively—such a literature would be wholly out of step with life. It could not represent the facts of life. Creative writers who approached life with this philosophy would have to avoid realistic, honest writing. However much they might feel ardent sympathy for the people, they would be forced into the position of ignoring reality—and hence their actual work would finally become indistinguishable from the empty literature to be found in the popular magazines.

This, with all of its implications, is the reason why a serious and sharp discussion was required of the ideas developed in my article.

Appendix 4

"Confessions of a Red Screenwriter"

by Richard Collins

Originally Published in New Leader *on October 6, 1952*

A COMMUNIST IS ALWAYS PREPARED. He, or rather his party, has an answer for everything. When I joined the party, I was handed ready-made: friends, a cause, a faith and a viewpoint on all phenomena. I also had a one-shot solution to all the world's ills and inequities. Then I went through ten years of constant reinforcement and re-commitment and education. I learned the party view on psychoanalysis, on existentialism and Sartre, on almost every writer living and dead, on folk music, on religion, on everything under the sun.

Suppose our Comrade keeps up with all the twists and turns of party policy, what is his reward? Why, peace of mind, of course. Since he has answers for everything, he has a great sense of personal security; the world is safe; everything is explained—his history and the future; and everything is also simplified—into black and white. This black-and-white world has appeal not only for oppressed, desperately poor Asiatic masses, but also for intellectuals weary of the mental effort necessary in a democratic or real world—a world full of complexities, without easy solutions, and sometimes without answers. The party member, on the other hand, has to make only one effort. He must be "flexible." "Flexible" means that you cheer for Earl Browder on his birthday and the next day you despise him as a "betrayer of the working class."

I used to sing lustily at Communist party conventions a song: "Browder is our leader, he shall not be moved . . . just like a tree that's standing by the river." After the Duclos letter, I had my private version: "Browder is our leader: he shall be removed."

By then, I was on my way out. But I was "flexible" for a long time. I, too, needed that feeling of always being right. Although denying religion, the Communists need it and express it in zealotry in relation to the party. This charge of religiosity angers the Communists a great deal. They answer that their position is based on reason. This is similar to their constant reiteration that Marxism is a science. If it is a science, it is a science without a provable body of facts, a science which has been incapable of correctly predict-ing anything within its field—history—ever since the Bolshevik Revolutions.

The Communists, for all their talk of reason and science, proceed on faith. And, as E. M. Forster says in his wise and delightful new book *Two Cheers for Democracy*, "to ignore evidence is one of the characteristics of faith."

As I say, I was "flexible" and full of faith. I made the jump from anti-Hitler and collective security to the Nazi-Soviet Pact on August 23, 1939, and from the Imperialist War to the People's War on June 22, 1941. The switch that threw me off the train of history started with the Duclos letter. Now how did I make those switches and why did it take me so long to recognize what I was doing? The answer is simple. I was thinking like a Communist. If you don't understand how a Communist thinks, I doubt you can understand his strength and his weakness.

This thinking is, actually, rather astonishing. The Communists attack Arthur Miller's *Death of a Salesman* because no reference is made to the working class. (To quote: "Monopoly and the working class disappear.") None of the motion pictures against Negro discrimination pleased them; they don't like Tennessee Williams because he is decadent and doesn't really confront the system. To them, T. S. Eliot, André Gide, and D. H. Lawrence are "reactionary, fascist and semi-fascist writers." Of Wagner they say: ". . . an anti-Semite and turncoat after the democratic struggles of 1848–9. His operas are a perfect expression of the petite bourgeois psychology which bows its head to reaction in real life and makes heroic gestures for 'freedom in art.'" They attack Picasso's art in spite of his personal adherence to their cause. The list of prejudices is endless, not only in the arts but in politics and international affairs. They cannot allow, for example the socialism of Sweden and Norway; only theirs is "true socialism." They cannot even allow Tito his Communist state since he refused to knuckle under to Moscow. In short, it must be their way or no way. Their excuse is that the Soviet state is protecting its citizens from unworthy and decadent works of art, music and literature and "incorrect" views on science.

Many Americans have never known a Communist personally. I'm afraid they won't recognize the girl next to them on the assembly line, or the nice old farmer next door as Communists because they haven't a real picture of what a Communist is. They have rather a bogey-man image. They expect a "Communist type." There is no such type any more than there is a Methodist type, or French type or capitalist type. *The only thing all Communists have in common is the way they think.*

At the last meeting of the Screen Writers Guild, in which their influence was pitiful, I realized why the Communists had exerted influence in the past:

In the first place, they weren't proved to be Communists, so they were accepted as "liberals."

In the second place, the ordinary citizen doesn't expect passion and conviction on democratic questions from persons so obviously anti-democratic.

In this last meeting, a Communist spokesman got up, after the question had been called on a motion to limit debate, and protested in passionate tones: "If there's no discussion, then the last vestiges of democracy have left the Guild." What most people don't understand is that he meant it. By a curious system of double bookkeeping, he was able to feel outraged for democratic America at this legitimate parliamentary denial of further speech, while at the same time he was completely prepared—at the point of his taking power—to silence any opposition in a far more brutal fashion.

Of course, I can speak only of the Communists I have known in Hollywood, in Los Angeles County, some on the National Committee and at least one from the Communist International. In the main, these men are neither stupid nor vicious, but, on the contrary, intelligent and well motivated. This doesn't mean they are not capable of stupid and vicious actions. Of course they are—but all the while they are convinced that their motives are idealistic and decent. It's the old story—a glorious end justifies despicable means.

One of the despicable means is the attack on individuals. Here the whole vocabulary of party invective as enunciated by Stalin is brought into play; "Trotskyites, spies, wreckers, Titoists, fiends, enemies of the people, murderers, agents, *provocateurs,* and diversionists." These labels, or their more euphemistic American equivalents, stick. They are used by intellectuals who have had contact with the party, and even have some effect for a time on ex-party people.

In my own case, I had made an irrevocable split with the party (in making an absolute declaration, first to the FBI and then to the Un-American Activities Committee), and yet I remember with trepidation over my first meeting with Roy Brewer [anti-Communist union leader]. I had never seen him, and would not recognize him on the street. Yet the voices of the past called to me—I expected to see in Brewer a local-type fiend, breathing fire and brimstone. When he opened his mouth, I expected a string of reactionary sentiments. Instead, I found him a quiet and reasonable man—and even more astonishing to me, he is on record as a liberal Democrat. He is also a good trade unionist, vitally concerned with the interest of his men. This was an extraordinary revelation to me, and I imagine it would equally confound a sizable portion of the Hollywood community. The Communists did that good a job on him!

The Communists believe that they alone have the solution to the world's ills, they alone really care for the toiling masses, the oppressed and under-privileged, that all others are imposters. The Communists can murder millions—in forced labor camps, in direct executions—firm in the belief that they are saving tens of millions. They are that positive that they are right. But how is it possible? If, as I say, they are intelligent and not consciously vicious, how can they behave this way? It is because they set up logic-tight bulk-heads, and these bulkheads are self-perpetuating. Once a Communist has looked at the world and achieved a given frame of reference—and the facts seem to fit—he cannot change, no matter how, under new circumstances, the facts stack up against him. Here is an example:

The Communists insist that the United States today is like Nazi Germany of the Thirties. Many of the Communists before the House Un-American Committee see themselves as Dimitrov defying the Nazi court. The facts don't bear this out. It is true that Communists are being attacked, and they were attacked in Nazi Germany; it is also true that, with the threat of war, there are dangers to our civil liberties. But, in a dozen other ways, the comparison falls to pieces. Why do the Communists believe that this period is similar to the Thirties? What is the reality behind this basic argument of the world Communist parties? In order to answer this, we will have to look at the 1930s, that period in which the Communist party, U.S.A., is still locked.

I want to tell how this period looked to me. In 1932, when I started at Stanford, the graduating engineering class had no work waiting for them, and no prospects of work—except for nine men who had jobs in Soviet Russia. Millions were unemployed, more millions were working half-time, factories were closing, terror was being used against the workers. Some industrialists were abusing their power and strikers were attacked by armed thugs. It looked as though a Mussolini or a Hitler could take over.

In Germany, the Nazis had taken power and the German Communist party seemed to be their prime adversary. There were Nazis in the United States too—not only Fritz Kuhn and the Bund, but the Silver Shirts, the Coughlinites, the Black Legion and others. Against them as well, the Communist party seemed the most active and militant force. The party enunci-ated a program against prejudice, for trade unions, for higher wages, social justice and civil liberties. Many of us took seriously Browder's slogan: "Communism Is 20th-Century Americanism." This was the Popular Front period, enunciated by the Seventh World Congress of Communist Parties in 1935. Revolution was forsworn, the Communist parties were to form a coalition with labor, the farmers and all progressives in order to stop Fascism and Nazism. The Communist party in America did not talk revolution, but day-to-day tactics.

I joined the party in 1937. At that time, the Spanish Civil War was raging. I was for the Loyalists as the democratic government of Spain. In 1938, the Gallup Poll showed 76 percent of the American people in favor of the Loyalists, so I was not alone. I was alarmed at the policy of so-called "non-intervention" because it was obviously intervention on the side of Mussolini, Hitler and Franco. I was alarmed by Munich, by the capitulation to and appeasement of Hitler. The Communist party presented itself and the Soviet Union as the great enemy of Nazism and the friend of the democracies. Collective security was supposed to be the union of the Western democratic nations with the Soviet Union against Nazi aggression.

Many of us had no idea that we were embracing, in whole or in part, another tyranny. And we were helped in making that mistake by a section of American liberals who unwittingly became an aid to the American Communist party because they overtrusted the Communists. They did not realize that Communists cannot be persuaded, that they who must dominate are deaf. The party people did not see the liberals as other men—they saw them first to be used and then as obstacles. *Between the liberal position and the Communist* (once both positions are seen clearly) *there is a gulf which can never be bridged.* Most liberals see that very sharply now, and those who do not are not liberals at all but crypto-Communists.

The Communists were also strengthened in their feeling of Communist righteousness by the absurd activities of some ultra-conservative groups who, to this day, lump all decent liberal opinion with Communism, thereby making Communism synonymous with social progress, all curiosity of the human mind, all change, and all difference of opinion. Although these groups use Communism as a dirty word with which to smear honest liberals and liberal opinion, the actual result is to give the Communist an avenue of approach to the liberal element—most often the youth—who, seeing injustice in the world, have a natural desire to change it.

So much for the Thirties. No matter what the Communists say or what they believe, the facts show that the Fifties are a far cry from that decade. My recognition of these facts is one of the things that started me out of the party. I hope what I have been saying has made my other reasons clear.

One reason I have not discussed was my increasing concern with the problem of writing. I realized that to be the kind of writer I wanted to be and a Communist at the same time was, for me at any rate, an impossibility. Even to be the kind of reader I wanted to be was becoming impossible. The Communist attack on "bourgeois" writing is absolutely necessary, because the great middle-class writers show the world in all its marvelous variety, and show man in all his intricate individuality—full of complex feelings, not routinized, not crass, but, as Pascal put it, "a thinking reed." If this is a man—this subjective as well as rational creature, this creature of dreams, strange desires, great spirit and curious contradictions—then the Communists are proven wrong. And this *is* man. The writer celebrates this man whose differences of opinion, of action and reaction, of sensation, are precious. They are signs of life—they *are* life.

The Communist, meanwhile, is too busy limiting what can be enjoyed, what is correct, right, proper. He is indulging his need to form moral judgments. As Silone has put it: "To the Communist there is no such thing as an adversary in good faith." The Communist, heroic as he can be, cannot allow others equal heroism—his opponents must be venal. He is therefore narrowing the world to his own image, trying to force it into the little black-and-white compartments he has fashioned. A world unified on theory is as fleshless, as bloodless, as deaf and as blind as the theory itself.

It was not only as a writer, but as a weeping, laughing man, that I left the party, as a citizen and as a human being. The idea of killing people because they do not agree with me is abhorrent. If we are prepared to take up arms against the Soviet Union, it is not because we disagree with them, but to protect ourselves. It is they who wish to impose their wills on us and on the whole world.

I am afraid of the Communists in the United States not only because I know that in such a war their loyalty is to the Soviet Union—their country right or wrong. I am afraid of the Communists because I am afraid of the Communist mind. And that mind, unfortunately, is not restricted to Communists. Anyone who cannot tolerate opposition, who is sure that he alone has the correct answers, who has moral superiority over his fellows because he thinks "properly" and they are in "error," any mind that approaches the problems of our time with prejudice and passion instead of reason—is basically anti-democratic.

But it would be absurdly abstract not to recognize that, of all intolerances, the Communist mind represents today, in our time, the most formidable opponent, because it is the only anti-democratic mind that can call upon a huge world-wide force, a mighty Soviet Army to support it. Nevertheless, we must not forget that it is this type of thinking—whether Nazi, anti-Nazi, Communist, anti-Communist or whatever—that in the long run represents the constant danger to American democracy.

As Jefferson put it: "I have sworn on the altar of Almighty God eternal hostility against every form of Tyranny over the human mind." Those are my sentiments exactly.

Appendix 5

Statement of Roy Brewer, Disallowed by the House Committee on Un-American Activities

October 28, 1947

PRELIMINARY STATEMENT OF ROY BREWER, International Representative in Hollywood of the International Alliance of Theatrical Stage Employees and Moving Picture Machine Operators of the United States and Canada.

IN RESPONSE TO YOUR SUBPOENA, I welcome the opportunity to present to this Committee the evidence which I have of Communist infiltration into the Hollywood studios. I am sure that the 30,000 employees now working in the Hollywood studios, of which our union represents approximately one-half, are fully conscious of the responsibility which the Committee has in this matter.

The story of Communist infiltration and intrigue which this Committee is revealing to the American people is not new to us. We have been resisting it for more than ten years. I shall present evidence which I think will conclusively establish the fact that there is and there has been a *real* Communist plot to capture our union in Hollywood, as part of the Communist plan to control the motion picture industry as a whole. The plan came dangerously close to success. I am happy to say that thus far it has failed.

The plan, as we see it, was for the Communist forces, led by Mr. Jeff Kibre, Communist agent sent to Hollywood in 1935, and his successor, Herbert K. Sorrell, to infiltrate and control Hollywood technical labor, while other Communist forces led by Mr. John Howard Lawson, whose activities have been described here, to infiltrate and control the talent guilds and so-called cultural groups in the industry. At the appropriate time these two forces were to be joined in one overall industrial union set-up under complete Communist domination. Our international union, the IATSE, found itself as the one real effective force standing in the way of this program.

Having failed to control our organization in Hollywood, the Communists found it necessary to seek to destroy it. Fomenting and aggravating jurisdictional irritations existing in the trade union structure in the studios, the Communists in 1944, 1945, 1946 and 1947 engineered and maintained a running series of jurisdictional strikes against our union. The real purpose of these strikes was the weakening and ultimate destruction of the IATSE, which was the recognized bulwark against Communist seizure of the studio unions.

Had those strikes been successful, and the IATSE been defeated, we are sure that the few remaining forces of resistance would have easily succumbed to the unbelievably effective machine which the Communist movement had built in Southern California in 1944. With a Communist-controlled union representing all Hollywood technical labor supporting a Screen Writers Guild, through which only pro-Communist writers could get into the Industry, we believe that the screen would have been effectively captured, notwithstanding the good intentions of the producers of motion pictures.

While this Communist plan has been defeated thus far, we have not been successful in this fight without tremendous efforts on the part of the real A.F. of L. unions in the studios and a tremendous sacrifice on the part of many of our members. Hollywood workers have fought valiantly to prevent their unions from becoming an adjunct of Soviet foreign policy. Hundreds have suffered personal injuries. Homes have been bombed, automobiles destroyed and children threatened. Intimidation and coercion have caused many to live for weeks in terror.

Some may say that the Hollywood story is a figment of a motion picture make believe, but to our members in the Hollywood unions, it is very real indeed. To them it has meant the pitting of worker against worker, brother against brother, yes and even husband against wife. Thus have the Communists sought to justify their slogan that the end justifies the means.

The trend of the times has aided our cause. Important persons in the industry who, a few years ago, greeted our story as too fantastic to believe, are now looking at it with recognition and concern. But we know from experience that the Communists will not give up—the prize is too great. We hope, therefore, that with the help of this Committee, the Communist menace in the motion picture industry may be successfully destroyed to the end that Hollywood labor may be spared in the future the strife and turmoil of the immediate past.

We shall continue to fight, to expose and to remove the Communist menace from our trade unions, so that, in keeping with our American system, our labor organizations may continue to be free, clean, progressive, patriotic and democratic, with continued improvement of working conditions and maintenance of adequate security for the may thousands of employees in this great American industry.

Appendix 6

"You Can Be Free Men Again!"

Motion Picture Industry Council Statement
in Support of Edward Dmytryk

WHEN THE COMMUNIST PARTY TRAPS AN AMERICAN into its unholy conspiracy, it is almost unbearably hard to break away. The Party sees to that, for the Party must enforce its discipline or die.

The Communist Party is now trying to destroy Edward Dmytryk for breaking with the Party and exposing its secrets to the proper government agencies. Dmytryk is not the first ex-Communist to be called "faker" and "liar" and "scoundrel" and "perjurer." These same accusations have been leveled by the Communist Party against such militant ex-Communists as Arthur Koestler, Louis Budenz, Elizabeth Bentley and Whittaker Chambers.

In each case, the records of these persons show that their disillusionment with Communism came slowly, but with it came determination to help destroy the menace which once had trapped them. The attack against Dmytryk merely confirms what veteran fighters against Communism already know, namely that the Party has been hit where it hurts.

Any American who associates with the Communist Party is befouled. He is befouled, not by the person who exposes him but by his own act in joining a traitorous conspiracy against his own country. This has been confirmed by the U.S. Supreme Court decision upholding the Smith Act. Read then a story which should interest you, a story of a person who finally realized that he had been besmirched by his association with the Communist Party and who sought our help in rising from Communist slime to cleaner ground.

We are just a few of the many loyal Americans in Hollywood who have helped bring about the complete frustration and failure of the Communist Party in the motion picture capital. On February 2, 1951, we met with Edward Dmytryk at his request. Dmytryk told us he wished to rehabilitate himself and he asked our advice and help. We questioned him and he asked our advice and help. We told him that we were not interested in him personally or whether he ever got a job again. We made sure in our own minds that it was not a principally economic pressure which had led Dmytryk to want to come clean, although, of course, that had something to do with it. We made sure that Dmytryk was really trying to escape the Communist trap.

The advice we gave Dmytryk was tough and drastic. No one without courage and sincerity could have followed that advice. An appointment was made for Dmytryk with the FBI. Another meeting was arranged with investigators of the House Committee on Un-American Activities. We suggested his voluntary appearance before the committee. We suggested a magazine article. In meeting after meeting with Dmytryk, we watched the man change and gradually lose his fear that for the ex-Communist there is no road back to decent society. We watched as, with his intellectual blinders removed, he slowly realized with growing anger the truth and the enormity of the Communist conspiracy against our land. We warned him to expect vicious attacks by the Communist Party.

Not one item of fact in the Communist Party line attack on Edward Dmytryk was unknown to us nor to the Federal Bureau of Investigation nor to the House Committee on Un-American Activities. Dmytryk himself told us the facts, in proper sequence and perspective and not pervertedly twisted to serve the Communist Party line. The one thing we could not know in advance, of course, was the one BIG LIE in the attack on Dmytryk, namely the unsupported claim that Dmytryk had said Progressives must go underground. We are certain Dmytryk never said anything like that. The BIG LIE was fashioned as the supposed "clincher" for a collection of half-truths and distortions in time and fact. The BIG LIE is an official technique of the Communist Party.

The attack on Eddie Dmytryk was not unexpected and it came as no surprise to those who know how the Communist Party operates. But the Communist Party has failed in its effort to destroy Edward Dmytryk. Were it otherwise, it would be a victory for the Communist Party and a defeat for Americanism.

We will be surprised if there are not other attacks by the Communist Party on other former Communists who have the guts to stand up and be counted and to tell the truth to the proper government agencies. It takes courage and desire and time for an American to work free of the tentacles of the Communist Party. And it takes help. But there is a way out. To any Communist Party member who may be seeking that way, we say: "You too can be free men again!"

Roy Brewer
I. E. Chadwick
Art Arthur
Ronald Reagan
Jack Dales
Alexander Kempner

THE MOTION PICTURE INDUSTRY COUNCIL, composed of Hollywood's key guilds, unions and management groups, endorses the above statement in accordance with the MPIC policy announced March 21, 1951 of urging all persons subpoenaed by the House Committee on Un-American Activities to tell the whole truth, and of offering "commendation and encouragement" to those former members of the Communist Party who have repudiated Party ties and who join their fellow Americans in the fight for freedom.

Notes

Chapter 1. Communism, Communists, and Cinema

1. S. J. Taylor, *Stalin's Apologist: Walter Duranty, the New York Times Man in Moscow* (Oxford and New York: Oxford University Press, 1990), 220.
2. Vladimir Pozner, *Parting with Illusions* (Boston: Atlantic Monthly Press, 1990), 109.
3. Vitaly Shentalinsky, *Arrested Voices: Resurrecting the Disappeared Writers of the Soviet Regime* (New York: Free Press, 1996), 222.
4. Sidney Hook, *Out of Step: An Unquiet Life in the Twentieth Century* (New York: Harper and Row, 1987), 493.
5. Dimitri Volkogonov, *Stalin: Triumph and Tragedy* (Rocklin, CA: Prima, 1996), xxvi.
6. Anna Louise Strong, *I Change Worlds* (New York: Holt, 1935), 348.
7. Many actual Comintern communications are included in Harvey Klehr, John Earl Haynes, and Kyrill M. Anderson, *The Soviet World of American Communism* (New Haven, CT: Yale University Press, 1998).
8. Benjamin Gitlow, *I Confess* (New York: Dutton, 1940), 217.
9. Klehr, Haynes, and Anderson, *Soviet World of American Communism*, 107, 148.
10. John Barron, *Operation Solo: The FBI's Man in the Kremlin* (Washington, D.C.: Regnery, 1996), 23.
11. Stephen Schwartz, *From West to East: California and the Making of the American Mind* (New York: Free Press, 1998), 338.

12. For Communist Party influence in American government, see Harvey Klehr, John Earl Haynes, and Fridrikh Igorevich Firsov, *The Secret World of American Communism* (New Haven, CT: Yale University Press, 1995).
13. Robert Vaughn, *Only Victims: A Study of Showbusiness Blacklisting* (New York: Putnams, 1972), 35.
14. Eugene Lyons, *The Red Decade* (Arlington, 1970), i, ii.
15. Hook, *Out of Step*, 255–257.
16. David Shipman, *The Story of Cinema: A Complete History from the Beginnings to the Present* (New York: St. Martin's, 1982), 294.
17. Cited in *Hearings Regarding the Communist Infiltration of the Motion Picture Industry*, Committee on Un-American Activities, House of Representatives, 1947, 172.

Chapter 2. Hollywood: The Dream Factory

1. Otto Friedrich, *City of Nets: A Portrait of Hollywood in the 1940s* (New York: Harper and Row, 1986), 14.
2. Hortense Powdermaker, *Hollywood: The Dream Factory: An Anthropologist Looks at the Movie Makers* (Boston: Little, Brown, 1950), 327.
3. Budd Schulberg, *What Makes Sammy Run?* (New York: Modern Library, 1941), 284.
4. Murray Ross, *Stars and Strikes: Unionization of Hollywood* (New York: AMS Press, 1967), 16.
5. Ronald Reagan, with Richard G. Hubler, *Where's the Rest of Me?* (New York: Duell, Sloan and Pearce, 1965), 130.

Chapter 3. "The Strategic Importance of Hollywood"

1. Ella Winter, *And Not to Yield* (New York: Harcourt, 1963), 149.
2. Natalie Robbins, *Alien Ink: The FBI's War on Freedom of Expression* (New York: Morrow, 1992), 93.
3. Testimony of Charles Bakcsy to California Senate Committee on Un-American Activities, July 30, 1941.
4. Nancy Lynn Schwartz (completed by Sheila Schwartz), *The Hollywood Writers' Wars* (New York: Knopf, 1982), 221.
5. Cited in David Saposs, *Communism in American Unions* (Westport, CT: Greenwood Press, 1967), 33.
6. *Hearings Regarding the Communist Infiltration of the Motion Picture Industry*, Committee on Un-American Activities, House of Representatives, 1947, 395.
7. Affidavit of Alex Saunders, County of Los Angeles, State of California, August 1, 1939, sworn and subscribed to Ursula Sitar. The entire affidavit is reproduced in *Facts*, Hollywood, California, August 3, 1939.

8. *Jurisdictional Disputes in the Motion-Picture Industry,* Committee on Education and Labor, House of Representatives, 1948, 1840.
9. *Motion-Picture Industry,* House Committee on Education and Labor, 1838.
10. *Motion-Picture Industry,* House Committee on Education and Labor, 1844.
11. *Motion-Picture Industry,* House Committee on Education and Labor, 2339.
12. Disney testimony from *Hearings Regarding the Communist Infiltration of the Motion Picture Industry,* House Committee on Un-American Activities, House of Representatives, 1947, 280–290.
13. William Mangil, "Little Willie in Movieland," *True Detective,* October 1944, 12.
14. *Variety,* August 2, 1937.
15. David F. Prindle, *The Politics of Glamour: Ideology and Democracy in the Screen Actors Guild* (Madison, WI: University of Wisconsin Press, 1988), 32.
16. "More Trouble in Paradise," *Fortune,* November 1946.
17. Interview, Roy Brewer.
18. Mason Wiley and Damien Bona, *Inside Oscar: The Unofficial History of the Academy Awards* (New York: Ballantine, 1987), 109.
19. Winter, *And Not to Yield,* 227.

Chapter 4. "The Communist Theatre Is Starting"

1. Nancy Lynn Schwartz, *The Hollywood Writers' Wars* (New York: Knopf, 1982), 44.
2. Elia Kazan, *Elia Kazan: A Life* (New York: Knopf, 1988), 101.
3. Kazan, *A Life,* 16, 117.
4. *Investigation of Communist Activities in the Los Angeles Area,* Hearings before the Committee on Un-American Activities, House of Representatives, 1953, 302, 303.
5. Morgan Y. Himelstein, *Drama Was a Weapon* (New Brunswick, NJ: Rutgers University Press, 1963), 17.
6. "Straight from the Shoulder," *New Theatre,* November 1934, 11–12.
7. Schwartz, *Hollywood Writers' Wars,* 49.
8. Kazan, *A Life,* 131.
9. Frances Farmer, *Will There Really Be a Morning?* (New York: Dell, 1972), 76.
10. Robert Vaughn, *Only Victims: A Study of Showbusiness Blacklisting* (New York: Putnams, 1972), 66.

Chapter 5. "The Industrious Communist Tail Wagged the Lazy Liberal Dog"

1. Patrick McGilligan and Paul Buhle, *Tender Comrades: A Backstory of the Hollywood Blacklist* (New York: St. Martin's, 1997), 150.
2. Bruce Cook, *Dalton Trumbo* (New York: Charles Scribners, 1977), 15.

3. *Hearings Regarding Communist Infiltration of Hollywood Motion Picture Industry,* Committee on Un-American Activities, House of Representatives, 1951, 1420.
4. *Communist Infiltration of the Motion Picture Industry,* House Committee on Un-American Activities, 1947, 177.
5. *Communist Infiltration of the Motion Picture Industry,* House Committee, 1947, 177.
6. *Communist Activities Among Professional Groups in the Los Angeles Area,* Committee on Un-American Activities, House of Representatives, 1952, 2444.
7. *Communist Infiltration of Hollywood Motion Picture Industry,* Committee on Un-American Activities, House of Representatives, 1951, 1590.
8. *Communist Activities in the Los Angeles Area,* Committee on Un-American Activities, House of Representatives, 1953, 945.
9. Neil Gabler, *An Empire of Their Own: How the Jews Invented Hollywood* (New York: Crown, 1988), 334.
10. Lester Cole, *Hollywood Red* (Berkeley: Ramparts Press, 1981), 95.
11. Cole, *Hollywood Red,* 138.
12. Cole, *Hollywood Red,* 159.
13. Cole, *Hollywood Red,* 177.
14. Quoted in Bruce Cook, *Dalton Trumbo* (New York: Charles Scribners, 1977), 162.
15. Nancy Lynn Schwartz, *The Hollywood Writers' Wars* (New York: Knopf, 1982), 88.
16. James Basset, "Communism in Hollywood: Why It Failed," *Los Angeles Mirror,* May 14, 1951.
17. *Communist Infiltration of Hollywood Motion Picture Industry,* House Committee, 1952, 3530.
18. *Communist Infiltration of Hollywood Motion Picture Industry,* House Committee, 1951, 368.
19. Schwartz, *Hollywood Writers' Wars,* 92.
20. *Communist Infiltration of the Motion Picture Industry,* House Committee, 1947, 239.
21. William L. O'Neill, *A Better World: The Great Schism; Stalinism and the American Intellectuals* (New York: Simon and Schuster, 1982), 244.
22. Richard Collins, "Confessions of a Red Screenwriter," *The New Leader,* October 6, 1952.
23. Victor Navasky, *Naming Names* (New York: Viking, 1980), 367.
24. Eugene Lyons, *The Red Decade* (Arlington, 1970), 27.
25. Norman Podhoretz, *Breaking Ranks* (New York: Harper and Row, 1979), 214.
26. Schwartz, *Hollywood Writers' Wars,* 88.
27. Alvah Bessie, *Inquisition in Eden* (New York: Macmillan, 1965), 25–26.
28. McGilligan and Buhle: *Tender Comrades,* 101.
29. McGilligan and Buhle: *Tender Comrades,* 204.

30. Sterling Hayden, *Wanderer* (New York: Knopf, 1963), 378–379.

31. Hayden, *Wanderer,* 328.

32. *Communist Infiltration of Hollywood Motion Picture Industry,* House Committee, 1951, 139.

33. *Communist Infiltration of Hollywood Motion Picture Industry,* House Committee, 1951, 146.

34. *Communist Infiltration of Hollywood Motion Picture Industry,* House Committee, 1951, 161.

35. Schwartz, *Hollywood Writers' Wars,* 89.

36. Schwartz, *Hollywood Writers' Wars,* 89.

37. McGilligan and Buhle, *Tender Comrades,* 541.

38. William P. Kimple, executive session testimony, Committee on Un-American Activities, House of Representatives, April 1, 1955, 118.

39. McGilligan and Buhle, *Tender Comrades,* 685.

40. William P. Kimple, executive session testimony, Committee on Un-American Activities, House of Representatives, April 1, 1955, 132.

41. John Cogley, *Report on Blacklisting* (New York: Fund for the Republic, 1956), 31.

42. *Communist Activities in the Los Angeles Area,* Committee on Un-American Activities, House of Representatives, 1953, 693.

43. *Communist Infiltration of Hollywood Motion Picture Industry,* Committee on Un-American Activities, House of Representatives, 1951, 1836–1849.

44 *Communist Infiltration of the Motion Picture Industry,* House Committee on Un-American Activities, 1947, 208.

45. Walter Bernstein, *Inside Out: A Memoir of the Blacklist* (New York: Knopf, 1996), 230.

46. McGilligan and Buhle, *Tender Comrades,* 591.

47. Cole, *Hollywood Red,* 168.

48. Philip Dunne, *Take Two: A Life in Movies and Politics* (New York, Limelight Editions, 1992), 128.

49. Cogley, *Report on Blacklisting,* 40.

50. Navasky, *Naming Names,* 244.

Chapter 6. "Communazis"

1. John Cogley, *Report on Blacklisting* (New York: Fund for the Republic, 1956), 36.

2. Nancy Lynn Schwartz, *The Hollywood Writers' Wars* (New York: Knopf, 1982), 150.

3. Cogley, *Report on Blacklisting,* 36, 37.

4. Cogley, *Report on Blacklisting,* 38.

5. Robert Vaughn, *Only Victims: A Study of Showbusiness Blacklisting* (New York: Putnams, 1972), 65.

6. Arthur Miller, *Timebends: A Life* (New York: Grove Press, 1987), 86.

7. Harvey Klehr, John Earl Haynes, and Kyrill M. Anderson, *The Soviet World of American Communism* (New Haven: Yale University Press, 1998), 299.

8. Schwartz, *Hollywood Writers' Wars*, 150.

9. *Hearings Regarding the Communist Infiltration of the Motion Picture Industry,* Committee on Un-American Activities, House of Representatives, 1947, 137.

10. *Communist Infiltration of Hollywood Motion Picture Industry,* House Committee, 1951, 1603.

11. Eugene Lyons, *The Red Decade* (Arlington, 1970), 342.

12. Earl Browder, *The Democratic Front* (New York: Workers Library, 1938), 84.

13. Benjamin Gitlow, *I Confess: The Truth about American Communism* (New York: Dutton, 1940), 333.

14. Schwartz, *Hollywood Writers' Wars*, 146.

15. Klehr, Haynes, and Anderson, *Soviet World of American Communism*, 73.

16. Benjamin Gitlow, *The Whole of Their Lives: Communism in America—A Personal History and Intimate Portrayal of Its Leaders* (Freeport, NY: Books for Libraries Press, 1948), 308.

17. *Communist Infiltration of Hollywood Motion Picture Industry,* House Committee, 1951, 4272.

18. Schwartz, *Hollywood Writers' Wars*, 147.

19. Schwartz, *Hollywood Writers' Wars*, 147.

20. Cogley, *Report on Blacklisting*, 39.

21. Schwartz, *Hollywood Writers' Wars*, 150.

22. *Communist Activities in the Los Angeles Area*, Committee on Un-American Activities, House of Representatives, 1953, 277.

23. Cogley, *Report on Blacklisting*, 25.

24. Philip Dunne, *Take Two: A Life in Movies and Politics* (New York: Limelight Editions, 1992), 114.

25. Patrick McGilligan and Paul Buhle, *Tender Comrades: A Backstory of the Hollywood Blacklist* (New York: St. Martin's, 1997), 423.

26. Lester Cole, *Hollywood Red* (Berkeley: Ramparts Press, 1980), 171.

27. Elia Kazan, *Elia Kazan: A Life* (New York: Knopf, 1988), 321.

28. Cole, *Hollywood Red*, 217.

29. *Investigation of Communist Activities in the New York City Area*, Committee on Un-American Activities, House of Representatives, 1953, 1465.

30. Dunne, *Take Two*, 112.

31. Dunne, *Take Two*, 128.

32. Schwartz, *Hollywood Writers' Wars*, 150.

33. *Jurisdictional Disputes in the Motion Picture Industry*, Hearings Before a Special Subcommittee of the Committee on Education and Labor, House of Representatives, 80th Congress, second session, 1948, 1550, 1552, 1554.

34. Wolfgang Leonhard, *Betrayal: The Hitler–Stalin Pact of 1939* (New York: St. Martin's, 1989), 163.

35. Schwartz, *Hollywood Writers' Wars*, 162.

36. Bruce Cook, *Dalton Trumbo* (New York: Charles Scribners, 1977), 38.

37. Larry Ceplair and Steven Englund, *The Inquisition in Hollywood: Politics in the Film Community, 1930–1960* (New York: Doubleday, 1980), 59.

38. Schwartz, *Hollywood Writers' Wars*, 185.

39. Dalton Trumbo, *The Remarkable Andrew* (New York: Lippincott, 1941), 112, 113.

40. Trumbo, *Remarkable Andrew*, 118.

41. Trumbo, *Remarkable Andrew*, 125.

42. Mikhail Heller and Alexander Nekrich, *Utopia in Power* (New York: Summit Books, 1986), 324.

43. Lyons, *Red Decade*, 82.

44. William Wright, *Lillian Hellman: The Image, the Woman* (New York: Simon and Schuster, 1986), 131.

45. Klehr, Haynes, and Anderson, *Soviet World of American Communism*, 84.

Chapter 7. War Party

1. Otto Friedrich, *City of Nets: A Portrait of Hollywood in the 1940s* (New York: Harper and Row, 1986), 106.

2. Friedrich, *City of Nets*, 189.

3. *Daily Worker*, October 25, 1942.

4. *New Masses*, February 1, 1944.

5. *American Legion Magazine*, December 1952.

6. *Current Biography*, Wilson, 1943, 351.

7. William L. O'Neill, *A Better World: The Great Schism, Stalinism and the American Intellectuals* (New York: Simon and Schuster, 1982), 78.

8. *Investigation of Communist Activities in the New York City Area*, Committee on Un-American Activities, House of Representatives, 1953, 1481.

9. Paul Jarrico, remarks at blacklist forum, January 19, 1989.

10. *Hearings on Communist Infiltration of Hollywood Motion Picture Industry*, Committee on Un-American Activities, House of Representatives, 1951, 235.

11. Dalton Trumbo, *Additional Dialogue: Letters of Dalton Trumbo 1942–1962*, Helen Manfull, ed. (New York: Evans and Co., 1970), 42.

12. Elia Kazan, *Elia Kazan: A Life* (New York: Knopf, 1988), 191.

13. Nancy Lynn Schwartz, *The Hollywood Writers' Wars* (New York: Knopf, 1982), 294.

14. *Communist Infiltration of the Motion Picture Industry*, House Committee, 1947, 111.

15. Transcript of executive session, U.S. House of Representatives, Committee on Un-American Activities, Los Angeles, November 23, 1953, 45, 48.

16. "Hollywood—The True Story," *People's Daily World*, special section, January 24, 1947.

17. Patrick McGilligan and Paul Buhle, *Tender Comrades: A Backstory of the Hollywood Blacklist* (New York: St. Martin's, 1997), 170.

18. Executive session testimony, House Committee on Un-American Activities, November 23, 1953, 52.

19. *Communist Infiltration of the Motion Picture Industry*, House Committee, 1947, 112.

20. McGilligan and Buhle, *Tender Comrades*, 612.

21. Dalton Trumbo, "Getting Hollywood Into Focus," *The Worker*, May 5, 1946.

22. *Communist Infiltration of Hollywood Motion Picture Industry*, House Committee, 1951, 1595.

23. *Communist Infiltration of the Motion Picture Industry*, House Committee, 1947, 132.

24. *Communist Infiltration of the Motion Picture Industry*, House Committee, 1947, 173, 174.

25. John Cogley, *Report on Blacklisting* (New York: Fund for the Republic, 1956), 226.

26. Morrie Ryskind, letter to William L. O'Neill, November 15, 1981.

27. *Communist Infiltration of the Motion Picture Industry*, House Committee, 1947, 138.

28. Dalton Trumbo, *Additional Dialogue*, 26.

29. *Communist Activities in the Los Angeles Area*, Committee on Un-American Activities, House of Representatives, 1953, 944.

30. *Communist Infiltration of Hollywood Motion Picture Industry*, House Committee, 1951, 265.

31. Schwartz, *Hollywood Writers' Wars*, 215.

Chapter 8. Taking It to the Streets

1. *Jurisdictional Disputes in the Motion Picture Industry*, Committee on Education and Labor, House of Representatives, 1948, p. 1967.

2. Father George H. Dunne, *Hollywood Labor Dispute: A Study in Immorality* (Los Angeles: Conference Publishing Company, 1951), 22–23.

3. *CLUV*, June 1945.

4. Victor Riesel and Murray Kempton, "Labor's Antidote for Communism," *North American Labor*, September 1948, 20.

5. Harvey Klehr, John Earl Haynes, and Kyrill M. Anderson, *The Soviet World of American Communism* (New Haven, CT: Yale University Press, 1998), 99.

6. Bella V. Dodd, *School of Darkness: The Record of a Life and of a Conflict Between Two Faiths* (New York: P. J. Kennedy and Sons, 1954), 181.

7. Dodd, *School of Darkness*, 187, 190.

8. *Communist Activities in the Los Angeles Area*, Committee on Un-American Activities, House of Representatives, 1953, 422.

9. Nancy Lynn Schwartz, *The Hollywood Writers' Wars* (New York: Knopf, 1982), 225.

10. Dalton Trumbo, *Additional Dialogue: Letters of Dalton Trumbo 1942–1962*, Helen Manfull, ed. (New York: Evans and Co., 1970), 163.

11. Schwartz, *Hollywood Writers' Wars*, 223, 225.

12. Trumbo, *Additional Dialogue*, 43.

13. See Allen Weinstein, *Perjury: The Hiss–Chambers Case* (New York: Knopf, 1977), 43, 205, 212, 361.

14. Trumbo, *Additional Dialogue*, 392.

15. Trumbo, *Additional Dialogue*, 512.

16 Bruce Cook, *Dalton Trumbo* (New York: Charles Scribners, 1977), 154.

17. Trumbo, *Additional Dialogue*, 37.

Chapter 9. Fronts, Fueds, and Blacklists

1. Ronald Reagan, with Richard G. Hubler, *Where's the Rest of Me?* (New York: Duell, Sloan and Pearce, 1965), 141.

2. "Stars Face Blacklist," *The Hollywood Sun,* June 15, 1945.

3. Reagan, *Where's the Rest of Me?*, 165–168.

4. *Investigation of Communist Activities in the New York City Area*, Committee on Un-American Activities, House of Representatives, 1953, 1168.

5. Elia Kazan, *Elia Kazan: A Life* (New York: Knopf, 1988), 191.

6. *Communist Activities in the New York City Area*, Committee on Un-American Activities, House of Representatives, 1953, 1156.

7. *Communist Activities in the Los Angeles Area*, Committee on Un-American Activities, House of Representatives, 1953, 967.

8. *Hearings on Communist Infiltration of Hollywood Motion Picture Industry*, Committee on Un-American Activities, House of Representatives, 1951, 416.

9. Nancy Lynn Schwartz, *The Hollywood Writers' Wars* (New York: Knopf, 1982), 228.

Chapter 10. The Battle of Burbank

1. *Hearings on Breakdown of Local Law Enforcement Authorities During Time of a Strike in the Hollywood Motion Picture Industry; from October 5 to October 28th, 1945,* Assembly Committee on Government Efficiency and Economy of the State of California, November 1, 1945, C. Don Field, chairman, 1.
2. Kirk Douglas, *The Ragman's Son* (New York: Simon and Schuster, 1988), 136.
3. *Breakdown of Local Law Enforcement Authorities,* California Assembly Committee, 23.
4. *Breakdown of Local Law Enforcement Authorities,* California Assembly Committee, 27.
5. *Breakdown of Local Law Enforcement Authorities,* California Assembly Committee, 9.
6. Douglas, *Ragman's Son,* 136.

Chapter 11. Hollywood Inquisition

1. *Hearings Regarding the Communist Infiltration of Hollywood Motion Picture Industry,* Committee on Un-American Activities, House of Representatives, 1951, 226.
2. James T. Bloom, *Left Letters: The Culture Wars of Mike Gold and Joseph Freeman* (New York: Columbia University Press, 1992), 7, 57.
3. Nancy Lynn Schwartz, *The Hollywood Writers' Wars* (New York: Knopf, 1982), 155.
4. Bloom, *Left Letters,* 14.
5. Bloom, *Left Letters,* 13.
6. Atlas's account from *Communist Activities in the Los Angeles Area,* Committee on Un-American Activities, House of Representatives, 1953, 945–947.
7. Patrick McGilligan and Paul Buhle, *Tender Comrades: A Backstory of the Hollywood Blacklist* (New York: St. Martin's, 1997), 698.
8. *Investigation of Communist Activities in the New York City Area,* Committee on Un-American Activities, House of Representatives, 1953, 1333.
9. *Life,* July 29, 1946.
10. *People's Daily World,* October 1, 1946.

Chapter 12. The Treaty of Beverly Hills

1. *People's Daily World,* March 21, 1946.
2. *People's Daily World,* March 14, 1946.
3. *People's Daily World,* March 26, 1946; June 25, 1946.
4. *People's Daily World,* March 2, 1946.
5. *People's Daily World,* May 20, 1946.

6. *People's Daily World,* April 29, 1946.
7. *People's Daily World,* June 25, 1946.
8. John Cogley, *Report on Blacklisting* (New York: Fund for the Republic, 1956), 160.
9. "More Trouble in Paradise," *Fortune,* November 1946.
10. *People's Daily World,* July 5, 1946.
11. *Jurisdictional Disputes in the Motion Picture Industry,* House Committee on Education and Labor, House of Representatives, 1948, 2304.
12. Ronald Reagan, with Richard G. Hubler, *Where's the Rest of Me?* (New York: Duell, Sloan and Pearce, 1965), 146–155.
13. *People's Daily World,* September 6, 1946.
14. *Los Angeles Times,* September 27, 1946. See also *Jurisdictional Disputes,* 1948, 2306.

Chapter 13. Technicolor Violence

1. "Rioting Marks Film Strike," *Los Angeles Times,* October 2, 1946.
2. "Hundreds of AFL Unionists Battle Furiously at MGM," *Los Angeles Times,* September 28, 1946.
3. "President of Film Actors' Union Condemns the Strike," *Life,* October 14, 1946.
4. "Studio Strikers Given Injunction Warnings," *Los Angeles Times,* September 29, 1946.
5. *Jurisdictional Disputes in the Motion Picture Industry,* Committee on Education and Labor, House of Representatives, 1948, 2124.
6. *Jurisdictional Disputes in the Motion Picture Industry,* Committee on Education and Labor, House of Representatives, 1948, 2124.
7. "Thirty-Eight Arrested in Renewed Studio Violence," *Los Angeles Times,* October 12, 1946.
8. *People's Daily World,* October 2, 1946.
9. Victor Riesel, "Film Strikers Out of Step," *Hollywood Citizen-News,* October 3, 1946.
10. *People's Daily World,* October 2, 1946.
11. *People's Daily World,* October 5, 1946.
12. "Win Peace Rally Echoes Reds Minus Marcantonio," *Los Angeles Citizen-News,* December 11, 1946.
13. *Hearings Regarding the Communist Infiltration of Hollywood Motion Picture Industry,* Committee on Un-American Activities, House of Representatives, 1951, 1843.
14. Ronald Reagan, with Richard G. Hubler, *Where's the Rest of Me?* (New York: Duell, Sloan and Pearce, 1965), 150.
15. John Cogley, *Report on Blacklisting* (New York: Fund for the Republic, 1956), 71.

16. Reagan, *Where's the Rest of Me?*, 152.
17. Reagan, *Where's the Rest of Me?*, 156.
18. Cogley, *Report on Blacklisting*, 72.
19. *Communist Infiltration*, House Committee, 338.
20. Screen Actors Guild, transcript of meeting at Hollywood Knickerbocker Hotel, October 24, 1946, pp. 79, 80.
21. *Un-American Activities in California*, Third Report of the Joint Fact-Finding Committee to the Fifty-Seventh California Legislature, Sacramento, 1947, 174.
22. *People's Daily World*, December 18, 1946.
23. McGilligan and Buhle, *Tender Comrades*, 523.
24. *People's Daily World*, September 9, 1947.
25. *People's Daily World*, September 20, 1947.
26. *People's Daily World*, September 27, 1946.
27. *People's Daily World*, September 8, 1947.
28. *People's Daily World*, July 30, 1946.
29. *Jurisdictional Disputes in the Motion Picture Industry*, Committee on Education and Labor, House of Representatives, 1948, 1681, 1682.
30. *Communist Infiltration*, House Committee, 518.
31. *People's Daily World*, March 4, 1947.
32. *People's Daily World*, March 11, 1946.
33. Reagan, *Where's the Rest of Me?*, 182–183.
34. Christopher Anderson, *An Affair to Remember: The Remarkable Love Story of Katharine Hepburn and Spencer Tracy* (New York: Morrow, 1997), 190.

Chapter 14. The "Reds in Movieland" Show

1. Walter Goodman, *The Committee: The Extraordinary Career of the House Committee on Un-American Activities* (New York: Farrar, Straus, and Giroux, 1968), 4.
2. Goodman, *Committee*, 16.
3. William F. Buckley Jr., and the editors of National Review, *The Committee and Its Critics: A Calm Review of the House Committee on Un-American Activities* (New York: Putnams, 1962), 101–103.
4. Goodman, *Committee*, 11.
5. Martin Dies, *The Trojan Horse in America* (New York: Dodd Mead, 1940), 11.
6. Buckley, *Committee and Its Critics*, 100.
7. Philip Dunne, *Take Two: A Life in Movies and Politics* (New York: Limelight Editions, 1992), 130.
8. Dunne, *Take Two*, 356.
9. *Hearings Regarding the Communist Infiltration of the Motion Picture Industry*, Committee on Un-American Activities, House of Representatives, 1947, 177.

10. *People's Daily World*, November 25, 1946.

11. *People's Daily World*, February 11, 1947.

12. *People's Daily World*, March 15, 1947.

13. *People's Daily World*, March 4, 1947.

14. Goodman, *The Committee*, 205; and Eric Bentley, *Thirty Years of Treason: Excerpts from Hearings Before the House Committee on Un-American Activities, 1938–1968* (New York: Viking, 1971).

15. Robert Stripling, *The Red Plot Against America* (New York: Arno Press, 1977), 63.

16. *People's Daily World*, February 8, 1947.

17. Stripling, *Red Plot*, 72.

18. Otto Friedrich, *City of Nets: A Portrait of Hollywood in the 1940s* (New York: Harper and Row, 1986), 307.

19. Friedrich, *City of Nets*, 344.

20. *People's Daily World*, October 4, 1997.

21. John Huston, enclosure to letter to G. R. Branton, January 29, 1953.

22. Nancy Lynn Schwartz, *The Hollywood Writers' Wars* (New York: Knopf, 1982), 256.

23. *People's Daily World*, May 22, 1947.

24. *People's Daily World*, February 4, 1947.

25. *People's Daily World*, September 3, 1947.

26. Francis Farmer, *Will There Be a Morning?* (New York: Dell, 1972), 227.

27. Lester Cole, *Hollywood Red* (Berkeley: Ramparts Press, 1981), 272.

28. *People's Daily World*, October 15, 1947.

29. *People's Daily World*, October 17, 1947.

Chapter 15. "The Glittering Names of Hollywood"

1. Gordon Kahn, *Hollywood on Trial* (New York: Boni and Gaer, 1948), 4.

2. *Hearings Regarding the Communist Infiltration of the Motion Picture Industry*, Committee on Un-American Activities, House of Representatives, 1947, 3.

3. *Communist Infiltration of the Motion Picture Industry*, House Committee, 9–15.

4. *Communist Infiltration of the Motion Picture Industry*, House Committee, 187.

5. *Communist Infiltration of the Motion Picture Industry*, House Committee, 71–76.

6. *Communist Infiltration of the Motion Picture Industry*, House Committee, 85–90.

7. *Communist Infiltration of the Motion Picture Industry*, House Committee, 101.

8. *Communist Infiltration of the Motion Picture Industry*, House Committee, 128–132.

9. *Communist Infiltration of the Motion Picture Industry,* House Committee, 136–159.

10. *Communist Infiltration of the Motion Picture Industry,* House Committee, 170.

11. *Communist Infiltration of the Motion Picture Industry,* House Committee, 195.

12. *Communist Infiltration of the Motion Picture Industry,* House Committee, 206.

13. *Communist Infiltration of the Motion Picture Industry,* House Committee, 218.

14. Patricia Bosworth, *Anything Your Little Heart Desires: An American Family Story* (New York: Simon and Schuster, 1997), 237.

15. *Communist Infiltration of the Motion Picture Industry,* House Committee, 221.

16. *Communist Infiltration of the Motion Picture Industry,* House Committee, 225–227.

17. *Communist Infiltration of the Motion Picture Industry,* House Committee, 179.

18. *Communist Infiltration of the Motion Picture Industry,* House Committee, 283.

19. Henry C. Rogers, *Walking the Tightrope: Confessions of a Public Relations Man* (New York: Morrow, 1980), 83.

20. David Caute, *The Great Fear: The Anti-Communist Purge Under Truman and Eisenhower* (New York: Simon and Schuster, 1978), 497.

21. John Cogley, *Report on Blacklisting* (New York: Fund for the Republic, 1956), 4.

22. Nancy Lynn Schwartz, *The Hollywood Writers' Wars* (New York: Knopf, 1982), 261.

23. Caute, *Great Fear,* 497.

24. Bosworth, *Anything Your Little Heart Desires,* 229.

25. John Huston to M. Hogan, January 7, 1953.

26. Stephen Humphrey Bogart, *Bogart: In Search of My Father* (New York: Dutton, 1995), 146.

27. Rogers, *Walking the Tightrope,* 84.

28. Rogers, *Walking the Tightrope,* 85.

29. *People's Daily World,* November 8, 1947.

30. *Communist Infiltration of the Motion Picture Industry,* House Committee, 293, 294.

31. *Communist Infiltration of the Motion Picture Industry,* House Committee, 312.

32. *Communist Infiltration of the Motion Picture Industry,* House Committee, 334.

33. *People's Daily World,* October 29, 1947.

34. *Communist Infiltration of the Motion Picture Industry,* House Committee, 363–366.

35. *Communist Infiltration of the Motion Picture Industry,* House Committee, 412–414.

36. Schwartz, *Hollywood Writers' Wars,* 281.

37. Bogart, *Bogart,* 146.

38. Bentley, *Thirty Years of Treason*, 976.

39. Friedrich, *City of Nets*, 256.

40. Patrick McGilligan and Paul Buhle, *Tender Comrades: A Backstory of the Hollywood Blacklist* (New York: St. Martin's, 1997), 714.

41. Paul Johnson, *Intellectuals* (New York: Harper and Row, 1988), 185.

42. Ella Winter, *And Not to Yield* (New York: Harcourt, 1963), 238.

43. *Communist Infiltration of the Motion Picture Industry*, House Committee, 491–504.

44. Rogers, *Walking the Tightrope*, 89.

45. *People's Daily World*, November 1, 1947.

46. William Wright, *Lillian Hellman: The Image, the Woman* (New York: Simon and Schuster, 1986), 212–213.

47. *People's Daily World*, November 4, 1947.

Chapter 16. "A Horrendous Story of the Persecution"

1. *Jurisdictional Disputes in the Motion Picture Industry*, Hearings Before a Special Subcommittee of the Committee on Education and Labor, House of Representatives, 1948, 2124.

2. *Jurisdictional Disputes*, House Subcommittee, 1884.

3. *Jurisdictional Disputes*, House Subcommittee, 1952.

4. *Jurisdictional Disputes*, House Subcommittee, 1899.

5. *Jurisdictional Disputes*, House Subcommittee, 1897.

6. *Jurisdictional Disputes*, House Subcommittee, 2069.

7. Interview, Roy Brewer.

8. Interview, Roy Brewer.

9. Victor Navasky, *Naming Names* (New York: Viking, 1980), 246.

10. "Anti-Red Labor League Holds Bull's-Eye Dinner," *Hollywood Citizen-News*, November 12, 1948.

11. Helen Gahagan Douglas, "My Democratic Credo," speech in California Assembly, March 29, 1946.

12. *Congressional Record*, 1949, 11903.

13. John Cogley, *Report on Blacklisting* (New York: Fund for the Republic, 1956), 92.

14. "A Case of Split Reasoning," *The Daily Bruin*, March 6, 1950. See also entry for Roy M. Brewer in *Current Biography*, 1943, 92.

15. Victor Riesel and Murray Kempton, "Labor's Antidote for Communism," *North American Labor*, September 1948.

16. Vladimir Pozner, *Parting with Illusions* (Boston: Atlantic Monthly Press, 1990), 76.

17. Steven Schwartz, *From East to West: California and the Making of the American Mind* (New York: Free Press, 1996), 468.

18. Howard Fast, *Being Red: A Memoir* (New York: Laurel, 1990), 345.

19. John Barron, *Operation Solo: The FBI's Man in the Kremlin* (Washington, D.C.: Regnery, 1996), 39.

20. Martin Duberman, *Paul Robeson* (New York: Ballantine, 1989), 352–354.

21. Stalin's earlier purges, during the 1930s, had claimed director Vevolod Meyerhold, whose confession had been obtained through torture: "The investigators began to use force on me, a sick 65-year-old man. I was made to lie face down and then beaten on the soles of my feet and my spine with a rubber strap. They sat me on a chair and beat my feet from above, with considerable force . . . For the next few days, when those parts of my legs were covered with extensive internal hemorrhaging, they again beat the red-blue-and-yellow bruises with the strap and the pain was so intense that it felt as if boiling hot water was being poured on these sensitive areas. I howled and wept from the pain. They beat my back with the same rubber strap and punched my face, swinging their fists from a great height.

"When they added the 'psychological attack,' as it is called, the physical and mental pain aroused such an appalling terror in me that I was left quite naked and defenseless. My nerve endings, it turned out, were very close to the surface of my body and the skin proved as sensitive and soft as a child's. The intolerable physical and emotional pain caused my eyes to weep unending streams of tears. Lying face down on the floor, I discovered I could wriggle, twist, and squeal like a dog when its master whips it. One time my body was shaking so uncontrollably that the guard escorting me back from such an interrogation asked: 'Have you got malaria?' When I lay down on the cot and fell asleep, after 18 hours of interrogation, in order to go back in an hour's time for more, I was woken up by my own groaning and because I was jerking about like a patient in the last stages of typhoid fever. . . . I began to incriminate myself in the hope that this, at least would lead quickly to the scaffold." Vitaly Shentalinsky, *Arrested Voices: Resurrecting the Disappeared Writers of the Soviet Regime* (New York: Free Press, 1996), 25.

22. *Russia's War*, a series seen in 1997 on the Public Broadcasting Service, documented these and other cases based on the most recent revelations from Soviet archives.

23. Boris Pasternak, *Doctor Zhivago* (New York: Pantheon, 1958), 503.

24. Shentalinsky, *Arrested Voices*, 303.

25. *Investigation of Communist Activities in the New York City Area*, Committee on Un-American Activities, House of Representatives, 1953, 1174.

26. For more on the Hiss–Chambers case, see Allen Weinstein, *Perjury: The Hiss–Chambers Case* (New York: Knopf, 1997).

27. Harvey Klehr, John Earl Haynes, and Fridrikh Igorevich Firsov, *The Secret World of American Communism* (New Haven, CT: Yale University Press, 1995), 317.

28. Kanfer, *The Plague Years: A Devastating Chronicle of the Era of the Blacklist* (New York: Atheneum, 1973), 91.

29. Edward Dmytryk, *Odd Man Out: A Memoir of the Hollywood Ten* (Carbondale, IL: Southern Illinois University Press, 1996), 115.

30. "Dmytryk of 'Hollywood Ten' Denies Communism in Oath," *Los Angeles Examiner,* September 11, 1950.

31. Alvah Bessie, *Inquisition in Eden* (New York: Macmillan, 1965), 90–91.

Chapter 17. Breaking Ranks

1. Richard Collins, "Confessions of a Red Screenwriter," *New Leader,* October 6, 1952.

2. *Hearings Regarding the Communist Infiltration of Hollywood Motion Picture Industry,* Committee on Un-American Activities, House of Representatives, 1951, 89, 107.

3. *Communist Infiltration of Motion Picture Industry,* House Committee, 119.

4. *Communist Infiltration of Motion Picture Industry,* House Committee, 465.

5. *Communist Infiltration of Motion Picture Industry,* House Committee, 1701.

6. *Communist Infiltration of Motion Picture Industry,* House Committee, 144.

7. Victor Navasky, *Naming Names* (New York: Viking, 1980), 133.

8. Patrick McGilligan and Paul Buhle, *Tender Comrades: A Backstory of the Hollywood Blacklist* (New York: St. Martin's, 1997), 36.

9. Nancy Lynn Schwartz, *The Hollywood Writers' Wars* (New York: Knopf, 1982), 284.

10. Dramatist Arthur Miller, who had achieved critical acclaim with his 1947 *All My Sons* and his 1949 *Death of a Salesman,* approached Elia Kazan with a script called *The Hook,* dealing with the "United Shoreside Workers of America." One character named Rocky is an agent of the employer and yet steps right in to run against Marty, the hero, at a union election. There is a sinister, behind-the-scenes villain named Jack Uptown who hangs out at the Waldorf, and one of the union leaders is in cahoots with him. At one point Marty screams, "This is Fascism! Let's bring America down to the waterfront!"

In his book, *Timebends*, Miller says *The Hook* was about Pete Panto's attempt to overthrow the "feudal gangsterism" of the New York waterfront—a "social issue" script, written and directed by "two minority men plotting to hit the American screen with some harsh truths." Mogul Harry Cohn liked the idea but because of the union angle ran it by Roy Brewer, who was wary of any project that might help Harry Bridges, then expanding eastward. Brewer met with Cohn, Kazan, and Miller, who suggested someone could accuse the hero of being a Communist, and then the hero would deny it. Brewer countered that, if the hero were a Communist, denying it is exactly what he would do. The IA man suggested that a representative of the *People's Daily World* could offer to help the hero, and then the hero would turn him down. Miller rejected the idea and later charged that Brewer had been brought in by the FBI.

"It's interesting the minute we try to make the script pro-American you pull out," Cohn said in a telegram to Miller.

Arthur Miller, *Timebends: A Life* (New York: Grove Press, 1987), 308.

11. *Hearings Regarding the Communist Infiltration of Hollywood Motion Picture Industry*, House Committee on Un-American Activities, House of Representatives, 1952, 2407–2414.

12. Lillian Hellman, *Scoundrel Time* (Boston: Little Brown, 1976), 103.

13. *Communist Infiltration of Motion Picture Industry*, House Committee, 410.

14. *Communist Infiltration of Motion Picture Industry*, House Committee, 225, 256.

15. *Communist Infiltration of Motion Picture Industry*, House Committee, 291.

16. *Communist Infiltration of Motion Picture Industry*, House Committee, 275

17. *Communist Infiltration of Motion Picture Industry*, House Committee, 1576–1606.

18. *Communist Infiltration of Motion Picture Industry*, House Committee, 621.

19. *Communist Infiltration of Motion Picture Industry*, House Committee, 644.

20. *Communist Infiltration of Motion Picture Industry*, House Committee, 1419–1442.

21. *Communist Infiltration of Motion Picture Industry*, House Committee, 1675, 1678.

22. *Communist Infiltration of Motion Picture Industry*, House Committee, 1674.

23. *Communist Activities in the Los Angeles Area*, Committee on Un-American Activities, House of Representatives, 1953, 909.

24. *Communist Infiltration of Motion Picture Industry*, House Committee, 1836.

25. *Communist Infiltration of Motion Picture Industry*, House Committee, 1687.

26. *Communist Infiltration of Motion Picture Industry*, House Committee, 1734.

27. *Communist Infiltration of Motion Picture Industry*, House Committee, 2417.

28. *Communist Infiltration of Motion Picture Industry*, House Committee, 3479.

29. *Communist Infiltration of Motion Picture Industry*, House Committee, 1586.

30. *Communist Infiltration of Motion Picture Industry*, House Committee, 3546.

31. *Communist Infiltration of Motion Picture Industry*, House of Representatives, 4475.

32. Navasky, *Naming Names*, 224.

Chapter 18. "Those Witches Did Not Exist; Communists Do"

1. Aline Mosby, "All Abroad! U.S. Tax Law Empties Hollywood of Stars," *Hollywood Citizen-News*, February 21, 1953.

2. Yves Montand, with Herve Hamon and Patrick Rotman, *You See, I Haven't For-gotten* (New York: Knopf, 1992), 238.

3. Patrick McGilligan and Paul Buhle, *Tender Comrades: A Backstory of the Holly-wood Blacklist* (New York: St. Martin's, 1997), 597.

4. Dalton Trumbo, "Blacklist = Black Market," *The Nation*, May 4, 1957.

5. Trumbo, "Blacklist = Black Market."

6. Margaret Truman, *Harry S. Truman* (New York: Morrow, 1973), 429.

7. James Bassett, "Communism in Hollywood," *Los Angeles Mirror,* May 14, 1951; May 17, 1951.

8. "Red Hollywood," *Morning World-Herald*, September 14, 1945.

9. Victor Navasky, *Naming Names* (New York: Viking, 1980), 107.

10. John Huston, Letter to M. Hogan, August 23, 1952.

11. Walter Wanger to Roy Brewer, undated.

12. Lena Horne to Roy Brewer, June 28, 1953; Carlton Moss is coauthor with Helen Arstein of *In Person: Lena Horne*, which appeared in 1950. The book gives a pos-itive portrayal of Paul Robeson and chronicles Horne's battles with prejudice but contains nothing overtly political.

13. Herbert Biberman, *Salt of the Earth: The Story of a Film* (Boston: Beacon Press, 1965), 32.

14. Michael Wilson, "Hollywood and Korea," *Hollywood Review,* January 1953.

15. Deborah Silverton Rosenfelt, *Salt of the Earth* (New York: Feminist Press, 1978), 157.

16. Biberman, *Salt of the Earth*, 206.

17. Pauline Kael, *I Lost It at the Movies* (New York: Bantam, 1966), 298–311.

18. Stefan Kanfer, *The Plague Years* (New York: Atheneum, 1973), 204.

19. John Howard Lawson, "Hollywood on the Waterfront," *Hollywood Review,* November–December 1954.

20. David Platt, "About Jules Dassin," *Daily Worker,* January 26, 1956, 6.

21. *Newsweek,* January 12, 1959.

22. Elia Kazan, *Elia Kazan: A Life* (New York: Knopf, 1988), 449.

23. Kazan, *Elia Kazan*, 508.

24. Lawson, "Hollywood on the Waterfront."

25. Lester Cole, *Hollywood Red* (Berkeley: Ramparts Press, 1981), 352.

26. Kazan, *Elia Kazan*, 529.

27. Marlon Brando, with Robert Lindsey, *Brando: Songs My Mother Taught Me* (New York: Random House, 1994), 195.

28. Navasky, *Naming Names*, 199.

29. *Communist Activities Among Professional Groups in the Los Angeles Area*, Com-mittee on Un-American Activities, House of Representatives, 1952, 4226.

30. *Los Angeles Daily News,* March 19, 1953.
31. *Communist Activities in the Los Angeles Area,* Committee on Un-American Activities, House of Representatives, 1953, 431.
32. *Investigation of Communist Activities in the New York City Area,* Committee on Un-American Activities, House of Representatives, 1953, 1192.
33. *Communist Activities in New York City,* House Committee, Activities, 1262.
34. Cole, *Hollywood Red,* 81.
35. *Communist Activities in New York City,* House Committee, 1353, 1364.
36. *Communist Activities in New York City,* House Committee, 1373.
37. "Secret Red Revolution School Near L.A. Bared," *Los Angeles Times,* March 23, 1956.
38. *Communist Activities in New York City,* House Committee, 1414.
39. William Alland, executive session testimony before HCUA, November 23, 1953, 48.
40. Alland, executive session testimony, 56.
41. Dalton Trumbo, *Additional Dialogue: Letters of Dalton Trumbo 1942–1962,* Helen Manfull, ed. (New York: Evans and Co., 1970), 345.
42. *Communist Activities in New York City,* House Committee, 1309.
43. *Communist Activities in New York City,* House Committee, 1445.
44. *Communist Activities in New York City,* House Committee, 1460.
45. *Hearings Before the Subcommittee to Investigate the Administration of the Internal Security Act and Other Internal Security Laws of the Committee on the Judiciary,* United States Senate, 1952, 175, 158.
46. *Internal Security Act,* Senate, 205–209.
47. Stephen Schwartz, *From West to East* (New York: Free Press, 1998), 469.
48. Paul Johnson, *Intellectuals* (New York: Harper and Row, 1988), 191.
49. Montand, *You See, I Haven't Forgotten,* 251.

Chapter 19. The Party's Over

1. James Bassett, "Communism in Hollywood," *Hollywood Citizen-News,* May 15, 1951.
2. David J. Saposs, *Communism in American Unions* (Westport, CT: Greenwood Press, 1967), 30–31.
3. Kenneth Anger, *Hollywood Babylon* (San Francisco: Straight Arrow Books, 1975), 286.
4. Alvah Bessie, *Inquisition in Eden* (New York: Macmillan, 1965), 137.
5. John Cogley, *Report on Blacklisting* (New York: Fund for the Republic, 1956), 160.
6. See "Legal Aspects" by Harold W. Horowitz, in Cogley, *Report on Blacklisting,* 174–180.

7. Patrick McGilligan and Paul Buhle, *Tender Comrades: A Backstory of the Hollywood Blacklist* (New York: St. Martin's, 1997), 343.

8. Stephen Schwartz, *From West to East* (New York: Free Press, 1998), 484.

9. Harvey Klehr, John Earl Haynes, and Kyrill M. Anderson, *The Soviet World of American Communism* (New Haven, CT: Yale University Press, 1998), 349.

10. *Time,* December 2, 1957.

11. Howard Fast, *The Naked God: The Writer and the Communist Party* (New York: Praeger, 1957), 3, 29.

12. Fast, *The Naked God,* 48, 171, 197.

13. Fast, *The Naked God,* 35, 64–66.

14. Fast, *The Naked God,* 110, 197.

15. Bruce Cook, *Dalton Trumbo* (New York, Charles Scribners, 1977), 271.

16. McGilligan and Buhle, *Tender Comrades,* 21.

17. *Hollywood Reporter,* September 18, 1959.

18. Anger, *Hollywood Babylon,* 220.

19. Larry Ceplair and Steven Englund, *The Inquisition in Hollywood: Politics in the Film Community, 1930–1960* (New York: Doubleday, 1980), 408.

20. McGilligan and Buhle, *Tender Comrades,* 347.

21. Dalton Trumbo, *Additional Dialogue: Letters of Dalton Trumbo 1942–1962,* Helen Manfull, ed. (New York: Evans and Co, 1970), 425.

22. Nancy Lynn Schwartz, *The Hollywood Writers' Wars* (New York: Knopf, 1982), 253.

23. McGilligan and Buhle, *Tender Comrades,* 695.

24. Robert Pitkin, "The Movies and the American Legion," *American Legion Magazine,* May 1953.

25. Ronald Brownstein, *The Power and the Glitter: The Hollywood–Washington Connection* (New York: Pantheon, 1990), 124.

Chapter 20. "The Chronicle of Some Mythical Kingdom"

1. Kirk Douglas, *The Ragman's Son* (New York: Simon and Schuster, 1988), 307.

2. Douglas, *The Ragman's Son,* 335.

3. Patrick McGilligan and Paul Buhle, *Tender Comrades: A Backstory of the Hollywood Blacklist* (New York: St. Martin's, 1997), 414.

4. *Halliwell's Film Guide* (New York: Harper, 1995), 203.

5. William F. Buckley Jr., "Who Is the Ugliest of Them All?" *National Review,* January 21, 1977.

6. William Wright, *Lillian Hellman: The Image, the Woman* (New York: Simon and Schuster, 1986), 355.

7. Victor Navasky, *Naming Names* (New York: Viking, 1980), 296.

8. McGilligan and Buhle, *Tender Comrades*, 161.

9. Lester Cole, *Hollywood Red* (Berkeley: Ramparts Press, 1981), 429.

10. Cole, *Hollywood Red*, 432.

11. Cole, *Hollywood Red*, 428.

12. "Maltz Letter to Communist Editor Bared," *Los Angeles Examiner*, May 23, 1960.

13. Griffin Fariello, *Red Scare: An Oral History* (New York: Norton, 1995), 266.

14. Navasky, *Naming Names*, 393.

15. McGilligan and Buhle, *Tender Comrades*, 739.

16. Navasky, *Naming Names*, 257.

17. McGilligan and Buhle, *Tender Comrades*, 53.

18. Edward Dmytryk, *Odd Man Out: A Memoir of the Hollywood Ten* (Carbondale, IL: Southern Illinois University Press, 1996), 200.

19. Howard Fast, *Being Red: A Memoir* (New York: Laurel, 1990), 27, 77, 138.

20. John Earl Haynes and Harvey Klehr, "The Communist Party of the USA and the Committees of Correspondence," *Problems of Post-Communism*, July/August 1996.

21. *Anaheim Bulletin*, May 26, 1960.

22. McGilligan and Buhle, *Tender Comrades*, 539, 717.

23. McGilligan and Buhle, *Tender Comrades*, 539.

24. McGilligan and Buhle, *Tender Comrades*, 625.

25. McGilligan and Buhle, *Tender Comrades*, 197.

26. Stefan Kanfer, *The Plague Years: A Devastating Chronicle of the Era of the Blacklist* (New York: Atheneum, 1973), 285.

27. McGilligan and Buhle, *Tender Comrades*, 555.

28. McGilligan and Buhle, *Tender Comrades*, 324.

29. McGilligan and Buhle, *Tender Comrades*, 28.

30. See David E. Scheim, *Contract on America: The Mafia Murder of President John F. Kennedy* (New York: Kensington, 1988).

31. Hecky Brown represents Phil Loeb, an actor from the Group Theatre who had a role in "The Goldbergs," an early sitcom. He committed suicide after wrangling with a government committee about Party affiliation.

32. Patrick Goldstein, "Hollywood's Blackest Hour," *Los Angeles Times*, October 19, 1997.

33. Philip Dunne, *Take Two: A Life in Movies and Politics* (New York, Limelight Editions, 1992), 7.

34. Dunne, *Take Two*, 205.

35. Elia Kazan, *Elia Kazan: A Life* (New York: Knopf, 1988), 566.

36. Yves Montand, with Herve Hamon and Patrick Rotman, *You See, I Haven't Forgotten* (New York: Knopf, 1992), 374.

37. Charlton Heston, *In the Arena* (New York: Simon and Schuster, 1995), 307.
38. John McDonough, "Kazan Outghta Be a Contenda for Film Award," *Wall Street Journal*, March 2, 1995.
39. John McDonough, National Public Radio, October 20, 1997.
40. Patrick Goldstein, "Hollywood's Blackest Hour," *Los Angeles Times*, October 19, 1997.
41. McGilligan and Buhle, *Tender Comrades*, xx.
42. Goldstein, "Hollywood's Blackest Hour."

Chapter 21. The Missing Cast

1. Harvey Klehr, John Earl Haynes, and Kyrill M. Anderson, *The Soviet World of American Communism* (New Haven, CT: Yale University Press, 1998), 87.
2. Yves Montand, with Herve Hamon and Patrick Rotman, *You See, I Haven't Forgotten* (New York: Knopf, 1992), 418.
3. Montand, *I Haven't Forgotten*, 368.

Index

343